I0749465

Giorgia V. Audino

LECHUZA

LECHUZA

Independently published.
ISBN 979-8-32391-026-7

Book design by Giorgia V. Audino
Cover design by Giorgia V. Audino

This is dedicated to my dear life companion, Arwen.

A special appreciation to two people in particular, who gave me the motivation to complete this important project of mine.
Thank you Kevin Roque and Bryan Gutiérrez.
I couldn't have done it without you.

Please, do not harm barn owls.

I

The echoes of a noisy bar in a quiet street faded, making way as the first storm of the month began to batter the windows of the establishment, drowning out the voices of the patrons, some of whom spoke in hushed tones while others boasted of their exploits, causing others to begrudgingly take part as a captive audience. Brida Castillo relished her own company, at the same time resenting her loneliness. The bar was pleasant enough, as it was the only place she could enjoy a calm evening without having to see a familiar face from work while still being distracted enough to not let her thoughts plague her.

Brida wasn't scared of her own thoughts, since it'd been some time since that underlying feeling of misery left her. The psychologist from the Counseling Program -a service provided at her workplace- called it an adjustment disorder. The mere name made her furrow her eyebrows, bringing an expression of shame to her eyes as she stared at the empty glass that was only getting warm in her hand. The bar was long and narrow, sporting a warmly colored, welcoming façade. The walls were decorated with old photographs, vintage signs, and the occasional neon light. Although the windows were closed, she could feel a cold breeze down the back of her neck, one of the few places her leather jacket didn't shield her from the chilly temperature of the bar. She placed one of her hands on the back of her neck, pressing it tightly in an attempt to ease the tension in her upper spine.

Normally, Brida was meticulous in her personal image. She tried not to linger on her reflection in the windows; she knew her image had changed since she started living alone, and her reflection disturbed her greatly. Her body was no longer athletic as before, and didn't fill out her clothes quite like she used to, having to tighten her belt to make them fit. Even if she had changed so much, she still retained a resemblance to her former image. Nights spent at the gym were once again bearing fruit, keeping her body in shape.

"You've been staring at that glass for a time."

The bartender stood right in front of her. His figure was making her eyes try to focus, but her sight wasn't the best when she had an unhealthy quantity of alcohol to herself. Gustavo Espinoza was an old friend. His gaunt face was accompanied by prominent cheeks, and with dark eyes reddened by the smoke of the bar. He somehow always managed to look his best. Gustavo was a man of many words with his feet always planted on the ground. A stable man.

"Hm. I got lost for a moment," she said.

Gustavo leaned on the bar, resting his body for the moment. He glanced at the glass and then at Brida, giving her a small smile. "Do you want me to tell you what happened to me yesterday afternoon? Also the other day on the radio, the announcer told some stories that made me laugh, I can regale you with some if you want."

Brida couldn't return the smile. She put the glass aside and improved her posture on the bench, leaning her arms on the bar for support. Gustavo was a kind friend, not an intimate one, for Brida, friends were never easy to make. The two had met by chance and for years maintained an aloof friendship at first, neither could say exactly when the other began to see the other's presence as a normal occurrence. "I've already listened to that channel. Never got a laugh out of it," Brida said, grimacing at the sound of her voice. She tried to clear her throat to no avail. "I think I'd like to know more about how your night is going."

"The same as any other night, with the same regulars. It looks like it won't stop raining tonight, the city only gets to have its fill every so often here," he said, smiling as he wiped down the bar table.

Right, insightful. The thought was laced with sarcasm; she couldn't remember the last time she'd spoken amiably to anyone outside of work. Her eyes fell on Gustavo again; in truth, she couldn't even remember the last time she had spoken to anyone in a familiar way in those past weeks. Her thoughts began to scatter, causing her mind to begin to go blank in an effort to regain control, her eyes becoming lost trying to fix her sight on Gustavo. Remembering where she was, Brida murmured in response.

"Are you alright?" Gustavo asked.

Brida frowned. She could tell exactly why she wasn't feeling well, but shook her head, massaging her eyelids with one hand in circular motions. Even she didn't feel like thinking about it. "Yes, the light hurt my eyes when I tried to look at you," she said, grabbing the forgotten bottle and pouring herself a new glass as Gustavo's gaze scanned her.

"Okay." He glanced at the windows and then down at the table bar, passing his finger along a scratch in the wood. "Come to think of it, Thomas hasn't come to the bar anymore. Did something happen to him?"

His smile was polite, but Brida couldn't help herself from gulping her new drink down in an effort to avoid his genial efforts. She didn't want to think about Thomas, not at that moment. "He's doing okay."

"You don't sound very convinced."

"I haven't talked to him these days, I wouldn't know."

"Just asking. Lately the city isn't even safe for cops. Every time I turn on the TV there's always some bad news, it never seems to stop."

"That's how it is now."

"Seems like it," Gustavo said. "The truth is that's why I have the TV off tonight, I didn't want to stress out people who already have enough in their lives to be stressed about. Well, also because I'm tired of the news. You know, misery attracts more misery. It's bad enough the island hasn't seen fit to give us better days."

She strained to listen to the conversation, but it was challenging when her eyes couldn't focus, and her mouth was starting to salivate a little too much. For a moment everything started to move in front of her. The corners of the ceiling started drifting to the side, dragging the walls along with them in the same slow movements. Her face didn't show any signs of dizziness, though her eyes needed a rest from the sliding walls and glanced at Gustavo once again.

"Maybe the drink is slowing you down, you know."

Brida gave a croaky laugh, pressing her lips against the rim of her glass. It wasn't funny, at all. Drinking was never an issue in her past, and indeed still is not. Gustavo was right about one thing; *something* was slowing her down. The only thing alcohol makes her do is think and get lost in her mind. Sometimes she couldn't grasp any coherent thought and stare at whatever was in front of her. Other times she would dwell on them, but that only made her drink more.

"I suppose," Brida said.

Time passed her by. The glass was empty again. She looked at her hand and played with the golden ring on her finger, toying with it, feeling the surface of it, the indents she's rubbed time and time again.

Then, she closed her eyes, exhaling all the air from her lungs. She took the ring off and put it on her ring finger of her right hand, but even doing that, her left hand still felt heavy. She lifted the bottle for another drink until a voice stopped her. It was Gustavo, as always. She hadn't even raised her arm to pour the liquid into her glass and Gustavo was quicker than her when she was in that state.

"That's enough for you," he said, taking the bottle out of her hand.

Brida was annoyed, observing how Gustavo put the bottle away, far from her sight. Gustavo glanced at her and smiled, prompting her to soften her gaze, but she didn't return the gesture. She took a deep breath. Gustavo was right, like every other night she came to his bar. She should stop for tonight. She knew it was still early, however, it was better to go back to her apartment and figure out what she was going to do with the free time she was going to have starting tomorrow. Fourteen days all by herself.

"You're right."

"I know you're having a rough night. Do you want me to call a taxi?"

"No, thank you. I'll sober up outside."

"Don't tell me you're going to drive in that state?"

"I'm not driving until I can clearly read the street signs."

Gustavo seemed to relax with her response, smoothing the lines of his forehead. "Do you want me to accompany you to your car, at least?"

"No, don't worry. I'll have a smoke outside."

"Be careful with the rain. Have a good night, Brida."

"Thank you."

Gustavo cleared his throat, smiling a little. "If you come by Friday, I can show you the new drink I'm trying to put on the menu. I've been experimenting. Maybe this way you can relax more by doing something new. What do you say?"

"Sure. I'll see you then."

She got out of her stool and headed to the entrance, feeling the chilly air of the city as she approached. She closed the door behind her, the difference of temperature making it a little difficult to breathe. The fog was heavy around the city and smelled of pure pollution accompanied by rain, mixing the odors, and clutching the air. Opening her jacket, she pulled out a pack of cigarettes and kept looking out at the surrounding area. The buildings were old, with only enough space between them to accommodate a sprawling network of narrow alleys that forced its citizens into neat rows below looming buildings, with the many eyes that resided within. One always felt like they were being watched. The city held on to an old style of architecture, which set it apart with decorative patterns, finials, and Tudor-style hood moldings that lent it the feeling of age held by its residents. Her hand twitched slightly as she lit her cigarette, now under those invisible looming eyes.

The rain had intensified. Brida made her way to her car, a dark Cadillac Fleetwood Brougham, remembering where she had left it. Her shoulders were getting soaked in the rain, with her hair already plastered against her skull and forehead. Just as she was about to unlock the Brougham, someone bumped into her, causing her to drop her keys. Frustrated, she looked to her side and saw a young girl with big doe eyes, and an anxious look on her face, clutching tightly an umbrella against her chest.

"I'm so sorry! I wasn't looking were I was going."

"Clearly." Brida blinked at her direction, taking a better look. The girl was looking at her as if trying to burn her image into her own mind. She took the cigarette out of her mouth and asked: "Did I burn you by accident?"

The girl was slow to answer, seeming to be lost in thought until she reacted and stopped staring. "No! No, not at all! It was close to my face but nothing serious happened," she said nervously, feeling a harsh gaze on her face. Brida hadn't meant to look at her that way. "Excuse me, I'm trying to find something, well, more like someone to help me with a problem."

Brida bent down to pick up her keys and, upon hearing this, turned to look at the girl, but in doing so she moved more aggressively than she felt, startling the young girl for a moment. Even if she was a little tipsy, she could still see how this girl was battling something in her thoughts, and she wasn't trying to make this girl more anxious than she already was. At least she was kind enough to shield her from the rain with her umbrella when she bent down.

Brida grabbed her keys from the puddle they had fallen into and stood up, looking back at the girl who had shielded her from the rain raise her umbrella to make room for Brida's full height, which made Brida smile. She slightly bent down, making the girl follow the movement, still trying to cover the two of them from the rain. "Who are you trying to find?"

"Someone who can help in a particular case," the young girl answered, a tremor creeping through her hand as she held the umbrella above them, arm outstretched. "Please, it's really important, could you hold my umbrella while I look for something?"

"Sure." Brida inclined her head, completely amused. Brida straightened up and arranged the umbrella so that the girl wouldn't be bothered by the heavy rain. She exhaled the smoke from her mouth, making the girl smile nervously as she searched for something in her purse. Now that she was close, Brida could see her better. Her face was soft, slightly sharper around the jaw. Her small nose was bright red and irritated, as if she had cleaned it many times. Her ginger hair was pulled back in a low tight ponytail. She was thin, which made her coat look much larger on her. Brida kept observing the girl, studying her face, and for a moment she thought of a mouse. She had the face of a little mouse. That thought made her smile internally.

"Here it is!" she exclaimed, producing a rather sad and wrinkly looking piece of paper. "I'm trying to find someone to help me find this person as soon as possible. I was told there were several private investigators here, but I don't know who to ask. I really don't know what to do."

Brida placed her cigarette in her mouth before grabbing the crumpled paper and reading what was written on it. It was a flyer for a missing person, alright. She gave a full glance at the information and zeroed in on the photo of the girl they were looking for. Brida handed the paper back to the girl and exhaled, removing the cigarette from her mouth. "And why are you trying to find this person?"

"I, well, it's personal," the girl said, glancing down at the flyer. "I'm a little apprehensive to talk to strangers, especially men, and since I bumped into you, well, I thought I'd ask you. If you could tell me what I can do to contact an investigator, I would be very pleased."

"Why do you need to find this specific person?"

The girl appeared to tense up still holding the wrinkled paper in her hand. "I don't want to sound rude, but I'd prefer to talk to an investigator about my situation, I'm sorry. I've been looking for some direction all day and I can't stay here very long, if you would be so kind as to tell me how I can contact someone who can help with this, it would be great. If not, then it's fine."

How ironic. Her work consisted of these types of cases, among others. "The only thing I can do for you is to give you directions to the nearest police department."

The girl nodded impatiently at the prospect of having an answer she was so desperately seeking. The girl had tender mannerisms that humored Brida, especially with such a red nose. "Anything, as long as someone helps me with this."

Brida considered what was happening. Now that she reflected on it, why was this girl wandering around alone at this hour? She could easily come up with several possibilities if she wanted to think coldly, except this girl didn't seem to venture out of the house much. If she was searching for the girl in the flyer, hunting for information at night wasn't the best way to go about it. "Hm. I work as a detective. I can only advise you on some matters. I'm Brida Castillo." Brida pulled her ID out her wallet to assure the girl she wasn't lying about her identity. The girl took the small card and carefully read the information under Brida's gaze. She saw the girl's face go from skeptical to astonished. Her eyes lit up as if Brida was the last piece of a puzzle. That confused Brida, who soon felt a smaller hand grab her arm. Brida couldn't keep herself from staring at the hand contrasting against her dark jacket, the knuckles were a bright rose color while the fingernails had a purple tinge, the usual signs of cold weather.

"You're a detective!"

Brida stopped eyeing the hand to look again at the girl in front of her. She tried to ignore the touch on her arm, leaving it tense and reluctant to move away from the petite hand. "I work for the SEPD. I'm not a private investigator."

"No, really! I thought I'd never find anything or, well, anyone. Please, I need your help with this. I don't know what to do. The truth is, this is actually scaring me, and I guess other people too, and I still can't believe I've found some help! You don't know how happy I am to finally meet someone like you, I hope you can help me with this!"

Brida winced at the high-pitched voice. A headache was making its presence known, pounding in the sides of her head. In this condition, she couldn't keep up with all the information and stopped the girl's rambling, putting her hand up in front of the shaking girl to take a pause. Brida was amused, but tired. She took her ID and put it inside her wallet, handing the umbrella back to the girl. "First things first, who are you?"

"I'm so sorry, I usually always introduce myself first. I'm Lisa Gallardo."

"Nice to meet you Lisa, but I can't help you like you want me to."

"But you have to!"

"I'm not a private investigator. The only thing I can do, as I already said, is to give you directions to the nearest department." Brida looked at Lisa's determined face. She had wrinkled her nose, which was charming in and of itself. "I'm sorry," Brida added.

Lisa kept silent. Brida waited for a brief moment until she shrugged the girl off, walking through the rain to get in her car, opening the door. She sensed a presence behind her and glanced toward the determined soul who gave chase. Lisa didn't seem quite as anxious as before. Deep down, she wanted to humor this girl.

"Yes?"

"I know you drank, I can smell it." Lisa frowned in deep thought. "You can't drive in that state. How about I buy you a coffee? There's a store around the corner. I think I saw one walking through here."

Brida exhaled wearily, locking the car door. She'd met strong-willed people before; it wouldn't be hard to drive Lisa away. "You know I can't help you, right?"

"I know. I'm trying to buy you a cup of coffee."

"Alright, a coffee sounds good. Give me the umbrella, I don't want to hunch all the way down there. The store you mention is around this corner."

Lisa smiled, showing off her dimples. She was shorter than Brida, making her have to work harder to keep pace. They were silent when they arrived at the 24-hour store. Brida held the door open for Lisa, who muttered a thank you as she hurried inside. Brida kept her gaze on Lisa's back, walking towards a small table near the window. She attempted to avoid her own reflection as she took a seat, but in the end she couldn't control her curiosity. Her eyes were strained, and some strands of her hair were plastered against her forehead. She passed her hand over, slicking it back. Brida waited for Lisa while looking out the windows, sitting in that table stained over the years. She checked her wristwatch and saw that it was eleven o'clock at night. It was late, but it wasn't out of the ordinary for Brida to be out at this time of night.

Lisa, for her part, was still thinking about how everything had lined up for her to finally meet someone like Brida. She turned her head slightly, and was intercepted by a pair of eyes that resembled a green tide, reminding her of all the green sights she had ever seen in her life. She had never seen eyes as beautiful as hers. She gave a sheepish smile to the detective and turned her attention back to the coffee she was preparing. She didn't even know how much sugar to put in the coffee as she was left feeling absent-minded, deciding to grab two sachets and a plastic spoon. She paid for it quickly, deciding to buy chocolates as she was feeling heavy from all the energy she had expended during the day. Finally, she walked to the detective, putting everything on the table. Brida didn't comment on the sweets, and accepted the coffee with a nod. She took a sip, making the bitter taste linger in her mouth.

"Thank you for the coffee."

"You're welcome, I didn't put any sugar in it if you wanted to put any yourself." Lisa opened one of her chocolates and looked out the window. She ate two pieces, wondering about what she was going to say. She meant to take another piece of her sweet, yet her mouth was quicker than her brain on decision-making. "I didn't like coming to the city. I don't like the buildings, nor how everything is stuck together. It seems like everyone is watching you walk around, although I think I'm a little paranoid. This is my first time in the city, you know."

Brida knew what she meant. St. Elkan was as abrasive as its patron saint and namesake. People would say the city was once a bright place to stay and live with all of your family, but for all the time she had lived in this city, Brida would say it's an unpleasant one. "Saint Elkan isn't exactly a wonderful place. You said you came from town, right?"

"Yes, Dameborne."

"Hope the city didn't give you too much trouble, then."

"Well… I got lost several times, but that's the least of it."

The old town was similar to the city, and although Dameborne was something of a mystery among the denizens of the city, their shared attributed remained. It was older, closed off, but just as unpleasant, surrounded by the same climate as St. Elkan, with the worst heatwaves, crackling thunderstorms, and depressive smogs all being collective trademarks. Brida couldn't think of much else about the town since she'd never been here. She took another sip of the bitter coffee. "Hm. I used to know someone from town. I want to know first why you're walking alone in the city, especially at this late hour."

Lisa gave her an embarrassed look and lowered her gaze to her hands. She should eat the piece of chocolate she had between her fingers, she was just dirtying her hand. "The truth is that I got a bit lost and I was looking for at least a place where I could rest my legs a moment and maybe take a cab if I saw one or continue walking my way to the motel I'm staying. I didn't really check the time for a while and everything went dark too fast. I didn't have a good day, but this has already improved my night a lot better, although I hope this never happens again."

"Alright," Brida said, giving her a small nod.

"I know the town is far away from the city, but I really need help with this. My friend is missing," Lisa said, taking a deep breath, squeezing the strap of her purse between her hands. "I don't know where she might have gone and I'd like for her to come home. Her full name is Elizabeth Montebrook Davis, as you saw in the flyer."

Brida felt her eyes grow heavier, contemplating the girl before her. She shouldn't even be contemplating asking about what was going on in town. Particular cases like this must go through her superior first. Perhaps getting her to talk about her situation and explain how she could handle it might help Lisa present her information and contact her respective jurisdiction. She shouldn't be doing this, expect she didn't want to leave the girl on her own. "Anything that jumps out to you about that time?"

"Um, well, she was acting weird the last few times we got together. We could be fine one moment and the next she'd be mad at me and everyone else. I didn't even know how to react when she got in that mood anymore." Lisa replied crestfallen, shifting on the chair. "It was about three weeks ago. The last time I saw her, we got into a big fight. We called each other names and said horrible things that I want to take back and the last thing I said to her was so awful. I've been thinking about that fight a lot and I admit I had my frustrations too, but none of that makes me feel any better." Lisa started to speak faster towards the end, until she stopped and took a breath to relax herself.

"I'm sure your friend knew it was a shallow fight. Tell me about the behavior."

"She had strange mood swings. I know everyone can get them from time to time, but she started to be too aggressive," Lisa said. "She would throw whatever she had on hand and then cry. Well, sometimes she'd cry, other times she'd laugh about it. I don't know when she started to behave like that. I never would have thought she would turn on me, too. At first it was over insignificant, small things, but eventually it got worse."

"Are you sure she never behaved aggressively before?"

"I'm sure. Elizabeth didn't break things out of anger, she would try to calm down when she knew she was getting angry. She started crying a lot and demand thigs from me and others. I don't know when she started to be like that, it's hard to pinpoint an exact date."

"Never had episodes like that before?"

"No, never."

"Her disappearance made everyone nervous, I suppose."

"I don't even know how to describe it. Some are nervous, but not about Elizabeth. My friend wasn't the only one who had strange mood swings now that I remember."

"What do you mean by that?"

"My neighbors, for example, are sweet people; the old lady used to bake sweet bread for the kids around town, but the last time I saw her she was trying to hit one of the kids. She was grabbing him by the shirt around his neck, shaking him and yelling at him. I feared she would do something worse to the child, so I ran for my grandma. When my grandma went to ask the lady what was going through her mind when she reacted like that, the lady was very frantic and upset, in the end we left her to calm herself down," Lisa sighed, putting her face between her hands. "I mean, sometimes kids can be a little too much, but, well, this old lady wouldn't even hurt a fly. I don't know if I'm explaining myself well enough."

"An out of character outburst like that could already be a sign of psychosis, but there's also the other the factor of old age, medication-"

"No, no, not only that lady. I've also seen other things happening in my town that shouldn't be happening! I seriously don't know how to explain it, but it's not normal that people who I know have never raised their hand to anyone are suddenly doing it all over, as if they could be flying off the handle at any moment. And then there are others who get sick and look like they are just waiting for… something, who knows what. I really don't know how to explain it. I just know that none of this is normal, or who knows. I don't even know what to think anymore."

Brida looked at Lisa, tapping her finger on the table. Three weeks. It was likely that Elizabeth Montebrook was already dead. If that girl was alive, it would be a miracle, a good one that many families and friends wanted to be true every time such a thing happened. But Brida had personally worked in disappearance cases, and most of them turned up dead at the end. Although who knows, there is also the possibility that the girl simply ran away from home. Moreover, she couldn't think of any feasible reason why the townspeople would be having these kinds of reactions. Perhaps the mania of the city was being passed on to the town.

"Let's put aside the neighbor's behaviors, did your friend have a boyfriend?"

"No… Not that I know of."

"Was your friend vulnerable at the time - drunk, medicated or anything?"

"I don't think so. I wouldn't know for sure."

"Do you have any reason to believe she was in danger?"

"I don't know, I don't think so." Lisa bit her fingernail, shifting her eyes elsewhere instead of the woman in front of her. "I don't want to think she was in danger. I thought she went with her friends, she spends a lot of time with them. Sometimes she would sleep over with them, so it wasn't that unusual for me not to see her at her home as much. I hadn't seen her for a while, so I went to her house to leave her a small gift. Her mother let me in reluctantly. She, um, she doesn't like me very much. I guess the lady assumed I did something to Elizabeth, because she kept mumbling some weird comments while I was there. In the end, surprisingly, she gave me permission to leave the gift in Elizabeth's room, but when I checked her room… it was as if she never lived there at all. I tried to ask her other friends, but they closed me off for some reason. None of them wanted to tell me what had happened or if Elizabeth had even gone home. My family had a small fight with her mother. My grandma heard her say she blamed me for her daughter's disappearance and they started arguing."

"That's the shock talking, don't listen to her," Brida said. She set aside the empty cardboard cup, her palate felt better with the aftertaste of the coffee than the alcohol. "Look Lisa, I can't help you. In fact, I'm taking an extended break from work. If you've already contacted everyone and checked the places your friend would frequent, then you have to file a missing person report here. Present all the information you told me to facilitate the search for your friend. I'm sorry about your friend's disappearance, but I cannot help you personally."

"I know they won't search for her."

"What makes you think that?"

"They already said I was wasting time doing this when they already had cases piled up. The case was closed and that was it for the time being." Lisa gazed out the window, noting the water slide from the glass. A heaviness settled in her chest, slumping her shoulders. "I'd prefer someone like you to handle the investigation."

"Do you remember who told you that?"

"Yes, but that doesn't matter. I want someone like you to take the case."

Ignoring the latter, Brida crossed her arms on top of the small table. Lisa turned her attention to her with that action which pleased the detective. The girl was attentive to her movements. "Listen, disappearance cases are opened and closed several times, it's too early to give up Elizabeth's case yet. We have cases from seventeen years ago and we reopen them when we find a new lead, even after such a long time."

Lisa grimaced at the response. Brida knew it wasn't something the girl wanted to hear. She couldn't take the case even if she wanted to, less when she was already on leave. Brida took a deep breath and regarded the girl in front of her. Lisa had her shoulders hunched and her face was pinched with anger and frustration, making her look like a child throwing a tantrum. Brida knew those signs all too well. Furrowing her eyebrows, her finger tapping the surface as she took everything into consideration.

"File a missing person report here."

"You're really not going to help me?"

"No. The only one who can assign me a case like this is my superior," Brida said as if what she had stated was a joke, receiving a worn look from the girl. It didn't help that Brida never had a particularly good sense of humor. "If you can manage to find help on your own, I wish you luck. Where are you staying?"

Lisa sighed, running her hand over her eyes. "I don't know the streets very well, but I can point it out if I see it."

"Come, I'll take you to where you're staying. It's late for you to be walking alone." Brida stood up grabbing the girl's umbrella and throwing the cup into the trash. Lisa hastily stowed her sweets inside her purse and almost grabbed the detective's arm out of inertia. She halted her action feeling her cheeks heat up with embarrassment. Brida merely tilted her head to one side. "They'll look for your friend. Sometimes it takes time, and that's the worst of it. The city shares cases with the town, and vice versa. You'll see soon they'll open the file again."

"No, they won't."

Brida passed her hand over her face and left it under her chin. "They will."

Lisa raised her eyebrows and followed the older woman in defeat. Soon they were in the Brougham in an awkward silence. Lisa stole a glance at Brida, her first real assessment of the woman. She was tall and looked healthy, yet there was something off about her that made her think she had something deeper afflicting her… she didn't know. Her posture against the seat seemed rigid and Lisa noted the glint of a ring on Brida's steering hand. Strangely, the ring was on the right hand and it looked very much like the ring her father wore with great fondness. She could notice an exquisite design on the ring in comparison to her father's plain ring.

"Are you married?"

There was a brief period of silence.

"No," Brida said, darting a sideways glance at Lisa.

"Oh," Lisa responded, feeling foolish. She blinked, unsure on how to apologize for the question, opting instead to look at the streets, hoping the detective hadn't taken offense to her curiosity. She pursed her lips, almost biting the inside of her cheek. Shortly she spotted familiar streets and pointed to the right path. "Turn here and we've arrived."

"Alright."

Lisa smiled. "Thank you for the lift."

"No problem."

Brida stopped the Brougham in front of a well-kept motel, the neon sign flashing and contrasting against the mist of the rain. Lisa took her umbrella, opening the car door and paused looking down, feeling the rain against her legs. Brida rested her arm on top of the steering wheel waiting for the girl to get her thoughts together. It didn't take long.

"Will you be at that bar these days?"

Brida blinked and shot a curious glance before turning back and nodding. "It's the only one I go to. Thank you for the coffee, it did me good." Brida smiled, wrinkling the side of her eyes. The first smile that hadn't weighted her down in so long. "Be careful, Lisa."

"I will, thank you for listening to me," said Lisa, wanting to add more, but eventually decided against it. She closed the car door and headed for the motel room she'd been assigned. Brida waited to see Lisa enter, resting a hand on the steering wheel while Lisa unlocked the door and waved goodbye. Once the girl entered the room seamlessly, Brida sighed heavily, her expression becoming serious. She dreaded going to the apartment she's staying at, but she had to if she wanted to be presentable tomorrow. Her friend, Thomas, had invited her to his house for lunch after he found out she was taking a break. Ever since Gustavo mentioned him, she couldn't help but miss him all the more.

Brida finally drove out, knowing tomorrow wouldn't be a good day.

II

She parked the Brougham in front of an imposing brick house and memories came to mind of when she and Thomas had scoured neighborhoods looking for a good house when they had been young. Ever since she met Thomas, he'd always had the idea of owning a fine house, fulfilling his dream years later. Now she knows if she dares to step foot into that doorframe, it'll cause a scene. Brida ran a hand through her mid-length hair and sighed, resting her hand on the steering wheel. She knew her image was better than yesterday, she had combed her hair, styled her choppy layers. Her bangs were long enough to comb over her ear. She had perfumed her neck and wrists with the perfume she favored most. There was no lingering scent of cigarettes.

It was two in the afternoon. The invitation said to arrive at least fifteen minutes early, but those minutes had already passed as Brida sat inside the car, waiting for a sign. Her pulse was frantic, and her mouth suddenly felt as if she had swallowed sand, passing her tongue against her lips. It was idiotic to wait. She picked up the bottle of wine she had bought as a gift, trusting that even Alina, Thomas' soon-to-be ex-wife, would like the brand. The man from the store had told her that it didn't have a strong flavor and would go well with most foods. She had believed him, as she didn't have the knowledge to determine which wine was the right one. All she knew was that white wine was for fish and red wine for meat. Resigned, she opened the door and locked the car. She stepped slowly toward the entrance until she stood near the synthetic mat that welcomed her, which was of poor quality and appeared to be on its last legs. She knew she had withdrawn from any social interaction since her supervisor authorized her vacation request, trapping herself in the same routine she had created. A memory of her former partner resurfaced, his mirthful chuckle calling her an animal of routine. Clenching one hand, Brida rang the doorbell and fixed her gaze on the nameplate, repeating the number in her head. The door opened and she could see Thomas surprised by her presence, unable to conceal his wide-eyed astonishment.

"It's been a while since I've been here." Brida grimaced at the gravelly tone of her voice. She cleared her throat. "I brought this. I was told it can go well with food." Thomas didn't reply right away. She almost got frustrated at the lack of response. Then Thomas smiled broadly, all his white teeth showing. He always had a warm smile, with the lines of his face rising, making his eyes draw more attention. Brida had missed seeing his face light up like that. It was a pity to no longer witness it. So much had changed.

"Brida!" exclaimed Thomas, going for a full hug, causing her to tense her muscles. She awkwardly patted his back. Thomas always had a pleasant natural aroma, her nose was close to his neck where it could concentrate and engulf her olfactory sense. Brida held her breath politely for as long as the embrace had lasted, until Thomas took her by the forearms. "I thought you wouldn't come."

"I thought so too, but I'm here."

"Come on in, we have a lot of catching up to do You shouldn't have brough anything, but thank you. We'll open it later." Thomas took the bottle, checking the name of the wine. It was a good brand. It must have cost her a pretty penny, which almost made him laugh. Brida had always been a bit old-fashioned in that respect. He and his family had met the Castillo's, they had been the most serious and polite people they had ever known.

Thomas was delighted to see his friend again. It had been a while since he'd last had her in his house, her presence was still guarded, her eyes looking at him and through him. Brida took her time entering the house, closing the door with a soft click. She took off her jacket and left it hanging on the coat rack, biding her time to keep up with Thomas later. For the moment it appeared to be just them. There wasn't much noise inside the house, only an electrical humming coming from the kitchen. Everything was illuminated with bright colors, a stark contrast with the façade of the house. It wasn't plain, but it didn't have a sense of coziness either. There were no extravagant luxuries, as Thomas always preferred to live with only the essentials. Thomas was waiting for her with a smile which made her dwell on all the mistakes she had made in the last few months. In particular, distancing herself from him.

It hadn't been intentional, but by the time she noticed it, there was already a considerable gap between them. Thomas, unaware of Brida's musings, steered the course of the conversation.

"Finally taking some time for yourself?"

"I'm trying," Brida replied. "Your house hasn't changed much since the last time I visited."

"I wouldn't know. You know I don't spend much time here."

"I thought you'd become homier by now."

"No, not at all," he said, lifting his eyebrows with a smirk. He took a cursory glance at the entryway and living room, and no, there was nothing homely about it. "Come to the kitchen with me, we can talk there while I'm finishing cooking. I made parmigiana today, it's already in the oven, so we can open this bottle and talk about what you plan to do." Thomas set the bottle down on the kitchen counter and picked up the corkscrew.

"Where's Alina?"

"She'll be a little late. I say she'll be here in ten minutes."

The kitchen was different from the other rooms, apart from the delicious scent coming from the oven, it had a warm, light energy that Brida always looked back fondly on their days past together. Brida sat in a chair at the small center table and stared at the kitchen window waiting for the glass of wine. The television was on, soundless, where Brida lost herself for a moment staring at the muted moving images on screen. Her senses returned as Thomas uncorked the bottle and handed a glass to her. She grabbed it and took a small breath, steadying her nerves.

"So, do you have anything in mind?" he asked.

"No, not really. I'll stay here and go for a walk in the park once in a while."

Thomas controlled his expression, keeping his smile. The answer had sounded automatic, and he didn't like that at all. Since when had Brida started talking to him like that, as if he were a stranger? Unfortunately, he already knew the answer, but it was impossible not to ask himself that every time they spoke. A feeling of sadness washed over him looking at Brida. Even at work, it was harder to go to her desk and spend what little free time he had with her.

"That sounds boring."

Brida shrugged. "That's my life now. A little bit boring."

"I wouldn't call your life boring," Thomas leaned against the counter, resuming his task in preparing several salami and cheese slices on a plate. "You've done a lot in your life. I was thinking of taking a break myself."

"You are?"

"Yeah, I think I will. The idea of having a vacation is nice, but I don't have to explain to you why it would be a bad idea for me to take a few days off. This house is driving me crazy and if I stay here, I'll become like my mother when she couldn't stand anyone in the house anymore. I don't want to start having to sneak out of the house at night just so I can have some peace."

"Why is the poor house giving you a hard time?"

He smiled at the remark. "It's not the house. It would be easier if it were the house giving me all this stress. Let me check the parmigiana."

Thomas turned to check up on his cooking. Brida couldn't keep herself from watching him closely and missing when she could watch him cook. There was a bizarre, mesmerizing factor in watching someone cook. When he opened the small oven doors, the aroma grew stronger, causing Brida to inhale it and remember all those good memories she had fondly stored in her mind. Thomas had always been better than her in the kitchen. When they had meals together in their younger days, Thomas had made the sacred rule that she couldn't touch the kitchen when he was present, unless she was preparing simple dishes or coffee as a joke. To be frank, it ended up being a necessity since Brida's cooking left much to be desired. She sipped from her glass and noticed the framed photos on the wall. Some were of the Cipriani family, others of Thomas in different locations. One in particular of them, smiling at work. Thomas always showed his teeth, smiling broadly, while she only sketched small smiles. One could tell it had been taken by Brida's desk, seeing her belongings unchanged over the years. She stopped checking the contents of her desk in the photo and her attention focused on Thomas's face.

"I thought you got rid of them."

"What?"

Brida pointed to the wall. "The photos."

Thomas followed the finger. "Why would I remove the photos?"

She remembered the last time she came, the photos weren't hung in the location she had become accustomed to seeing them. Now they were held proudly up on the wall. Returning to their place, as if Thomas was finally doing justice to something she didn't know about. The nails were different, noting how they had a white ring around breaking the paint. "Never mind. Yesterday a girl tried to convince me to help her on a disappearing case."

Thomas wanted to ask her why she had thought that, contemplating what she might been thinking until he decided to play along. "And what did you say?"

"That I couldn't help her."

"How did this girl find you?"

"We bumped into each other outside Gustavo's family's bar. Apparently, this girl had been searching for a private investigator to help her with her friend's disappearance. According to this girl, they already closed the investigation over in Dameborne."

"I haven't heard of this, those are supposed to come by our desks."

"Elizabeth Montebrook. It's the name of the missing girl."

"Doesn't ring any bells."

"It'd better if I returned to work."

"No, no, you still need to take your leave."

"We're already struggling-"

"And I still think you should take a break from such work," he interrupted, sketching an apologetic smile. "Besides, you can't say no to already authorized vacations. I don't know what those morons in town are doing, but eventually the file will get here."

Brida nodded, running her index finger across her lip. "So that we're even more short-staffed here when that case comes around?"

With an exasperated sigh, Thomas replied, "Good to see you can still be stubborn, but you have to remember why even Ortiz wanted you to take some time off. And speaking of him, Ortiz called the other day and asked me how you were. I didn't know what to answer him."

"Ortiz called you?"

"Of course, I guess he wanted to hear from you after everything."

Brida opened her mouth and then closed it just as quick. She shook her head and tapped the table with her index finger. It was a subtle quirk that Thomas knew well. He smiled a little as he took the dish out of the oven. He was satisfied with how the recipe had turned out. He kept thinking the fact that Brida was in his kitchen and not avoiding him was already a special occasion, so he took out the ceramic plates given to him by his grandparents long ago.

"I think you should call him if you want to," he said, leaving the appetizers on the table. "He's called me twice now and you know Ortiz doesn't exactly have me high up on his social calendar to do that for me."

"Maybe I will. I haven't seen him since he retired."

"That's because you locked yourself up. You were hard to talk to."

Brida looked away. "I know."

"I didn't say that to make you feel bad. I'm happy you're here," Thomas smiled, being quite sincere achieving to make his friend smile. He felt the nerves of his hands jump, there was no need to mask his emotions. "You'll see, it'll be better this time. I have a great suspicion that good things will happen to us soon, and I think it's only fair after all the problems we've had over the years."

"Is that what you call everything that's happened?"

Thomas glanced at her, leaving the food to cool down on the table. He watched as Brida ran her forefinger along the ripples on the plate. He took a seat next to Brida, embracing the small liberty that still belonged to him. "What do you want me to call it? Because it's been problem after problem these past few years. I'm not saying it with malice, don't get me wrong, but I feel it's the right word for all of this."

"You may be right."

"Of course I'm right."

Brida smiled and raised her eyebrows at Thomas' matter-of-fact tone, she intended to test that notion, but was interrupted by the sound of the front door opening. Brida reverted to her serious expression, observing a silhouette she had known for years. Alina was a slender woman with a delicate neck, graceful posture, her head tilted in a manner Brida thought arrogant. Admittedly, Alina was beautiful, albeit her personality made her beauty diminish and bizarrely, Alina reminded her of a porcelain doll, the kind antique stores put on display, lovely and almost perfect, easy to break at the slightest push. Alina's eyes narrowed as she stared at Brida in the kitchen.

"I thought we'd have a meal with someone else, not her."

Brida knew her presence was unwelcome. She didn't need Alina's exaggerated glances or passive-aggressive behavior to know that. There had been a period when she used to dine with them freely, but ever since the 'incident' happened, it ended up driving up a wall between her and her regular life. Alina was antsy in her presence, she couldn't blame Alina for her apprehension. Brida liked her frankness, that's why she always found her a pleasant company ever since she met her. Now she was the one on the receiving end of the 'bad' comments and it didn't bother her, on the contrary, she appreciated the open hostility. Thomas shot a scathing glance at his wife. Alina didn't want to have the decency to be polite and show a neutral expression. Brida felt how what little energy she had vanished. Still, she was amused by how Alina was upfront in her displeasure.

These occurrences and many others like it were what had made her weary of this house. Although it amused her, it was tiring. Brida stared at Alina, the way her whole demeanor became aggravated by her presence. She considered staying. Then again, she had no inclination to put up with the palpable tension in the air and preferred to be in that dingy apartment or somewhere else in the city.

"I told you we'd eat with a friend," Thomas said. "And you agreed."

Alina glared. "You didn't tell me you were going to invite *her*."

Thomas frowned at his wife's imprudence. He nodded to Brida with a strained smile, leading Alina out of the kitchen and into the living room. He felt his hands tingle. "Don't speak like that right in front of Brida." Thomas took a breath, wondering if he should stop before things escalated. Impulses getting the better of him, he continued, "If you don't want to have a meal together, then you can go eat somewhere else. It wouldn't be the first time you leave when I invite someone to the house. When have you ever seen me say something like that to you in front of your friends?"

"Don't talk to me like that."

"Then don't be like this, Brida is your friend too."

"You're out of your mind if you think that, I'd rather leave."

Unbeknownst to the two of them, Brida could hear the couple's heated whispers. It had been a mistake to assume things would work the way they had before, Brida realized now. Apparently, she had a lot to dwell on. She waited for Thomas to return to the kitchen, noting how his posture had changed to a tense one. For just a moment, she wanted to be selfish and stay. It only lasted a moment.

"Thomas, I have to go now." Brida stood up, setting her plate aside. "I came to see you both for a moment, I couldn't stay even if I wanted to. Thank you for inviting me anyway, it's good to know I still count on your friendship." Alina felt Brida's gaze on her, and tried to be indifferent to those eyes. "It's good to see you well, Alina."

"You don't have to go," Thomas tensed. "I really want you to sit down and enjoy this with us. It's been a long time since you've been here. Alina didn't meant it-"

"Another time."

"You really don't have to go."

Brida ignored him, shifting her gaze back to the shorter woman. Alina displayed her irritation at her presence. Brida interpreted the possible twisted thoughts running through her head. She wasn't interested and, after all, it was no concern of hers. Thomas knew Brida wasn't going to put up with this kind of attitude, even he wouldn't put up with it. Not even if he pleaded could he make his friend stay, he knew that, but that didn't stop him from following Brida to the door, completely ignoring Alina's presence, walking behind Brida who was already at the entryway, grabbing her jacket.

"At least call me if anything happens, please."

Brida didn't want to make a promise. "Sure, I'll call you."

"Take care."

Thomas knew it wouldn't happen. Thomas waved his hand, but Brida didn't take him into account as she strode away. The clicks of her boots against the pavement of the driveway only made him slump his shoulders. His face tightened as he clenched his hand into a fist, the air beginning to feel colder with the dark clouds overhead about to burst. He closed the front door and went to the kitchen, Alina was no longer there. He stared at the plates and drew his lips in a straight line. He took them and returned the food to the ceramic mold. His hunger had gone after such a spectacle. He washed the plates, running his hand through the old patterns. Alina seemed to have returned, her voice similar to a buzzing noise in his ears.

He wasn't listening to anything Alina was saying.

"Why are you always like this?"

Alina sneered at him. "Like what?"

"You know what I mean, you aren't dumb." Thomas dried his hands with the dish towel, pausing for a moment to think his next line. He didn't want another fight. His lawyer wouldn't be happy to know they had argued again. "There was a time you liked Brida. You used invite her over and even once you gave her a gift. What's changed?"

"Yeah, I liked her. Not anymore. You know what happened to her and that makes her dangerous to us, to me! Didn't you think of that when you invited her over?" Alina grabbed her purse and headed to the stairs. "You can invite anyone, but not her. Who knows if that man is still out there. What if that man comes to this house looking for her? Haven't you thought of that? I'll go and see a friend in a moment, don't wait for me."

"You can't start deciding who I keep as friends, Alina." Thomas pinched the bridge of his nose. How could she even mention that man? Although he didn't know if that man was still- He wasn't going to start thinking about that now. "And you know I stopped waiting for you a long time ago. What I don't understand is why you made all that fuss about Brida being here and decide to go out to meet your *friend*?"

No response.

Thomas tried not to explode in that moment, taking a deep breath looking at this left hand, the ring there shinning in the light. He ran his thumb over his ring finger. He knew they should have divorced the same year Brida suffered the incident that almost took her, and he also knew his own marriage wasn't doing neither him nor Alina any good. Thomas glanced at the photos Brida pointed out earlier. He didn't understand why she thought he would throw his photos away. There were family photos he occasionally liked glancing at, all of good memories. He was fond of that picture of him and Brida, since it was when his friend became a detective assigned to her first division. Brida had been his friend going back all way to their time in police academy together. The only one who stayed by his side. Brida was always there as a strong presence that he knew would take care of him, but also push him when he needed to be pushed. Just like family. He liked to think he was the same for her. He knew Brida was going through a difficult time, that she needed to heal. At least she had come to visit him. He heard Alina's footsteps coming down the stairs, which he chose to ignore. He didn't even want to look at her.

Instead of keeping quiet and waiting for her to leave, he decided to speak up.

"I can't live like this, Alina. I don't know why you're waiting so long to sign the divorce papers. We can't even sleep in the same room."

"I thought you were joking last time you mentioned it."

"Why would I joke about- You know what, just go with that man."

"How did you…" Alina grimaced, "You're sick, Thomas."

He heard the front door slam shut and couldn't stop the snark from his thoughts that this potential lover was going to have to put up with Alina's nagging at some point. He knew Alina hadn't taken any steps beyond what was necessary, she still respected the union they had formed. He was aware she was doing it to make him jealous, or at least make him open his eyes to the fact that he was losing her. He didn't know how to tell Alina that it wasn't the typical complications of an early marriage, but that he had apparently made a big mistake in misunderstanding their dating relationship. He didn't want to whish her ill, but he also didn't want to be in this kind of union where tall the foundations were already broken by pure insecurities.

Thomas stood alone in the kitchen, wondering if their relationship had always been like this from the beginning. He had enough of his mother's silent stares when he visited her. Divorce wasn't a taboo in his family. What his parents had against him was that, for them, he didn't give due importance to the consequences of this marriage. How could he be the object of ridicule, solely because he failed to control his wife. Thomas never had the need to restrain anyone. His nonno often reminded him that when a woman truly loves, it makes any man ask heaven to die at the same time so as not to leave the other alone. He thought about his wedding day, all had been happy for them. How Brida had looked at him with pride, where now she saw him as if he were a stranger. But sometimes, that old look comes out. Thomas remembered how delighted he had been that day, seeing Alina in her white dress, laughing when he dropped his piece of cake by accident. Now, they couldn't even stand being in the same place.

He missed those bygone times.

III

He couldn't stop thinking about apologizing to Brida. Thomas turned off the radio and parked the car silently in front of the apartment building. With his hand gripping the steering wheel, he glanced at the old wooden door of the apartment building. Of course he knew where Brida was staying at the moment, although he had kept away to respect the distance Brida had wanted. Seeing this building, so lacking in character, made Thomas think of the beautiful house he had grown accustomed to; old-fashioned, dark, filled with greenery, inside and outside, the numbing perfume of roots filling every hallway. He always joked that he had to strain his eyes every time he entered her house. It was a memorable place for him. Now Brida stayed in this building, where she surely no longer had the same comforts she enjoyed months ago. Inwardly, he knew she was distancing herself from the -he still didn't know how to call it- 'incident'. He didn't know if Brida still had the intention of selling that house.

Thomas took the sweet he had brought from the passenger seat and got out of the car, the cold, damp air outside buffeting his face, causing him to cough. He already knew the treats, as they often seemed to be nowadays, were an excuse for Brida to accept his apology. He checked the dessert in his hand, a simple cheesecake with whipped cream on top. He knew his wife -well, soon-to-be ex-wife- had made the sweet for a social gathering she had planned that evening, but he was long past caring about the details, so he didn't ask her anything and grabbed one of the custards and his car keys. After checking the entrance for visitors, the old building manager let him pass, having already recognized Thomas from the moment he parked. Thomas gave him a polite smile and climbed the old stone stairs. He found Brida's room easily. The door was distinguished from the others by a severe crack on the frame, the number marking the apartment practically hanging off the door. He ought to tell the old man he had to screw the numbers better, knowing Brida didn't care much for it. He took a breath and knocked.

"Brida?" Thomas glanced at the corridor, then back at the door, knocking again. He really preferred the house to this dump. He hoped Brida wouldn't sell the house.

Brida didn't answer.

"It's me Thomas, I came here to apologize."

No answer. He stubbornly waited. Brida couldn't ignore him all morning. He was going to wait. Minutes passed as he obstinately waited outside the door until he heard distinctive footsteps. He turned his head and saw his friend walking down the hall with a serious face, her gaze focused on him. He tried to smile, leaving the bad mood that had started taking root in him behind. He saw she had a coffee in one hand and a paper bag of groceries in the other.

"Brida, good morning. I was waiting for you."

"Morning." Brida furrowed her eyebrows slightly, hiding her suspicion. "What are you doing here?"

"I came here to apologize." Thomas showed her the custard in his hands. Now that he reflected on it, he felt like an idiot for bringing a cheesecake. "I brought you a cheesecake."

Brida looked at the dessert expressionlessly. "You didn't have to get me anything, and you don't have to apologize for what happened at your home. Alina's comments weren't hurtful."

"She was rude, but I didn't come here to apologize on her behalf. Alina knows why she does it and to be honest, it's not the first time. It's me who I wanted to apologize for and start anew with you. You came to my house and tried to hang out with us like old times. Why are you so surprised to see me here? We're friends."

"No, we haven't been for a time."

Thomas decided to keep quiet and wait for her to open the door. Once it was open, he stepped inside and looked carefully at the humble room. It was small. The kitchen was connected to a small living room sporting a small table with two chairs in the center. There was no television, just a clock on the wall and a radio on a shelf that, by the looks of it, he knew wasn't working properly. He wasn't shocked by the sparse decor, Brida was never homely in that regard. What kept him uptight was the lack of greenery around, knowing Brida was particularly fond of them. At least now he knew what to get her the next time he sees her, instead of bringing her a sweet that Brida was going to throw away sooner or later. Feeling anxious to be in this room again lacking in character, his hands began to sweat.

"Why are you still standing there? Come on in."

Thomas felt apologetic and tried to ignore the remark, entering the apartment fully, and leaving the custard on the table. He moved the chair, which creaked as he sat on it. He waited for Brida to close the door, sensing her presence at his side. "Are you okay? It seems like you haven't been sleeping well."

Her eyes narrowed as she asked, "Why are you here?"

Thomas waited to give a convenient answer as Brida took a seat across from him. He decided to go with the truth. "Because I miss you, Brida, I really do. You should drop your guard with me, at least a little bit. It hurts me seeing you like this."

Brida stared at him and then slumped her shoulders. "You know I don't like sweets."

"I know. I remember how you used to complain about how my desserts made your mouth dry. I didn't want to come here without giving you something."

"And your excuse was this."

"I didn't say it was a good one."

Brida smiled faintly, making Thomas feel gratified. Finally, Brida was beginning to look less cautious around him. He regretted their friendship stranded in this way, but now he was trying to mend it. He knew a friendship this sturdy would soon come together again, perhaps not quite the same, but just as good. What gave him hope was that Brida wasn't averse to his presence. Or so he imagined, assuming Brida wanted to reconnect just the way he wanted to, it wasn't right to assume the other person's actions, he reminded himself.

"I kept thinking about what you said. Do you really want to go back to work?"

Brida shrugged her shoulders tiredly. "Perhaps I made a mistake in requesting all these days for myself, but I have nothing to do, and work, even if it's paperwork, has kept me entertained for a while."

"Well, I really don't know what to tell you," he said, staring at her. He crossed his arms on the table. He had many opinions on the matter, but kept them to himself. "If you want to come back, who am I to say no to you. Maybe then I'll go bother you when I stop by to your desk to say hello."

"You've never bothered me."

Thomas smiled in surprise at the sincere response, not knowing what else to do in the face of such frankness. It reminded him of when his nonna complimented him and he would only thank her politely. No one liked persons who couldn't appreciate a compliment. "Glad to hear that. Anyway, it's true that I miss you. I made mistakes with you and I hope you can forgive me for listening to bad advice." Thomas places his hand in Brida's shoulder, making her observe his movements. Her skin tingled with the new feeling of warmth emanating from him. She felt pitiful at how enraptured she was by a simple touch.

She patted his hand making Thomas give a soft laugh. He removed his hand, settling back in the chair, lowering his gaze to the table. Brida sighed, wanting to squeeze her temples. "You made a decision, and you know our friendship isn't the same anymore."

"I didn't know what to do."

"Nobody did." She glanced at Thomas' disappointed look. If she wanted Thomas in her life, she had to be genuine. She hardened her gaze, clenching the hand she kept under the table. "All I needed from you was for you to stay a little longer."

"I was with you."

"You weren't."

"I'm your closest friend, Brida. I think the only one you have who knows you as you are, and how could I not be with you?" Thomas glanced at her. He controlled his racing thoughts, not wanting to focus on bad memories, but rather on the conversation they were having. He took a deep breath, experiencing a heaviness in his chest. "I was with you from the beginning."

"It didn't stop. The screeching."

"Why didn't you tell me? I could've stayed with you longer." Brida was hurt badly close to a year ago, and deep down he knew she wasn't improving fully. She had a scar to prove it, a reminder of how close it came to killing her. He was so familiar with that scar. He had cleansed that scar, changed the bandages, and placed his hand over it making sure it was closed. He had- Anxiously, he swallowed the saliva that had built up in his mouth and decided to change the subject. "Do you want me to talk about my shift?"

"Alright."

"It was pretty uneventful. I was patrolling around this area, and I had to detain an intoxicated person that was resisting arrest, causing a whole scene. At the end it was a busy day with paperwork," Thomas smiled apologetically. He, too, was easing his mind as he recounted his shift. "I even had to miss lunch and head over to that place we used to eat together. The old lady still remembers me, surprisingly. The food was less greasy too."

"Sounds like a normal day."

"It was, it was."

A silence formed between them.

"I started dreaming again," she admitted.

Thomas grimaced. He had many reasons to feel ashamed, and in that moment he would've liked nothing more than to excuse himself. He wouldn't do it as the excuses were simply empty words. For the moment he had to content himself with the knowledge that Brida had allowed him this conversation.

"I'm trying to improve," she said.

"I believe you." This time he really did.

She missed him too, yet her pride didn't allow her to say it aloud. Thomas saw how her eyes were vacant, fixed on a point, and his heart clenched. He was about to check her pulse, but controlled his impulse. An unconscious habit that had stuck with him since he had tended her during the time she remained bedridden. He controlled it each time he saw her unwell. When Brida placed her other hand on the table, -the one she had been clenching into a fist under the table-, he frowned as he noticed an object he thought already trashed. She still had that awful ring. It was the ugliest thing in Thomas' eyes. The man's last gift after the incident.

"You didn't throw it away."

Brida glanced at the ring on her finger. "No, I didn't." She didn't know why she hadn't been able to throw it away, it was something she was mulling over.

Thomas was vexed, not with her, but at the ring, at the man behind the ring. He consulted the plain clock on the wall, taking note of the elapsed time with a weary sigh. He had imposed himself for too long and he needed to get home. Nothing but trouble awaited him there. "I have to go, but call me if you need anything. If you need anything, just give me a call. I'll be glued to the phone."

A feeling of nostalgia made her sigh. "I'll try."

Thomas smiled in reply.

Brida waited for him to leave and locked the door. She stood there, unwilling to move. Thomas' reactions made her reflective. She looked at her right hand where the ring was and removed it. Thomas was right. She should've thrown the ring away when she had the chance, yet there was *that* something preventing her from doing so. She thought she'd gotten rid of him, the old Brida, too, but she couldn't.

She turned around, surveying the apartment. At the end of the line, she had been left alone just like her father. Hurt people who isolate themselves and close off their thoughts to others. Her father had lived cloistered with his many regrets. She took a deep breath and let it out abruptly, observing the dessert Thomas had brought, recognizing it wasn't one of his recipes. Thomas didn't tend to decorate his desserts. She sighed, placing the ring on the table, and stared at the object.

IV

Adam H. Ortiz pulled out a box of mints from his jacket and passed them to Brida, who took it without much thought. Former Captain Ortiz appeared to have calmed down since the last time she saw him. Although his complexion had changed with time, as it happens to everyone in life, he still looked younger than his sixty-six years. He was robust now, and his droopy eyes made him look fatigued, but there was a stillness about him anyone could see as an attentive and focused man. Brida sat next to him on the park bench, watching people go by, remembering when they used to talk during and after work. Ortiz had the fortune to have known Mr. Castillo, thus he had recognized the family name when she joined the station.

Ortiz observed the horrendous panorama in front of them in the park, full of tall weeds, the rusty playground equipment with the image of the saintly Elkan that seemed to attract all manner of buzzing and chitinous insects, obscuring its face. A sense of loss resurfaced within himself, experiencing the oppression of his musings. The distinctly unpleasant smell of dampness reached his nose, causing him to exhale the odor out of his nostrils. "They told me you resumed your counseling."

"That is confidential information."

Ortiz chuckled at the dry response. Only because he has known her for years can he tell her type of humor consists of monotone answers. "Thomas mentioned it to me the last time I called him. If you must know, only Thomas and I are aware."

"I considered it necessary if I wanted to perform well at work."

"If I were you, I wouldn't worry so much about work. You should start writing, it's helped me a lot, personally. My daughter-in-law gave me one of those small notebooks that you can even leave in the glove compartment. Whenever I have to wait for my grandchildren at school, I take out the notebook and write down whatever comes to mind."

Brida looked at him pointedly. Ortiz had retired months ago, now enjoying spending time with his grandchildren alongside his wife, Gene. He had reminded her of what the psychologist had encouraged her to do, to find a pastime to reduce stress. She had no inclination for art, no inclination for writing either. She exercised regularly to maintain fitness and considered it her method of stress relief, but even Thomas didn't see it as much. It was routine, the psychologist said. "At least one of us is doing a better job of spending his free time."

"I even thumbed through my old notebook on a whim and found some interesting writings. I didn't remember that I used to write poems before. It was as if all those memories hit me in the face when I started reading them. They were horrible. I don't know why my Gene told me she liked them," Ortiz said, passing his hand over the back of his neck and then straightened up. "We need to stop dwelling on the past. It only makes you stagnate. I realized this when I retired and didn't know what to do."

"I'm progressing on my own."

"That's good. I've seen colleagues reject the idea of seeking help, thinking they don't need it, that it'll slow down their careers. I'm glad you're not like them. You don't know how many good friends I lost." Ortiz glanced at her out of the corner of his eye, smiled, and looked away. "Have you been taking care of yourself?"

Brida inclined her head. "Yes."

"That's good," he repeated.

In a way, Brida felt reassured, yet a sense of self-consciousness persisted, only increasing with Ortiz's inquiry. Ortiz rested his hands on his thighs, causing Brida to unwittingly copy his movement. He caught wind of this, observing the natural shape of her fingernails. Now he understood why Thomas was odd when he phoned him. She was wearing the ring. He personally didn't have any strong concerns seeing the ring, for he knew it was a simple object now. But he also knew Brida still gave it undue meaning by holding on to it.

"When I retired, I didn't know what to do with myself," began Ortiz, who continued to look at her hands with even eyes. "I think I drove everyone crazy the first few weeks. And at one point, I went through a period of time where I felt something like what I see in you now. Listless, with no direction."

Brida inclined her head in his direction.

"You know," Ortiz started again, "I listened to the radio on my way here, there's a storm coming. It'll pass through Dameborne and hit the city. Seems like a big one. Gene and I were planning to visit that town, but this might put a damper on it. We'll see. Looks like a good place to gaze and stay for a few days. Gene has always wanted to learn more about our saint and founder, and I've been told Dameborne retains that historic air. I never gave a second thought to the historical figures here, but I guess it's never too late to start reading and getting to know what's around here."

Brida was never a history buff. It was common knowledge Saint Elkan was intimately connected to Dameborne. *He* had filled her in on many interesting facts about the city itself, but rarely spoke of the town. Brida shut down those specific thoughts. "Everyone seems to be talking about that town lately."

"What do you mean?" Ortiz asked, genuinely curious.

"A few days ago I met a girl from there. She told me about some problems happening in town."

"What kind of problems?"

Brida ruminated on the disappearance of Elizabeth Montebrook. How they had already 'closed' the investigation, which actually meant it remained open until solved. Brida ran her tongue behind her teeth, debating whether she should tell Ortiz everything about that night. "The usual issues that happen here. Psychosis attacks, violence, among other types of incidents."

"Ah, those kind of problems. They sound serious."

"They can get serious." A brief silence formed between them. Brida changed her position on the bench. "I was thinking of going to Dameborne myself." It was true. She had thought it through. She lowered her gaze to the box of mints in her hand. Perhaps that was what she lacked, the very interest in knowing something new. Every place had its stories, even the roads themselves had stories to tell. As much as the city had its historic value, it had nothing to offer her. Every detail was tied to *him*. It didn't provoke any strong reaction in her, on the contrary, it made her pensive about how she had lived in direct and short-term interests. A routinized life.

"Maybe we'll meet you there."

"Maybe."

"Gene asks about you often. She wants to invite you over for dinner, but you know she's overcome with shyness thinking she'll bother you. If it were up to her, she would've called you a hundred times by now. What do you think about coming to the house and share a meal with us?"

"Are you sure?"

"I came with the intention of inviting you."

Brida looked sharply at Ortiz, then averted her gaze. "Alright."

"Come by at six. Gene will be looking forward to seeing you," he said with a smile, pronouncing the crow's feet forming next to his eyes. "Thomas is worried about you, but I can see you're doing better from here."

"Thank you."

"You're welcome," Ortiz said, eyeing Brida with gleeful eyes. "I'd like to stay longer, but I have to pick up my grandkids. You know how they get if I don't come early, they start telling their grandmother I don't love them anymore and stuff like that. They know Gene spoils them rotten, that's why they hang on her like monkeys. I'll tell her you'll come for dinner."

Brida watched him leave, noticing his measured, long strides. As always, his presence had brought her comfort. She straightened her posture on the bench and looked up at the sky. The clouds were greyer, rolling and slowly twisting, threatening to break soon. She wondered if that girl, Lisa, got the help she needed.

V

Lisa surveyed the patrons of the bar she had been visiting lately until she found the person she was looking for. Sitting in front of the bar table, alone with a bright drink in hand was Brida with a vacant stare. Lisa seized the opportunity without a second thought and advanced to the older woman, sitting next to her, causing Brida to stiffen and glare at the new presence. Lisa felt a heavy gaze land on her and, to her surprise, Brida was already staring at her out of the corner of her eye. Her eyes looked wary. She tried to speak, to say something, at least a greeting, except her throat had closed up from the nerves.

"I thought you would've left town."

Her comment caught Lisa by surprise, making her choose her words carefully. "I told you they wouldn't listen to me. It's not that surprising to see me here." She coughed, struggling to get the feeling out of her through. Eventually, she succeeded, but even so her voice didn't come out the way she would like it to, losing intonation on the first few words.

"What makes you say that now?"

"Because they didn't listen, like I said they wouldn't."

Brida kept looking at her, setting the colorful drink away from her. She knew they were understaffed right now, few people wanted to be cops in the city no matter how much money was poured into attempting to beautifying the place. She had discussed it with Thomas, how it was becoming increasingly difficult to recruit new police officers. At the moment the job didn't look appealing. Each time the recruiting events went by, out of approximately five hundred interested, only a third turned up, ultimately leaving less than twenty people in assessment phases. Therefore, in the end, fewer were left, knowing what the job entailed, putting one's life at risk several times and not to mention the pay. Most had families and the pay wasn't enough to make them stay. Many knew how erratic the city was becoming. She didn't know whether to believe the girl, but something inside her told her to take into account what she was saying. If they hadn't paid attention to her, it was because they had other cases on top of others, and sometimes, sadly, the townspeople weren't given priority.

"I want to buy you a drink as a thank you for the other day."

Brida blinked wearily, taken aback by the sudden gesture. "No."

"I want to."

Electing to ignore her made the girl take her silence as approval. Lisa rummaged through her purse while Brida was left wondering why she had to deal with this kind of situation, eyeing the girl's movements with disinterest. Gustavo, who was chatting with someone else at the bar, spotted Brida's new companion and smiled at her, raising his eyebrows in question. He excused himself from the conversation and walked over to where his nightly regular was. Brida watched Gustavo approach and narrowed her eyes at the arrival of a third party.

"Your niece, Brida?"

Brida merely snorted in response.

Gustavo took the abandoned glass. "What did you think of it?"

"Too sweet."

"I'd like to order a tequila shot for her, please," requested Lisa. "And a lemonade for me, without ice, please."

Gustavo smiled at the girl. "Sure, I'll be right back." He threw a glance at Brida, who shrugged. She wasn't going to explain to him why this girl wanted to buy her a drink. The situation itself was already odd, she didn't need Gustavo's opinion. Gustavo rolled his eyes and promptly prepared the order.

"Is he your friend?"

"Yes."

Lisa waited for Brida to say more, but there was only silence, which caused her to laugh softly. "I thought you were going to say something else."

"I don't have anything to say."

"It's okay," said Lisa, nervously clenching the strap of her purse. "I came here hoping to see you. I started to think I wouldn't see you again, but here you are! So much has happened to me and I thought I wouldn't be able to get help here either. So, you've changed your mind about this?"

"I'm not a private investigator," Brida said eyeing Lisa, who looked back at her frustrated. Again, Lisa scrunched up her nose slightly, returning to that mental image Brida had catalogued as that of a little mouse. "I'm on vacation."

"You've told me that before."

"And yet you want me to help you."

"I do, I still do," Lisa said quietly. "I'm desperate and finding you that night was a stroke of pure luck. In town, a man told me how I could get help here to find my friend. He gave me directions on who might help me. Coming here didn't seem to help much as I wanted it to. I knew it was going to be hard to find someone like that, but later I realized there aren't that many private investigators or even detectives here." She didn't want to admit she didn't have enough money to hire a private investigator either. She didn't want to recognize how meaningless everything she had done was. Lisa turned to the detective, eyeing her discreetly. Now that she thought about it, the detective's name sounded familiar. She knew she had heard the detective's name before, so when she saw the older woman's ID she hadn't even remembered her manners in quickly returning the card. A strange sense of déjà vu came over her. It didn't feel like she was making it up, but she wasn't certain.

Brida felt each word drain her energy. "Who?"

"Mm?"

"Who was this person you're talking about?"

"Oh, sorry. His name was…" Lisa frowned, concentrating on the memories of her conversation with that man, but nothing came to her mind. She couldn't remember anything, only the image he had projected. "I don't remember what his name was for some reason. I can't remember much, although I know he and I talked a lot."

"Can't remember his name?"

"No, I don't know why."

"If you talked to him that long, then you can describe him to me."

Lisa stammered, fiddling with her fingernails. "I can only remember his demeanor. I don't know why I'm having so much trouble remembering something so simple." Why couldn't she remember something so easy? She felt worse realizing the detective was humoring her and she couldn't even recall such basic details. "All I remember is that he listened to me, saw me cry… He comforted me by telling me that I could find someone to help me with this. I don't know. I really don't remember much. Most of the last conversations I had with him at the end were about what to do to get someone from here to help me with this. I should've asked him more, but I was- I am desperate to find Elizabeth."

Lisa tried not to show how Brida's silence had affected her. She wanted the support of the only person she believed could help her, since she mentioned that man from the park, the older woman became aloof. Lisa kept silent not wanting to bother anymore, she knew how often asking the same question many times always made people lose their patience. Elizabeth had told her several times she had a bad habit. The drinks arrived. Gustavo placed the respective drinks to each one, noticing the change of mood. He raised his eyebrows at the girl who didn't even know what to do with her herself and determined to leave them alone. He knew Brida was going to handle the situation. Lisa, who was already upset, reached for the tequila glass, but something stopped her. Brida had grabbed her wrist, smiling only with her lips in a playful way that reached her eyes. The sudden contact made Lisa jump, causing the drink to splash onto the bar. Lisa felt flustered for a second, raising her gaze to the detective who suddenly let go of her, seeming to realize her action.

"You are a minor."

"How could you tell?"

"A hunch." It was untrue. Brida remembered well the information from the flyer Lisa carried in her purse. Elizabeth wasn't old enough to buy alcohol, but she was old enough to vote. She merely connected the information presented and that was it. Nothing special.

Lisa fell silent and suddenly started to giggle, her cheeks coloring to a pinkish tint. She looked sheepish. "I've already had my share of alcohol, but it's actually pretty reassuring you saw through me like that. Sometimes it feels really nice when they pay attention to you."

"What do you mean?"

"Many seem to ignore me."

"And I don't?"

"No, you don't. At least not like the rest."

Brida frowned, bewildered, then smiled. It was a private smile, in which her eyes went from a dark green to a playful flash of other myriad shades of green. Lisa assured herself it was a trick of the light. Leaving the glass alone now, her courage resurfaced again asking the same request. She placed a hand on the detective's arm as she had done the first time they encountered each other.

"Please, Miss Castillo," Lisa said, turning fully to the detective with a worried frown. "I don't want to push this hard, but I need help with this, can you look at this? I know I'm being pushy, but I need to know where Elizabeth might have gone. She's not one to just leave, she always comes back in the end."

Brida grimaced at hearing her last name that way, she had never liked being called that. The only Miss Castillo had been her grandmother and she was long dead. A headache was building up. "I'm not Miss Castillo, call me Brida. Castillo, if you really want to. The only title I allow others to call me is Detective Castillo, and you know I can't allow that right now either."

"Because you're on vacation?"

"Exactly."

That short answer ended the conversation with a tone of finality to it that seemed definitive. Brida took note of how Lisa was biting her nails from asking her again to look at her friend's case again. It was good that Lisa was fighting for her friend, that she didn't forget her and give up, but her insistence and desperation was making her feel dejected. Gustavo returned and again raised his eyebrows at the sight of the liquid spilled across the bar. He gave the detective another oddly colored drink making Brida sigh and take whatever her friend had given her. She ended up being his guinea pig. Lisa observed as the bartender asked Brida for comments and she tried to be descriptive, however, her answers didn't seem to help. It was entertaining to watch them interact. Gustavo glanced at Lisa with a smirk and she returned an awkward smile feeling her hands tremble. When he left, Lisa felt her mouth salivate from nerves.

"I've been thinking about it and I don't care if you're on vacation or that if you work for the police exclusively. I need help and the police in my town don't do much. The last time I went to have Elizabeth's case reviewed, they pulled me out and told me the file was already closed."

"You're persistent, aren't you?"

"When I need to be, yes."

Brida passed her hand down the back of her neck, rubbing her fingertips over her tense muscles, trying to soothe them. Talking with Lisa, she couldn't help but think that she had taken some time to rebuild herself, to try to heal and that this had become a part of it. Brida looked at Lisa. "I shouldn't be talking about this, least of all to someone like you."

"What do you mean?"

"For starters, I don't know you. Secondly, I'm taking time off because work lately is giving me trouble. And lastly, those in town are still going to send the case here, it will just take time. I won't be the one handling the case, it'll be someone else. Another detective will take over the investigation. The point is, be patient."

Lisa stared at the bright glass, feeling lost, twisting the frills of her long skirt. She wasn't angry at Brida for not helping her, but she wasn't feeling well either. Her stomach twisted nervously. All the sacrifice she made for nothing. She began to feel her throat closing up. Taking a shaky breath, she rubbed her hands together and then pinched the corners of her fingernails to soothe the nausea she was experiencing.

"There is another way I can help you."

Lisa jumped and looked at Brida with wide eyes. "You will?"

"Not in the way you think."

"Thank you so much!" Lisa smiled, taking Brida's hand between her own. It was such a sudden gesture of gratitude that Brida couldn't stop herself from focusing her gaze on the pale hands encircling hers. Lisa's hands were tender and gelid, so unlike the warmth Thomas's hands held. Brida tried to ignore the touch and palmed the small hands in a gesture of indifference.

"Don't thank me."

"Why not?"

"Because I won't help you with your friend's disappearance per se. The case may come up for review in the next few days. My superior will review it and assign it to an available detective. What I can do for you is to make you talk about it and understand your emotions so you can be calm. Do you understand?"

"Yes, I think I do."

"We'll see," Brida said, peering at her wristwatch. She felt apprehensive for the girl, knowing she hadn't fully understood. "Are you still staying at the same motel? I can give you a ride."

"Yeah, I'm still staying there."

"Let's go then."

"What about your drinks?"

"I've had enough."

Brida paid her tab along with the drinks Lisa had ordered and straightened her jacket as they left the establishment. Gustavo merely gave Brida a knowing look and accepted the money without comment, for which Brida was grateful. All the way to Lisa's place for the night, Brida listened to various little anecdotes about what the girl did in her free time in town, about how she liked to go fishing with a friend who always got her into innocent trouble and other stories of the like. Brida listened to it all and as Lisa dozed off, memories flooded back of when she and Thomas used to go dancing together when they were younger, much younger. They had known each other for a long time. They both liked to dance to the occasional song, although Brida didn't dance willingly, if Thomas wanted to and asked her to, she almost always accepted. Those had been good times. Other vivid memories she had were of *him*, how even in touch he sought permission wordlessly. Simple touches or the so-called 'butterfly touches' initiating on her arms and going down to her hands. He-

"I never thought I'd like to spend so much time in the lake," Lisa said, looking at the blackened sky through the car window, unnoticing how Brida clenched the steering wheel. "When I was a kid I was afraid of fish. I don't remember who told me that fish bite your toes, but it really stuck with me and I thought that if I went in they'd eat my whole foot! Come to think of it, it's really silly, but sometimes that thought comes to me when I stick my feet in the lake."

"Sounds nice."

"It is." Lisa yawned, rubbing her face, and hugged herself for warmth, feeling a shiver run through her body. She stared at the older woman with tired eyes. It felt good to be next to the detective. Even though she didn't know her, she felt something comforting coming from being around her. "Have you been told you're a bit intimidating?"

"Sometimes."

"I wish I had a more serious face."

"Your face isn't bad."

"I don't think so. I would like to be tougher, so I wouldn't have so many problems."

Brida turned to look at her and returned her gaze to the road, debating in her mind whether she should open up a little with the girl. Trouble comes to everyone no matter who they are in life. Regardless of who one was, if life intended to put one through it, the logical step to take was to adapt and move on. "Even if you had a sterner face, you'd have the same problems."

"You think so?"

"I know so."

Lisa remained silent leaning her head against the car window, watching the motel sign approaching. On one hand she didn't want to leave Brida's company, but on the other she didn't want to bother the detective more than she had today. The motel where she stayed wasn't dangerous, at least it didn't seem so and she didn't feel so afraid of staying alone in the room she booked alongside with her aunt. Her motel neighbors were an elderly foreign couple and, in the other room, a businessman who always talked on the phone at high hours of the morning. Surely her aunt must be worried about her by now. "You'll help me with this, won't you?"

"In a way," Brida said, then gave a stern look at the girl. "Are you staying alone at the motel?"

"No, my aunt is waiting for me. I didn't come alone to the city." Lisa let out a small laugh at the question, unlocking the seatbelt. She didn't move from the seat, beaming at the detective. "We got a ride into the city, but I think my aunt wants to stay with a friend of hers. I could stay a little longer, but I'd rather go home. I think my aunt will see who I can go back to town with that's safe."

Brida pulled a pocket notebook she kept for her notes out of the glove compartment, holding a pen between the pages as a divider. She quickly jotted down her phone number and the apartment address under the girl's curious stare. "If you need anything, whether it's a ride around here or to go back to town, don't hesitate to call me or you can also come to this address. Your aunt can talk to me if you want her to be reassured of your safety. After all, I'm still a stranger."

Lisa stared dumbfounded at the piece of paper she had received and turned to the detective. She didn't even know how to react to this gesture, shifting her gaze to the paper. "You would really do this for me?"

Brida assented, raising an eyebrow. "It's not safe for you to go so far alone."

"Thank you, really, thank you. I'll tell my aunt about this."

"Go to your aunt then, it's late."

Lisa grinned at the older woman, thanking her for everything again, getting out of the car and headed to the assigned room she shared with her aunt. Brida kept looking out the window until the girl was already inside before starting the Brougham and driving off to her own apartment. She took the scenic route through the city, maintaining her mind empty. When she arrived at the apartment, she left her jacket on the kitchen chair, picked up a bottle of whiskey with a glass in hand and went to her room. Inside the small space there was no light other than what peeked through the window at night. There was a wooden chair in front of the window, where she poured herself a glass and sat contemplating the city. The clouds were streaked and heavy, slowly sending droplets of water that began to hit the window, lulling her.

A great clap of thunder startled Brida out of her seat, causing her to jump up and stare out of the window with wide eyes. There was a particular sound in the rain: the hooting of an owl. She frantically searched for the owl, but the rain and the fog building up on the window obscured it while taunting hoots were heard far away. Brida began to break into a sweat, feeling her stomach twist with nausea until she couldn't stand it any longer and vomited a mix of alcohol and bile on the floor. Brida touched her face, running her fingertips over her nose and mouth, trying to take in her surroundings. Shaking, she took in the shattered glass now accompanied by her own refuse. Carefully, she got up and stumbled to the bathroom. She dreaded to turn on the light, not wanting to create more opportunities to see her own reflection. Even still, with the glimmers and flashes of light coming through the window she could see herself in the mirror, and recognized she was no longer the same woman she had been some time ago. A flash of lighting thundered across the sky, washing the whole room in white light for a few seconds. Brida sat down on the cold floor, waiting for the rain to stop.

VI

Brida Castillo Gallagher was worn out. She hadn't had a coherent thought the past days -she reckoned she hadn't-, but here she was futilely raising the hopes of a girl desperate to find her missing friend. She was in the same wooden chair facing the window, a new glass in her hand. Even with the window closed, a draft entered through the parts the frame that failed to seal properly. Saint Elkan's air wasn't pleasant, far from balmy. It carried a humidity characteristic of the coasts that lay only half an hour from the city. Her eyes wandered around the room and noticed the dampness in the corner; the rain was starting to be a problem, staining the cheap paint of the apartment with mildew creeping from the edges.

She wondered what state that house might be in since she hadn't checked it for a month. Her late father had chosen it for its skylights and the small inner garden space the house had in its center. Over time, the care they gave the initially neglected and overrun space became a charming garden. Her father had spent a lot of time in that garden while she continued her patrols at the time. Both had enjoyed that new pastime, becoming a shared habit. They had even planted azaleas in honor of her grandfather. She was disappointed in herself for leaving the house.

It had been a long time since she'd heard the hooting. Brida's fists clenched tightly as a knock resounded at the door. With a sharp intake of breath, Brida relaxed her hands and checked the time on her wristwatch. It was too early for visitors. She strained to get up, but her legs didn't react in time and she nearly fell off the chair, her joints aching from being in the same position most of the night. She hadn't been able to sleep. Not when there was a chance she could still hear that animal. She ran her hand through her hair, her mouth dry struggling to pass saliva, except her mouth simply didn't want to produce any. She had no desire to see Thomas. Apprehension manifested itself as a knot in her chest. Hurriedly she cleaned her face, experiencing again the same nausea she had felt last night. The hooting had been close, closer than previous nights. If she closed her eyes, the fluttering could still be heard. Another knock on the door forced her to open her eyes, realizing she hadn't moved from the bathroom in her room.

Lisa knocked once more on the door, peering anxiously into the hallway. She didn't know how the detective might react to her presence, she knew she was troubling her greatly. She clenched the strap of her purse between her hands and turned her attention back to the door. The door opened, revealing a miserable Brida, the green of her eyes feeling shallow to Lisa. Where before those eyes were rich, vibrant, and deep, a pallor had taken over, leaving pools of pale, bottomless moss. "Good morning."

Brida stared at the girl, unresponsive. This wasn't the visit she was expecting. Brida took a deep breath trying to appear composed, answering in a low, polite voice, not wanting to startle Lisa with the tension she had felt moments before. "Morning."

"May I come in?"

"Yes?"

"Yeah?"

Brida huffed and opened the door to invite Lisa inside, which made her expression transform from a grimace to a full, wide smile that revealed her dimples. Brida surveyed the apartment and was ashamed of the state it was in. It wasn't cluttered, but it was a spare and bleak room. She couldn't beat her chest for not having the comforts she had a while ago. Lisa, for her part, was more embarrassed for entering a private place. "Why did you came here so early?"

"I wanted to talk to you about several things, but I guess I didn't think through my decision. I guess I got overexcited and didn't want to miss the opportunity to, well, spend more time with you. I told my aunt all about yesterday and she calmed down a little on the issue about me going around the city completely alone." Lisa smiled at the detective, leaving her purse on the small kitchen table. "My aunt works a lot and was nervous about leaving me alone at the motel. Can you open the window? It smells so musty in here."

Brida raised her eyebrows at the change of subject. She stayed quiet for a brief moment and answered with a curt reply: "Sorry about that."

"Don't worry about it, sometimes my room gets something permeating throughout it too."

Brida nodded, puzzled that a simple suggestion from this girl was putting her in a flustered state. She didn't open the window all the way, not wanting the temperature in her apartment to change so drastically. She cleared her throat, causing Lisa look at her quizzically. "I'll take a shower before anything else, make yourself comfortable," Brida said, feeling a twinge of internal discomfort once again at the state of the apartment.

"Okay, I'll be waiting here."

Without further ado, Brida returned to her room and closed the door. She stood there, contemplating the chair in which she had spent the night and sighed, pressing a hand to her temples. A sudden thought came to her in her father's voice. If her steps had gone wrong, then all she had to do was to hurry along the path she knew now was right. Ignoring her reflection as she entered the bathroom, she turned on the shower faucet and took off her clothes, leaving them inside the hamper. Brida stepped into the shower, tensing her muscles at the contact with the cold water. She picked up a sponge and scrubbed it over her body, carefully passing it over her stomach, feeling the scar that lay there. The cut had slashed all the way across her low stomach and reached deeply, having pierced her uterus. Brida ran her hand over it, feeling the raised skin. It had a different color than the rest of her skin, paler and pink.

A memory she could never get out of her mind, just as she could never get it out of her body.

She changed into her usual attire and applied her makeup in front of the bathroom mirror. She combed her hair and styled her layers the way she liked it. Brida came out of the bedroom and watched what Lisa was doing, swallowing saliva, running her hand through her damp hair. Lisa was waiting for her in the kitchen, throwing shards of glass in the trash. The glass she had broken, forgotten in her obsessions with the owl the night before. She observed the care Lisa took in picking up the pieces, however, she didn't want the girl to cut herself, not feeling like dealing with someone else's accident. "Leave it, I'll deal with it later. I'm ready."

Lisa raised her eyes and let out a sound of approval, fully turning to the detective. "You look better."

Brida tilted her head, no longer attentive to the girl's hands, seeing that Lisa had already distracted herself and set the glass shards aside. "Thank you. Sorry for the state of my…" Brida flicked her eyes around the room making Lisa understand the message.

"Don't worry, I don't think much of it." Lisa felt like she was soothing a wounded animal, one that could still lash out if one got too confident. She intuited Brida was a tough person to deal with, but she also now knew the detective seemed to be averse to her presence. Brida glanced away at some random place in the apartment, nodding to what Lisa said, making Lisa smile every time it happened. Perhaps the detective wasn't inclined to social interaction, or maybe Brida was too serious of a person. She shouldn't assume.

"The kitchen has no food, so we can go somewhere to eat if you're hungry."

"Where to? I don't know the city very well."

"I know a few places to grab a good bite. I'll pick one."

"Okay, let's go."

Neither of them minded the silence that had formed. Lisa followed the detective, always careful not to take a step further than her, something Brida took into account and stopped walking slowly to resume her normal pace and make Lisa comfortable. Lisa let out a small laugh, skipping a little when she got off the sidewalk.

"You have lion steps," said Lisa.

Brida huffed at the comment. They reached the Brougham, where Lisa surveyed the streets with curiosity, hugging her purse to her chest as she leaned a little to see better through the window. Brida drove through narrow streets till she found a relatively quiet part of town, where a lady was fanning herself outside of a diner, sitting at what looked like an iron chair.

"Where are we?"

"I used to come here to buy bread."

Lisa nodded at the straightforward answer and got out of the car while Brida shut off the engine. They were in what looked like an old alley, where the floor consisted of large cobblestone. The same lady fanning herself gradually became recognizable with each step. Lisa watched as Brida greeted the lady. Brida leaned on the wall with her arm stretched out, observing the lady straighten up in her seat to see her better. She appeared to be in her seventies with short, curly, gray hair, wearing a modest floral dress with a long-sleeved sweater on top.

"Look who's here," the old lady said.

"Morning. How are we feeling today?"

"Oh, you know, same old, same old. You know nothing happens here," answered the lady a bit bored.

"As it should be."

The old woman nodded, rubbing her knee, and wincing in pain. "It's going to rain soon, you know. My knees haven't stopped hurting since I got up. My son told me that we were going to have some terrible days, lots of rain and wind."

"That's how the weather is going to be all week."

"Now that I'm seeing you, I remember your friend Thomas came by the other day. I asked him about you, but he told me you had taken time off from work, what a drag." The lady then frowned, tapping Brida's leg with her fan causing Brida let out a small husky laugh. "You'd better take care of yourself. You should be grateful they're at least giving you some time off," she said, waving the fan and stopping when she saw Lisa, who was standing there looking into the alley. "And who is this girl?"

"Hm." Brida glanced at Lisa, who smiled nervously, stepping closer to her. Brida placed a hand on Lisa's shoulder, easily feeling her bone over her sweater. "Her name is Lisa. I invited her to have breakfast with me and decided to bring her here."

The lady fanned herself again and leaned back in her chair, stretching her legs. The sound of her knees popping could be heard, making Lisa tighten her lips thinking that it must've hurt. "She's kind of shy, isn't she? Nice to meet you Lisa, come on in. I won't keep you any longer, enjoy your breakfast. Say hi to Thomas for me when you see him."

"I will. C'mon Lisa."

Brida entered the small eatery, passing through the old door with a new chip one of its corners it had acquired since the last time she was here. Lisa, who had remained quiet thus far was ashamed of her manners and thanked the lady before entering. Inside, the diner was cramped, but resplendent with vibrant colors and ceramic plates hung on the walls. Pictures and statues of roosters were everywhere, including some of the plates. Lisa leaned over to get a better look at the handmade drawings on the plates while Brida sat at the familiar table she always chose when she stopped by for a bite. Lisa walked over to the table and sat down, not taking her eyes off all the pictures of roosters that surrounded them. An almost comical level of roosters, really.

"You'll like the food here."

Lisa nodded, looking around. "They seem to be fond of roosters."

Brida ran her eyes over all the images of the roosters, some of which she had personally met thanks to the lady outside. "The owner was involved in cockfighting when she was younger. Her father had the best fighting stock. I accompanied her once and didn't much care for it. Well, now that we're here, I recommend the chilaquiles, they make them well and always make sure you've got a full plate."

"Ah, that explains all the roosters," Lisa said. "Do they have hotcakes?"

"Yes, with plenty of bacon."

Lisa couldn't contain her blissful expression at the prospect of a filling meal leading Brida to feel a sense of protectiveness over her innocence. A boy came out of the kitchen, closing the door behind him and smiled broadly when he saw Brida making a gesture for him to come over. Lisa got a chance here to see how the detective interacted with people she knew as the boy and the detective exchanged pleasantries and orders. It gave the impression the older woman was trying to be social -and that she could be-, but she would politely cut the conversations short, didn't ask too many questions and didn't drag out her answers. The boy nodded at the order, jotted it down in a small notebook and left them alone, returning to the kitchen once again. Lisa stared again at the images of the roosters, resting her chin on her hands, her mind lost in the images of those animals. She really couldn't imagine someone like Brida in those places where she knew there was the familiar 'black hand' her dad always warned her about. Soon she remembered what the lady outside had told Brida.

"Who's Thomas?"

"My friend."

Lisa snorted. "Do you always answer like this?"

"Yes."

"Okay, now you're just messing with me!"

Brida smiled, a slight lift of one corner of her lips making her look both sincere and sardonic. She tapped the table with her index finger. She couldn't find any reason against simply answering the question. "Thomas is one of my few friends and the only one I'd consider close to me. We used to come here to eat right before our morning shifts." And when they had fewer years in their lives, less stress.

"That sounds nice."

"It was."

Lisa observed how Brida's eyes became distant, maybe lost in a memory of her friend. She wondered internally what had happened to Thomas. Brida talked about him as if everything was in the past and they were no longer friends. She wanted to ask a little more, but it wasn't her place to ask those kinds of questions; she'd been chastised about it before. Elizabeth at times would tell her to stop asking so many questions, that it pissed people off. At first she hadn't believed Elizabeth if she actually bothered the rest of the group -Elizabeth's group-, it was just questions. Over time she noticed how Elizabeth's friends would get annoyed when she asked certain questions, to the point where, when she walked with Elizabeth, the group would ignore her presence to focus only on Elizabeth. Oftentimes it confused her as to why they didn't tell her anything and at others she just accepted it. Lisa pressed her lips together and tried to distract her mind by looking back at the roosters. Soon they were served; Lisa with her hotcakes and Brida her coffee with a homemade sweet bread. In silence, Lisa cut a piece of her hotcake, feeling the taste of butter and honey that brought back memories of the breakfast she always ordered in her hometown.

"I want to go home. I can't stand another day in this city," began Lisa, pressing the bacon strips with her fork against the plate. She cleared her throat, feeling it closing in on her. "I've been here for days and I can count on my hands the trees I've seen outside the park. The only thing I liked were the bridges, we only have the one in town."

"And what's that one like?"

"It's near the lake. If you ever decide to come to town I can show it to you sometime. My friend, who I told you about last time, shows me the places where fish go and we feed them if we bring food. I can even show you where all the fish gather to eat the kelp thanks to him."

"Maybe."

Lisa smiled in amusement. "Although, I can say Saint Elkan may have a charm other cities don't. You know, the city feels different, like there's no life here. There isn't much color, and if there is, it's well hidden. But it does have some nice bridges. I'm a fan of them if you couldn't tell. I don't know why I've always liked them so much, although it scares me a lot when they fall down."

"In my experience the city always wakes up at night."

"It does look different at night."

Brida reached for her coffee and mulled about what she was going to propose, inhaling the smell of the espresso in the process. It wouldn't hurt to spend time in Dameborne. She had already told her former superior and his wife she could see them in town if they were up for it. She looked at Lisa who was finishing her breakfast with pleasure. Along the way she could also give a ride to this girl who gave the impression of getting lost again and this time she wouldn't be so lucky. "Do you need a ride into town?"

Lisa stopped eating and looked at Brida confused. "What?"

"I can give you a lift."

"Are you going to help me?"

"I asked if you need a ride, that's all."

Lisa narrowed her eyes and then laughed, covering her mouth with her hand. "You're the best cop I've ever met. Seriously, If I meet that man again, I'll thank him forever! Thank you, really."

"I'd like to meet this man you've been talking about so much," Brida said looking at those glinting doe eyes. She really did have the face of a little mouse. "Tomorrow we can go. I'll pick you up, but I'll talk to your aunt first."

"Sounds good to me. I was already running out of money and I think my aunt was getting exasperated with me. Not in the bad way, but let's just say she's very concerned about leaving me alone. She knows I'm careful, but still," Lisa shrugged. "I don't want to inconvenience her so she can finally do her business and work in peace."

"Hm."

"Besides I'm the best company you could've asked for."

Brida huffed, amused as the girl laughed at her own comment. "I'll see for myself." Inwardly, Brida hoped she was doing the right thing as she sipped her coffee, allowing herself to smile a little and revel in the moment. The memory of a younger Thomas surfaced, and felt her heart weigh heavily on her.

VII

Brida prepared her soft-sided luggage with the essentials: her makeup and toiletries bag, underwear, shirts, pants and two leather jackets. The shoes she would carry in a duffel bag, so as not to dirty her clothes. She finished packing and checked the hour on her wristwatch. It was time to stop by Lisa's. She sat on the bed surveying the apartment, resting her arms on her thighs, interlocking her hands. She didn't have any personal belongings in the apartment. Everything was stored in the house, accumulating dust. Since she decided to distance herself from the house, the only items she took were her clothes and the ring that laid heavy on her hands ever since then. Brida glanced at the landline wondering if she should call Thomas or even her former superior to let them know she was going to the old town. Brida decided it was best to leave. She had already told Ortiz she would see him in town and Thomas- Well, Thomas was busy with his share of worries. She took her luggage and left the apartment, handing the spare key with the old building manager in case Thomas came to visit and could give it to him.

"How many days will you be gone?"

"I don't know, Don. Maybe two weeks at the most."

The manager looked at the detective over his glasses, taking the key and putting it away with the other listed keys. "Be careful over there. I've heard a lot of stories about that town ever since I was a kid. My mother always used to put the sign of the cross over me when we went on vacation there. We only went there once or twice, but my dear mother always made us pray in the car."

"Nothing will happen, hopefully. In two weeks I'll be back."

"I'll keep the key for you if Thomas doesn't come. God bless you."

"Thank you, Don."

Brida headed to her Brougham to pick up Lisa. She didn't feel like pondering about whether what she was doing was right or wrong. Throughout the year she had questioned herself plenty and now she was allowing herself to take a break from that. Lisa waited patiently outside the motel alongside her aunt, Maureen, hands tucked in her coat, smiling as Brida's car approached. Parking in front of them, Brida let the engine die and got out to greet them, opening the trunk in the process. Lisa's aunt returned the greeting and helped her niece put her bags together with Brida's luggage.

"I'm so sorry for the inconvenience," Maureen said, bringing her hand to her mouth unconscious of her nervous gestures. She hugged Lisa's shoulders, looking up at Brida who was closing the trunk. "Thank you for doing us this favor. I didn't know who to call and I didn't want Lisa to go back to town alone."

"It's not an inconvenience."

Lisa rolled her eyes as Maureen started chatting with the detective, who politely remained silent listening to her aunt's ramblings. The girl found it a little funny how Brida just assented to whatever her aunt had to say. The detective listened to Maureen's divagations, surprising Lisa the patience Brida had in not voicing anything against the way her aunt could jump from one point to another. Lisa was grateful when her aunt realized how much time had passed and, in an embarrassed voice, she apologized to Brida for talking so much. Brida replied again that it hadn't been a problem.

"I think my nerves are eating me up." Maureen let out a shaky laugh. "I'd better shut up because otherwise I'll never let you go. Drive carefully, I mean, I think you're going to drive fine, but you know what I mean, you never know."

"We will," replied Lisa wearily.

When they said their goodbyes and Lisa promised to call Maureen when she got home, she climbed into the car and eagerly buckled her seatbelt while she waited for the detective. Maureen had already parted with the same comment to the detective to be careful on the road. Before entering, Brida pulled out her pack of cigarettes and lit one for herself, looking at the pay phone in the corner of the motel. No, she wouldn't call Thomas. She inhaled the smoke and exhaled it abruptly, quickly discarding the rest of the cigarette. Maybe she'd call him when she was in town.

"Did you check you brought everything?"

"Twice and yes, everything is in my bags," Lisa said, smiling. The detective saw the genuine pleasure radiating from the girl and couldn't help but smile a little herself. Lisa turned to the older woman, hesitated, and then smiled sheepishly. "Before hitting the road, can we get some snacks? I'm craving chips."

"We'll see."

On the highway, Brida began to feel apprehensive about going to Dameborne. She hadn't lied when she mentioned she knew someone from that place, her former partner was from there. She never thought she would know the origins of the person who had betrayed her, even if it was to help another, and she was wary of it. Lisa was asleep with a bag of chips in her lap and a small unopened soda beside her. Brida smiled at the image as she drove. Lisa's mouth was ajar, letting out little nasal sounds as she snored. Every time she spent time with Lisa, she felt a horrible desire to protect her from everyone and everything. It reminded her of the good times and kept her thoughts away from stagnant friendships and old bonds. Brida drove leisurely, watching the landscape change, how the forest surrounding the road grew thicker and thicker. She couldn't help but glance in the rearview mirror, trying to retain the image of the city in her mind. Brida controlled her breathing and felt the air getting colder, prompting her to turn off the air in the car. As she drove on, a sense of isolation crept in which made here pay closer attention to her surroundings.

They were close to old Dameborne.

At the entrance of the town stood a statue of a stone dog, which seemed to smile at her as she approached it in an unsettling display of welcome. When she passed it, the town appeared in front of her, covered in mist. It was so still, so quiet that for a moment it felt like it was stuck in time. Brida slowed down to take a good look at the surrounded mountain range, which embraced the whole town. The entrance was old and made of stone with large pillars for support. It was quite low, as if designed with only the clearance of antique wagons in mind. As she passed the entrance, old houses came into view. A few had modern facades, but most still looked like colonial-era houses. The same could also be seen in the city, only without the cultivated land and chicken coops sprinkled about that Brida was beginning to notice. She took in the scene, continuing driving at a low speed, noticing a rooster escaping from the fence of a house. She could see that some parts of the streets were unpaved in the distance, but the entire center of town had cobblestone lanes.

"Lisa, wake up, we're here." Lisa didn't answer, prompting Brida to touch her arm to rouse her awake. Lisa's eyes fluttered open, straightening herself to get a good look of the surroundings on all sides. Her brain didn't seem to have fully awoken with her, making Brida smile as she observed the ritual. "Wake up, dormouse. We're here."

"We are?"

"Yes. Where do I drop you off?"

Lisa looked out the front window and pointed to a narrow street. "Ah, yes. Continue straight ahead until you see a sign that says Gallardo's Inn, it's the only one in these parts of town. There's a motel across the road, away from the lake. I really recommend you stay at our inn, it's centrally located. Finally, I got back home. I couldn't stand the city anymore. I don't know how they do it."

"You get used to it."

Lisa stretched her arms, trying to shake off the drowsiness. She blinked several times and said, "I wouldn't like to live there, everything is close by here and you don't get lost so easily. At the inn we have a map set up inside if you want to see it, my dad came up with it when he went to look at other inns." Lisa ran her hand over her face and watched the town through the windows, calling to Brida when she saw the inn's welcome sign. The neon light contrasted against the fog, where at times the Gallardo's Inn sign was clear and in periods the letters were blurred by the haze.

"You didn't tell me your family owns an inn."

"It didn't used to be an inn, but my dad turned it into one."

Brida passed under the entrance of the inn and parked in the vacant lot, turning off the car's engine. Lisa immediately jumped out to take stretch her legs and take a big breath of fresh air. The inn was a modest one, clean and well kept. There were only eight numbered rooms, attached to each other. Brida opened the trunk and took her bags, and also helped Lisa take hers out.

"Looks like I'm going to rent a room off of you."

"No, I'll lend it to you."

"Nonsense."

"Seriously, you brought me here without asking for a penny and invited me to breakfast last time. You never let me pay for anything. It's the least I can do. I'll lend you a room if you promise…" she took a breath, looking at Brida who was frowning, already anticipating what she was going to say next. "If you promise to solve whatever happened to Elizabeth."

"You know I can't promise that."

Lisa grimaced, furrowing her brows. A moment later, she realized she had no choice but to accept that the detective couldn't help her, not in this way. She hadn't accepted the detective's past words, but now that she was at home, the weight of the situation had fallen on her. "Sorry, I'm sorry, I'm being too pushy. You don't have to promise me anything, I just hope you can hear from Elizabeth while you're here," Lisa said, looking down at her shoes. "Also, be careful if you want to go sightseeing around town. People aren't behaving very well, like I told you."

Brida nodded. "I remember."

"Let's go to the office."

Brida took in the place while Lisa fumbled for her keys in her coat. When she finally found them, she unlocked the door and entered the quaint small office. The office was illuminated by the only window near its entrance, sporting a classic walnut desk with a round lamp, littered with papers and books, connected to a dark hallway where potted plants seemed to inhabit the corners. Family photos hung on the wall in a sporadic fashion. A calendar could be seen along with a few diplomas, seemingly from Lisa's father; Martin Oliver Gallardo. There was no photo on any of the diplomas. Lisa put her bags behind the desk and picked up a worn-out book, quickly jotting down the date and handed the registration book to the detective. "You'll see me around here a lot in the afternoons and evenings, my grandma only takes the morning shift. I seem to recall room three is one of the best rooms, well, I like it myself. You can take that one and put your stuff in there at once."

"How much is it?"

"Fifteen bucks the night. One hundred for the entire week."

Brida pulled out her wallet and took out the money to cover the week, placing it on the desk where Lisa took it without looking at it, scribbling in the registration book. Lisa grabbed a key from one of the desk drawers and gave it to Brida, who put it in her jacket.

Lisa smiled at the older woman. "Watch out for the next-door neighbor if you see her, it's the old lady I told you about days ago. I'd like to say she won't try anything if she sees you, but I'm not so sure anymore. Remember my friend who takes me fishing from time to time? His name is Collin, he lives near here, but he's out of town right now. Maybe he'll come by in the next few days."

"Alright, I'll go put my things in my new room."

"Hey Brida," Lisa started with a shyer voice, trying to maintain eye contact with the detective. Playing with the pencil in her hands, bending it without wanting to break it. "Thank you for the ride and again I'm sorry for always nagging you, but I really want to know what happened. So I can accept-"

"I understand the sentiment. That's what my job was all about."

"Okay," Lisa smiled, feeling better already. "I'll be here if you need anything. Just knock on the door and I'll open it. I lock it for security."

Brida nodded. "I'll see you later. I'll try to rest for the time being."

"Do you want some chamomile tea? It helps me sleep better."

"Don't worry about me, go tell your family you're here and call your aunt."

"Oh, yeah. Almost forgot."

Lisa chuckled in embarrassment and walked down the dark hallway in dismissal. Brida left the office and opened her new temporary residence, Room 3 at the Gallardo's Inn. It was relatively compact, not quite as cramped as the dingy apartment she stayed in back in the city. The windows had long, heavy green curtains, hiding the outside world and leaving the room in shadow. On the walls were several paintings of hares in chiaroscuro. The room had a particular painting of a mountain hare that contrasted with the others, centered above the bed. She sat with her back to the painting of the white hare and inhaled deeply, closing her eyes. For a moment she felt familiar with the place. It seemed to her not new at all, but rather old and nostalgic. A place she already knew.

Brida settled down for a nap, feeling her eyes burning. She ran her fingers across her face as she laid down, closing her eyes. Restless minutes passed, which turned into a full hour, until Brida got out of the bed in annoyance. She ran her hand through her hair, combing it and left the room to de-stress with a smoke. She gazed with weary eyes at the town she had initially ignored. The church stood in the center, occupying it as a place of importance for the town. Houses seemed to surround the large church, making her think perhaps the church was built first and then the houses around it. From the inn she could see it had a somber façade, made of stone, with long, narrow dark windows. The peculiar thing about this church was that there was no cross at the top as they were commonly built. She consulted her watch, noticing it was almost nine o'clock at night. The sky was awash in orange and purple hues, staining the gray clouds with soft colors. Brida walked to the office and saw Lisa writing in a notebook and tapping away on a calculator; it looked like she was doing some accounting. Brida tapped on the glass, calling Lisa's attention, who jumped a little and smiled when she saw the detective. She waited for Lisa to unlock the door and stepped inside.

Lisa raised her head and couldn't contain a grin. She imagined herself having a sore neck every time she wanted to see the detective. She closed the door without returning to her seat at the desk. "Did you have a good rest?"

"I couldn't sleep, so no."

"I told you chamomile tea would've helped you out."

Brida raised her eyebrows and limited herself to a small smile. She appreciated the frankness of her innocent remarks. "Any place you'd recommend for a bite?"

"There's a small diner nearby. I don't know if you're in the mood for something specific, though. There's not much variety here, not like the city." Lisa soon had an idea. "I stayed here doing the numbers of what I lost these days. My family already had dinner and I forgot to grab a plate. My grandma doesn't like to listen to me cook at this hour. She's strict with her sleeping schedule. How about I buy you dinner for all you've paid for me?"

"I don't think that's a good idea."

"Why not?"

"Lisa, I'm still a stranger and older than you."

Lisa shook her head. "You're older but you're not a stranger. You know my Aunt Maureen and you two were talking for quite a while… well, my aunt was talking for quite a while. My aunt talked to my dad and mentioned you." Lisa saw the detective place her hands on her hips, staring her down, intimidating Lisa under the stern gaze. "Besides, I was also thinking of going to get something to eat. With you I wouldn't have to go to the diner alone anymore. I'd feel safer."

Brida didn't even have the energy to lose her patience. She accepted in the belief Lisa would leave her alone when once they arrived at the establishment, which prompted the girl to grab her sweater and reach for the office keys with a big smile on her face. She took a sheet of paper from her notebook and wrote a message for her grandmother in case she came to the office to check on her. If she was still awake. "There's no need to take the car. We can walk over to the dining place, plus it's a good chance for you to see more of the town. C'mon, let's go," Lisa said, locking the office door.

The two walked at a leisurely pace. At times, Lisa would point out to the most relevant parts of the site, such as the park where a copper statue of Elkan lay, the lake with the bridge Lisa had mentioned before, and the central church connected to a recluse monastery, among other places. However, once Brida's attention had been brought to the church, she had a hard time paying heed to anything else Lisa showed her until Lisa took her arm to enter the small diner. It had a sign on top labeled Uncle Rhys' Diner. Lisa opened the door, ringing the front doorbell. Inside there were only two occupied tables and an old man on the bar stool. No one bothered to see who had come in. The eatery had vibrant colors and religious ornaments adorning the walls. In one of the corners lay a small jukebox. There were only three tables available, of which Lisa was going to choose one, but the detective had already chosen her seat at the bar stool. Lisa was a little stumped, but prevailed in her plan to engage Brida in a conversation.

"So, what do you think of the place?" Lisa asked.

Brida regarded the girl. "We'll see about the food first before I say anything."

An elderly man came out of the kitchen. His serene look changing to one of joy when he spotted Lisa. He immediately gave her a hug with one arm patting her back. Lisa hugged the man with a big smile as he let out a small chuckle. "We've missed you around here!" he said. "How did it go with your aunt?"

The man was short in stature, with white hair and thick bushy eyebrows. His countenance was pale with moles scattered over his skin, a clear sign of his age. He seemed to be quite a character. His cheeks flushed rosy, possibly from the heat of the kitchen itself. His eyes roamed over Brida with suspicion. Lisa stopped hugging him and settled back in her stool to get a clearer view of him.

"It went fine. I didn't like it very much," Lisa said awkwardly, noting how Rhys warily regarded Brida from his spot. "Grandpa, this is Brida, she's a cop. She gave me a ride back to town since Auntie Maureen couldn't come earlier. I've been safe all this time. Brida, this is my grandpa Rhys, he's the owner of the place and a friend of my grandma's."

Seeing that she'd been introduced, Brida acknowledged Rhys with a cool nod. "Pleased to meet you, sir."

Rhys seemed surprised by the information Lisa dumped on him. "Pleased to meet you too, Brida. Thank you for returning my little girl safely." His expression had changed from one of distrust to acceptance, relaxing his features. He hummed thoughtfully, observing Lisa with a stern look. He put his hand on Lisa's shoulder in a reprimanding way. "I'm glad Lisa found someone who decided to help her, but even I know no one does these kinds of favors. My little girl here got the idea of going to the city and joined Maureen on her trip there. We knew she'd be fine with her, but one can't help but worry."

"It's understandable." Brida glanced at Lisa. The girl had her eyes on the bar table. "I met Lisa by chance. I had planned to come to town for a few days and decided to give her a ride with Mrs. Maureen's permission."

"Ah, so you know Maureen. Then it's all right, Maureen is a bundle of nerves, if she didn't see any issue with Lisa coming with you then there's nothing to worry about." He patted Lisa's shoulder causing the girl to smile tensely. "Well, I hope you enjoy your stay here and if Lisa starts bothering you, just let me know and I'll give her a few slaps on the wrist. She couldn't stop pestering people here about what happened to her friend. We know it's a horrible thing to happen and many of us are saddened by it. Lisa was affected more than others. The good thing is that we were relieved when Lisa decided to go with her aunt to see what's in the city to distract herself from- well, you know. Now, what would you like to order?"

Lisa, who was silent throughout the conversation, glared at Rhys. Rhys let out a small laugh and patted Lisa's cheek, who looked like a scolded child. She had a pinkish tint to her cheeks and shrunk back in embarrassment. Lisa asked for what she preferred from his recipes and Brida opted to have Rhys recommend a dish. The senior excused himself to go to the kitchen to prepare their dishes, leaving a fidgety Lisa on the receiving end of a verdant stare. The detective's face was serious without any lines of anger.

"I don't like to lie," she said, defensively. The stare continued. "I know I was wrong to lie to everyone here. I know something could've happened to me when I searched for help, but I was as careful as possible. It was just that day where the night caught up with me."

"You were lucky."

The detective's scant words made her understand how severe it all was. Lisa already knew what she did was wrong, hearing it from an official was worse. An officer who had been kind to her without wanting anything in return. "I know. I'll never do it again, no matter how much it hurts," she said, playing with the buttons of her sweater. At least the older woman wasn't angry at her. "Remember I mentioned my friend Collin earlier? He was the only one who helped me when Elizabeth went away. Elizabeth's friends started shutting me off and no one wanted to talk to me at the end. They don't even bother to look at me when I see them at the park."

"Do you know why they do that?"

"No, not really. It's true what I said about only a few people pay attention to me or want to talk to me. I'm really happy you're here. You may not be my age, but I feel better talking to you," Lisa admitted with a shy smile, looking down and now fiddling with her long skirt.

Brida observed the girl's nervous movements and considered letting out a sigh, but instead she inclined her head in a courteous gesture to her honesty. She wasn't going to repeat what Lisa already regretted having done. It would be counterproductive. The food arrived and a comfortable silence formed shortly after as they enjoyed their meal. Lisa broke the silence with a small cough.

"I think I need to tell someone about this without feeling judged." Lisa stopped eating and wiped her mouth with the napkin she was holding. "I know you're not here for this, but I'd feel better if I told you. Elizabeth became pretty rough in our last meetings. Sometimes I didn't know what to say or how to act without overthinking her reactions. When our last fight happened, Elizabeth came by the office to reproach me for asking about her with her friends. She started yelling at me and I got nervous. Collin was outside listening to everything and suddenly I saw him peeking through the door right as Elizabeth started pulling my hair. We started to fight until Collin pulled her off of me. Elizabeth kept screaming and tried to hit Collin too."

"Did she harm you?"

Lisa nodded. "She never hit me before. I started crying. She, um, wanted to grab me. I think she wanted to hug me, but I was too upset to let her. Collin took her out of the office. If it hadn't been for him, I think I would've had ugly bruises all over my face. I don't know. I never would've thought that in the end I'd be hurt that way too."

"Did Collin say anything to you afterwards?"

"He told me he'd had enough of her being like that with me, that friends shouldn't treat each other like that. He also told me to stop being her friend. At that time I didn't want to see anyone. My dad probably knew what had happened because he only asked me that one time and then never mentioned it again. Then days went by and I told Collin I was going to see Elizabeth at her house. I wanted to talk to her about what happened. Collin didn't like me going alone." Lisa coughed, putting her hand to her mouth. Her throat was getting tired from talking so much however, her mind felt like it was relieved of a burden. "I went to her house only to be told by her mom she wasn't home. I tried to reach her several times. At the park, her friends, her mom, places she might go here in town and nothing. Her mom also looked anxious those days. Then one day, when I saw Elizabeth's mom with the police, I knew something bad had happened. There was a long investigation, but they never issued a verdict…"

"Sometimes cases are closed when there are no leads to follow. It's too early to say," Brida said, thinking it would be something she should take into consideration the next time she returns to work if the case isn't assigned to anyone during her leave. "They might have exhausted all trails for the time being, and have already sent the case to the city."

"You think so?"

"It has always been done this way."

Lisa nodded, understanding better how they were organized. "I'm pretty sure I made the police here hate me. I kept asking about Elizabeth several times during the first week and the officer told me that if he saw me in his office again, he was going to scare me off!"

"I'm sure he told you that so you'd leave him alone with the investigation."

"He could've said it nicer!"

Brida laughed huskily, half-closing her eyes. Lisa watched the scene with a big smile, thinking the detective should laugh more. When it was time to pay, Lisa expressed her indignation after Brida paid for everything once again without giving her a chance to even take out her wallet. As they left the diner, bidding their goodbyes to Rhys, they headed down the same streets they had passed through to get to the inn. Brida walked absentmindedly, keeping all her focus on the church, which Lisa took notice of.

"If you want to go to church, the day after tomorrow you can visit it," Lisa said, pulling her sweater tighter against the cold air. "It isn't open to the public usually. It's very beautiful inside, unlike the outside. It's a little somber, isn't it?"

"I think I'll go."

"I didn't know you liked churches."

"I've never been interested in them, but this one appeals to me."

They arrived back at the inn, where they went their separate ways: Lisa to her office, waving goodbye and Brida to her new room. Brida took off her jacket and laid it on the back of the chair by the window, massaging her neck for a moment to relieve some tension before settling in for sleep. The room felt familiar, yet it was still something new unsettling her mind. Now was when Brida began to notice the stillness of the town, in the silence of her own room. She changed into loose fitting dark blue sweatpants along with a lightweight short-sleeved shirt. She laid on the bed, feeling her back rest after a long day. Brida kept her eyes closed, relaxing little by little, taking deep breaths listening to the gentle breeze outside accompanied by rustling sounds that sounded like tree branches swaying in the wind.

In her dreams, a rotting, acrid stench overcame her and began to disturb her deeply, accompanied by the grinding of teeth on flesh and the clacking of beaks. Widening her eyes startled by the sudden pain, she hunted for the source of the sound, but she didn't have to search far. What she saw left her transfixed on the bed. A writhing mass of owls feasted and clawed at her open stomach, raising their bloody heads to stare at her with human eyes, pupils dilated so wide she couldn't even see the color of their eyes. They screeched, beating their wings showing their deformed beaks, baring human teeth. Brida tried to protect herself from the owls' assault, groaning in pain as her arms were scoured by their talons. One last time, she saw her rent stomach before she lost consciousness in the dream and awoke with a start in the waking world. She opened her eyes with a sharp intake of breath and touched her stomach, feeling the scar. There were no owls, only that damned scar, the slash that almost disemboweled her. Brida grimaced with her hair sticking to the back of her neck from sweat. Her hands were still on her stomach.

VIII

Tommaso "Thomas" Cipriani was tired of the same routine. The alarm buzzed him awake at five in the morning, as per usual. Familiar with the morning darkness, he probed for the button to turn it off and lay in bed with his eyes open, staring at the ceiling. He didn't feel like starting his day. He was still bothered by what had happened days before, feeling things had somehow gotten worse. Pushing the covers aside, he got out of the bed, ignoring the presence of Alina next door, who slept without a single worry, or so he assumed. How much he envied her at that moment but, deciding that dwelling on that thought would only hurt him, he quickly ignored it. He felt his bones throbbing and went to take a brisk shower. He prepared for his workday by partially putting on his uniform, undershirt, pants, and boots. He always put everything else on when he arrived at the station. Thomas set his moka pot on the stove and picked up the phone dialing Brida's number, holding out hope till he heard the last ring die with no response. He did this twice until he left the phone with a frown. He thought they'd gotten off to a good start last time he'd visited.

He continued his day, mind wandering as he patrolled routes. Crossing the narrow streets of the city, he looked at his wristwatch: it was only twelve o'clock in the afternoon. Maybe he could check on Brida quickly and buy something to eat while he was at it. With that thought in mind, he drove to the apartment building. Thomas stepped down from the police car, receiving stares from the civilians who expected trouble from the law. He zipped up his jacket, adjusted his radio on his shoulder and headed to the reception desk, where the manager was reading the newspaper. He could make out a forecast for Dameborne, a downpour was coming.

"Good afternoon, Don. Is Brida here?"

The old man looked up from his glasses and put the newspaper aside. "No, she left yesterday. She told me she would stay in town for two weeks. She also asked me to give you the spare key if you came over. Do you need me to leave a message for when she gets back?"

"No, that won't be necessary, thank you. I just wanted to know if Brida was here." Thomas didn't know how to feel about the news. He was clearly confused, yet comforted that his friend decided to take a little trip into town, the farthest away from home she's been in years. He glanced at the newspaper and recalled Ortiz also wanted to go to the old town with his wife, Gene. Maybe that made her want to travel there. "Did she tell you why she was going to town?"

"No, she didn't tell me anything. Let me give you the key before you go," the old manager said, opening his drawer where he kept all the keys to the building. Numbered and systematically sorted. Thomas could see the key with the number of Brida's apartment. "Here it is."

"Well," Thomas began with a polite smile. "It was good to see you again, Don. If Brida's not around, then I'd better go buy something to eat. Say hello to your family for me."

"Likewise. Are you sure you don't want me to leave a message?"

"No, it's fine."

Thomas returned to the car and wondered whether he was trying too hard to be part of Brida's life again, but at the same time he didn't want to miss the opportunity for them to be a real part of each other's lives again. When Brida last told him she had started dreaming, he knew firsthand how heavy those particular dreams were. If the screeching hadn't stopped for her, that meant only one thing: Brida was becoming unbalanced again. She didn't sleepwalk at night, but he knew that, at worst, she would wake up not knowing where she was at first and ask for the specific time. There was a period where Brida consulted her wristwatch regularly. She had inquired once about that man -whom he didn't want to remember- and he answered candidly, knowing she wouldn't forgive him if he tried to shield her from the truth, no one knew where he had gone. Vanished like those scorpions scurrying among the rocks and just like that animal, which hides in the crevices, Thomas was on the alert for this man to come out of hiding. He knew he had resorted to a curious analogy, but that was how he thought of things.

He clicked his tongue and went about his routine until he got home in the evening, tired and stressed. Thomas left his keys on the front table and went to sit in the kitchen, resting his chin on his palm, staring blankly without a fixed point. Maybe he was to blame for not having many friends in the first place -although he admitted he didn't know what the right number of friendships one should have was-, finding it somewhat difficult to find the good kind of friends, the kind who show honest respect and share deep understanding. His coworkers didn't count, they were just that, coworkers. He looked at the photograph he had with Brida, smiling at the camera and hugging Thomas by the shoulders. He couldn't remember the last time Brida had smiled like that. He knew the nature of their chosen work and the experiences they had endured had hardened them both in their own way. Knowing how to relax and communicate was something the retired Captain Ortiz came to discuss with them at a meeting. It was something they'd been discussing for some time, as the suicide rate among the island's officers had increased. They didn't have a high population rate, so it had been something to be aware of.

Lost in his memories, he recalled all the times he had visited Brida in the hospital. Ortiz had been there too, glued to the door, just as furious and shocked as he was. Ortiz had always been a composed captain, but when he found Brida bleeding to death in her own home, he had been shaken by the sight one of his own officers in that state. He was grateful Ortiz didn't send him away when it happened.

The room where Ortiz had found her had a skylight overhead, bathing her in light as if she were a living grotesque sculpture. Thomas grimaced at the morbidness of the description, but it was impossible not to think of her that way when he himself saw how her skin resembled the same white marble. Her hair had stuck to her face and her lost, glassy eyes led Thomas think she was already dead, but when Ortiz touched her, Brida collapsed as she gave signs of life. The illusion of statuesque beauty had been shattered, leaving a wretched woman with an open stomach. Thomas had never in his life felt so disturbed as he had that day. He knew why, the reason being that he was seeing the body of someone he considered family in that state. He so vividly remembered every detail. She was lying on that floor, trying to hold Ortiz's arms unable to even squeeze her hands tightly for all the blood she had shed. Her eyes had shifted at that moment and he could identify the intense anguish she was feeling, her teeth clenched, her eyes crossing his. Her eyes were unsettlingly luminescent. Thomas could see Brida felt wrath beyond anything he could ever understand.

His eyes lowered and saw the stomach out- Thomas tried to get that image out of his head again, feeling guilty for not being able to forget it completely. It was an image that had scarred him.

When it was his turn to look after her in the hospital -it was always his turn, Brida had no one-, on occasion she would hold his hand, sometimes it wasn't even his hand, she would take his wrist and massage over his veins wanting to feel his pulse or try to be near him to center her mind. She had described to him that in those moments when she awoke she didn't feel alive. This type of behavior persisted in some form after she returned to work. At times when she happened to pass behind his cubicle in the department, Brida would run her hand across his shoulders and squeeze his bone. Whenever it happened, Thomas could only manage a smile. He felt bad every time Brida felt the need to reassure herself that he was there. That she was there too. Clearly it wasn't always that way, and he hadn't always been so protective until the 'incident'.

He had spoken to Gene on a rare occasion at the hospital, about his thoughts and she had qualified all of his reactions natural. He had been soothed by her. Mrs. Gene Lombard Ortiz was like fresh air in the morning every time he got to see her. The lady bore a serene image, which made it obvious why his former captain's demeanor changed every time she was mentioned. If it hadn't been for her, he might had been overbearing and wouldn't have known how to cope with the first few nights in the hospital. He was grateful to her whenever he recalled her.

When Alina arrived at the house, she found Thomas still sitting in the kitchen with his uniform on, looking at his photographs. She frowned and hung her long coat on the coat rack. She wasn't in the best disposition to deal with Thomas' mood, let alone when he was looking at old photos. Alina took a big breath trying to relax her nerves. "What do you have now?"

"Nothing."

"Right."

Thomas watched her as she set her bag down on the living room couch and walked over to where he was, getting everything ready to make dinner. He didn't even feel sorry that he hadn't prepared anything prior. He didn't even know what time it was. The silence was tense as Alina prepared a simple dinner, the smell of ham frying with eggs was presently turning Thomas' stomach.

"Are you still mad at me?"

Thomas with all the little calm he had while still trying to control what he was feeling at the moment because of the memories, he answered. "I'm not mad at you, but I'm tired of always hearing the same thing. Since she suffered the..." he passed his saliva, still not knowing how else to call that horrible episode. "That incident, you've been rude. I wonder if it's a fear or something else. I don't understand what happened to make you start behaving like that. Then, when I try to reconnect with her, you start with your passive aggressive comments and make it all go to shit."

"Oh, I made everything go to shit?" Alina said, mockingly. "Every day you had to go see her. It seemed like you never wanted to leave her side, even when I tried to reach out to you, your answer was always that she might need something. You seemed obsessed with her! Brida this or Brida that! Do you know how that made me feel?"

Thomas stared at her, shocked at the nonsense coming out of her mouth. "What the hell are you even saying?" Thomas asked, confused. Had she been jealous all this time of the time he had spent with Brida at the hospital? Was it all just jealousy? It was too idiotic. Jealousy for taking care of someone who had the stomach- He couldn't believe it. "Alina, please tell me you don't think that way. Tell me all your behavior isn't based on stupid, pointless jealousy."

"At first it was, but now it annoys me how much you prioritize her over everything," she said, turning to look at him. "You were never like that with me. You never left your job when I needed you to, but you could make all the time in the world when she fell off her pedestal. Your actions only made me think that you actually love her and not me."

"What?" Thomas regarded her as if she were now a stranger. He couldn't recognize his wife after what she had confessed. He ran his hand over his face, combing his hair in the process, leaving his hand on his neck, feeling like an idiot for not noticing sooner. He didn't even want to answer because he didn't know what to say, his mind was still grasping that all this time what Alina had been feeling was jealousy, as if everything they lived together as a couple had never mattered. There was a point where he loved Alina as one should love a woman, but since everything went downhill it was impossible for him to ignore certain attitudes. He understood Alina was saying all that out of her insecurities, to prove to everyone that what she had always said about him was true. "Are you listening to yourself?"

"I'm right in saying you never paid the same attention to me as you did to her," Alina said, continuing cooking, glancing at Thomas, who was looking back at the photos. "Maybe at first you paid attention, but ever since she was put in a hospital, that changed."

"Brida was a victim," Thomas gulped his saliva, controlling his rising emotions even in light of their argument. It seemed odd to him that Alina, being a woman, wasn't understanding, since the victim had been another woman. "Imagine if *that* happened to one of your friends, you would be there for them too, wouldn't you? She needed support, you should've understood that from the beginning!"

"And I did!"

"No, Alina, you never did. It annoys me when you tell lies. Falling off the pedestal? Alina, you of all people know in what state we found her in. You of all people should understand that. You think that's falling off the pedestal? What do you mean? You think I was having something more with her when I was taking care of her in the hospital. She had all her stomach op- You think I was having an affair with her, when she was deeply wounded, with her stomach… stitched up. You don't understand anything." He looked at Alina, who had already finished cooking her dinner. Alina didn't even dare to look at him. It wasn't right to have a discussion like this, without being able to see each other's faces. Thomas noticed Alina's tense posture, her shoulders contracted.

"I'm really tired, Thomas," she started, putting her plate aside. "You always try to make excuses for her and want to look good for your *friend*. As far as I know this isn't how friends treat each other, you treat her differently than me and I don't deserve this, Thomas. You always do the same thing, you always do whatever the fuck you want and I'm tired of it! Once or twice was fine, but you always had to go see her."

Thomas gave a grim look to her. "I can't believe the crap you say."

"What?" she asked, tauntingly, turning her head to see him, believing she was winning the argument. "You know I'm right, because otherwise, you wouldn't be reacting this way. I knew it would always be the same with you. I knew there was something wrong with this *friendship* you two have. I don't know why I didn't realize it before. I even knew when a man has a *friend* like that he can't be trusted, but I did trust you, Thomas, because you were different but you are just like everyone else!"

"You really don't know what you're talking about."

"Think what you want, but you're not her friend either. If she still considered you her friend, she would have called you by now, right? But she hasn't because you're no longer anything! Don't think I haven't noticed how many times you have tried to call her since that day you went to see her. Just admit that you're in love with her, that you've always been in love with her all this damn time!"

Exhausted from the moronic argument, Thomas got up and headed for the entrance, grabbing his keys and wool jacket. "Look, I don't feel like arguing anymore. You're out of your mind, Alina. Every time you said I was having an affair with Brida, you were actually seeing some coworker because in your rotten head you wanted revenge for something that didn't happen, hasn't happened, and never would. Your sister? Apparently her conscience bothered her and she told me all about what that guy was gifting you. You try to make me jealous, but all you manage to do is make me see you for how immature you are. Here, the one who's doing everything you accuse me of doing is you."

Alina looked alarmed, opening her mouth in shock and then turned her expression into a sneer. "Go fuck yourself! I regret meeting you, I regret talking to you, I regret saying yes to everything, I hate you Thomas! I fucking hate you!"

Thomas left the house, closing the door harder than usual, not wanting to hear any of her comments. He was frustrated by everything that had happened. Alina knew nothing of his friendship with Brida, the two of them had lived through moments together that can forge inseparable bonds between people. They have always respected each other and had great communication since they met. Their friendship had been made rockier thanks to the events of last year, but he knew that if they reconnected they could at least try to bring back some semblance of normalcy. Once again they could support each other as they had always done and trust each other. It became apparent Alina never had a friendship this sustaining and memorable, he wasn't surprised. He knew firsthand how Alina treated her friends. He wasn't going to go into that thought, as it wasn't his problem. Thomas took a deep breath, keeping his eyes trained on the narrow street outside his home as he walked along the sidewalk. It hadn't been a good idea to leave the house in uniform, but he didn't feel like going back even to change. In his mind, he just hoped he wouldn't run into someone who felt like stabbing a cop, it wouldn't be the first time. He let out a small snicker at his thoughts. Maybe he could go to Gustavo's, he hadn't seen him in a while. Gustavo was another good friend with whom he should communicate more.

He put on his jacket, zipping it up to his neck and tucking his hands into his pockets maintaining his body heat from the damp cold of the city. He crossed the street quickly, reflecting on the years he had shared with Alina. They had met through a mutual acquaintance and, as in all relationships, things worked out so well they ended up marrying. His family had congratulated him when he shared the news of his upcoming marriage, except his mother hadn't smiled at him at first and had even looked at him doubtfully. Alina had reproached him for his mother's behavior. Thomas approached his mother that same day when Alina kept bringing up how his mother wasn't happy with the news. His mother had been arranging some vases and without even glancing at him, she pointed out the decision he was undertaking was too big for a girl like Alina. A *girl* like Alina. At first he hadn't understood her words and, after his marriage, every time he went to see his mother, he felt humiliated. He knew what was going through her mind, that he too was a boy. A *boy* who hadn't measured his choices. Thomas stopped dead in his tracks, nauseated by his thoughts, and coughed to mitigate the sensation. At that moment he hated himself, this was nothing new. Maybe it was better to return home.

He needed to ask for time off. He was so tired.

IX

The hare stared at her from above, its black eyes seeming to bore into Brida's own. The only thing she knew about hares was how they hid during the day and were active at night. She didn't even know if that was entirely true. She had never been interested in those animals. Her head was throbbing against her skull. All those times she only drank, ate once a day, and didn't sleep well were taking their toll. She picked up her wristwatch she had left on the bedside table and saw it was eight o'clock in the morning. At least she didn't wake up any earlier than that. Brida took a deep breath and proceeded to change her clothes, leaving the room with her leather jacket in hand.

Brida smoked peacefully, sitting on one of the benches outside the inn. She heard water running and turned to see an old woman walk with a hose in hand and a concentrated look, watering the plants and cleaning the pavement with the pressure of the water. The old woman had a face similar to Lisa's, though her hair was greyer than the young girl's characteristic carrot red. Her complexion was thin and her hands still held a youthful delicacy. The old woman felt a glance and nodded to the stranger as she went about her morning routine. Brida thought she was going to ignore her presence, yet every time she moved on the bench or grabbed herself a fresh cigarette, the old woman glared at her. "Morning." Brida curtly greeted, already tired of the lady's accusing stare. The old woman didn't respond to the greeting. Brida disinterestedly observed her. It was obvious Lisa hadn't grasped her grandmother's personality, but who was Brida to judge the lady when perhaps she had done the same when she was on the job.

Brida took her time to think about whether she should visit the church, remembering Lisa had remarked it would be open today. Her curiosity had intensified since then. She had never been interested in religious sites -she herself wasn't religious- but something about the one in town had been drawing her attention recently. Brida got up from the bench and headed in the direction of the church, passing the park, leaving Elkan's image behind. The church had an old colonial quality to it, akin to the rest of the town's oldest buildings. Brida took notice of its form, seeing that it was molded after a cruciform plan, a characteristic feature of the Anglo-Saxon churches; something she had learned with *him*, a fact that forced her to steady herself as she recalled it. The small windows with triangular lintels had stained glass windows with images of animals on them, wild, unrestrained. At each corner of the towers there seemed to be several statues of ravens, positioned as if to protect the sanctuary. Brida noted the church attentively, walking slowly towards the entrance.

The entryway had two stunted columns and a door of the same aged green cooper that distinguished the Elkan statue in the park. The doors had two worn out dog heads on each side biting a hoop. Their furious eyes seeming to glare at visitors, but upon closer inspection they shared a smile akin to the statue at the entrance of the town. Brida pushed the door expecting to see a religious beauty, but there was only darkness. She slipped in slowly and the door closed behind her, chasing away what little light there was from the outside and leaving her in shadows. It seemed impossible, since the church had several windows, but no light came in at all as if the church itself repelled it. She didn't move from her spot until her eyes became accustomed to the gloom. She could now see the hidden magnificence of the place. There was a large, old cradleless chandelier hanging low in the center of the chamber. The wooden benches lined up on the side of stone pillars that supported the ceiling.

On the walls were paintings depicting the deaths and ruin of holy women. One was decapitated, another was mutilated and mauled, and another simply presented her head to the viewer. The paintings were done in chiaroscuro like the paintings of the hares in her room. The images seemed to be captured at the exact moment where they were being executed by men in armor and beasts, yet they seemed barely present even in the scenes of their own murder, as if at any moment they could disappear into the darkness that surrounded the image. Their agonized faces seemed to have a light of their own and every detail of their tears could be seen from where she stood. She could tell through their faces that they were experiencing a betrayal she could never forgiver herself for, their expressions emerging from the darkness with clarity as they looked at the visitor to the church. Brida looked down, feeling ashamed of her own past as those paintings made her remember the moment she was betrayed by her own partner, when he had left her with a gaping stomach. She could never forget it, never forgive it. She let out a heavy sigh and kept walking away from the paintings. She didn't want to keep looking at what she could've possibly been in the past.

At the end of the hallway, there was a quartz altar, with a holy mantle on it. There were no saints, nor any sign of the Messiah in the church. The only image behind the altar was a large painting of angels piercing demons with their lances, stepping on them with serene faces, seeming to have a faint smile as the demons agonizedly burned in the living fire. Brida clenched her teeth, feeling for a moment as if the painting had come to life. Her footsteps echoed as she took a seat in the first row of pews, unsure of what to do in such an esoteric place as this. She wondered if people had thought the same thing when they entered a church of this kind. Every little movement made the wooden benches creak, echoing in the desolate space. She didn't know how long it took before she felt herself relax as she looked at the painting behind the altar.

"Welcome to our church, woman."

A soothing voice startled Brida, making her turn her head to discover the source of the voice, where she found two nuns were standing like figurines in the middle of the aisle. A young nun stood next to an older one, both holding the same position, their hands adorned by large rings resting intertwined on their lower bellies. They wore the typical religious garb Brida was familiar with, the long black veil accompanied by the white bandeau, and the white coif and guimpe over the habit. They didn't have the usual crucifix on their chest, nor the chaplet on their hips. Instead, they wore necklaces of viridescent gems seemingly twinkling with every breath they took, a medallion of a bird Brida couldn't make out in the center of their chest. On their hips they wore an elaborate belt of small beads that fell to the end of the skirt, with several golden tawny feathers touching the ground.

Brida stood up, almost stumbling in her haste. "Thank you… for receiving me."

The younger nun smiled tenderly at Brida's trepidation. Brida could see their faces better now, entranced by their appearance. The young nun was beautiful, with marble-black eyes, a straight nose, and thin, elegant lips. The older nun shared much of the same features, matured by age. Their skin looked like it had been painted by a Renaissance artist, pale and without any hues of pink on their otherwise pale skin.

"What is the reason for your visit?"

It was hard to tell which of the two had spoken. They had the same eerie smile, their lips never parting. Their eyes were pitch black, they seemed to be mirrors that Brida could see herself in. She tried to dismiss those hallucinations from her head by clearing her throat.

"I wanted to get to know this church, but if I'm intruding I can leave."

"No need for that. We were only asking what your reason for being here is. We all have one. Stay if you wish, we won't bother you while you are here." The voice had a low, almost hoarse timbre.

"No, no need to concern yourselves," Brida politely replied.

"Do you like it here?"

Now Brida could identify who had spoken. It was the young nun, who had a more melodious timbre than the old mother. She asked herself if she liked a place as strange and intoxicating as this one. She had never seen anything like this in her life. She had never seen a church where they shared images of slaughtered women and demons being sentenced in such obvious and vicious ways; it was typically more subtle, but this church was unusual. She was never one for religion and the only religious building she knew perfectly was the chapel her old school had with its saints and virgins. Even so, she couldn't give a clear answer, she was ignorant of several factors of churches and thus her opinion didn't carry as much weight, at least, in her perspective.

"So far I'm liking it."

"We're glad to hear it."

"Good..." Brida said slowly, gazing at the narrow windows. "I noticed there isn't much light coming in here. I hope you don't mind, but when would the altar candles be lit?" She didn't want to keep focus in the dim light on images that only brought delirium. A candle could make her focus, give her some guidance.

"It won't be necessary, your eyes will soon get used to it. The light only harms here."

Brida nodded, trying to understand what they meant without success, while the sisters walked towards the altar with the same serene pace they had approached her with before. Brida followed them with her eyes. The older nun pointed to the candle on top of the ancient metal ornament. The younger nun took one of the candles from the altar and gave it to the older nun along with the table runner, who took it and left them. Only her footsteps were heard in the quiet altar room, followed by a creaking of an old door.

"We can compromise by lighting the altar, since we see you like the light so much."

"Thank you for being kind."

The young nun smiled lovingly at her, causing Brida to tentatively smile back. She felt herself relax again with the new religious presence in front of her, observing how the nun cleaned the altar. Brida couldn't stop glancing at her and felt rude for staring too much. She heard a soft chuckle coming from the sister. The nun seemed to have realized what was happening, causing Brida to control her expression, maintaining her face earnest.

"Come, approach the altar."

Brida took a moment to comply with the order, leaving her place. Her footsteps echoed throughout the church and positioned herself at the side of the altar, observing the nun. As she stood close to her, she could perceive a peculiar, yet oddly familiar numbing smell. The scent was thick and strong, and lingered in Brida's nose. Brida tried to resist her urge to inhale the aroma again, breathing softly, shifting her head to one side in a courteous manner, lowering her gaze. She betrayed herself in her distraction, inhaling the scent of plants and roots. Others would think it was an oppressive odor, but for her, it was like something she knew. Something she missed dearly.

"Forgive me, I wanted to see you better."

Brida gave a curt nod, keeping her eyes lowered.

"You have a beautiful pair of eyes."

Brida glanced at the nun who was staring directly at her, the pupils appearing to be the same color as the iris, making them look intensely black up close. She had never witnessed anything like this before. The brown of the iris could always be seen no matter how dark it was. The nun moved noiselessly while Brida watched her curiously. "Thank you."

The young nun, who was satisfied with her response, turned to continue arranging the altar, bending down slightly taking what she needed from inside the altar. Taking a new table runner for the altar, which was decorated with weavings of snakes with fanged, agape maws, the young nun draped it overtop the bare ornament of worship. Now that she was closer to the sacred place of the church, she didn't see the tabernacle her former school chapel even had. She knew churches weren't the same, perhaps they were managed differently. "My companion will be back with your lit candle."

Brida assented silently. Soon she caught another scent. The older nun approached with a candlestick in one hand and a lit candle in the other. Now the humid and putrid smell that had lingered in her nose mingled with the odor of the candle flame. The older sister took on the task of illuminating the altar. She was wrong, the light gave greater life to the paintings. As each candle was lit, the angels smiled more. Their lances glowed and tingled with radiance. The condemned demons were now mere people falling off precipices. They had no wings, no horns, much less the goat's feet she had heard so much about from the elders since she was a child. The altar had taken on a different air now that it illuminated. The snakes decorating the center took on a vibrant color. Another person might have felt all this peculiar, perhaps excommunicated the church for not having any image of a saint, virgin, or the Messiah himself. She didn't know what was worse, to see a dead man in the center of the chamber or the violent paintings shown here.

"Have you been in a church before?"

"Not like this one." Brida turned her head to the younger nun. She couldn't tear the faces of agony from her mind. "My grandparents went every Sunday without fail. My father, on the contrary, never had a strong opinion about religion and, to be honest, I don't like the concept of it." The words had escaped her mouth, falling in an uncomfortable silence at the information she had blurted out.

"Sounds like a father who had his mind focused on other present matters."

"I wouldn't call it that," said Brida softly, looking down at the altar. If she had already spoken, better to finish what she had started. "When my grandmother was still alive, I remember she used to tell me if I prayed at night my sins would be forgiven. My father disagreed with her and told me good deeds born out of one's own free will were best seen."

The elderly nun smiled placidly at her response. "We have always liked people who are able to see beyond simple fanaticism. People who see beyond merely individuals telling them and making them act in some way for their benefit, that they stop following the sheep horde and leave the shepherd aside… we've always liked them."

"I couldn't comment on that, but I have seen cases of fanaticism in my work."

"No need to be so formal with us," said the younger nun, finishing the last touches on the altar. She picked up the dying flowers from the vases, resting them on one of her arms. "Think of this old place like your second home."

"Thank you for your hospitality."

"You're welcome," said the older nun. "We have enjoyed your company. Would you like to stay and eat with us? We know it's an unexpected invitation, but it's been a while since we've had a visit that interests us. Before you came in, we were already preparing the meal. We always overdo it."

"If you are sure."

"We are."

The nuns turned to walk away and Brida followed them, passing through the doorway and smelling once again that damp aroma permanenting and impregnated in the very walls of the corridor. They reached the dining room, where there was a long, old wooden table with eight chairs, high-backed and made of a deep, dark wood that echoed a powerful scent Brida had been surrounded with during her time in the church. The room was cold and humid, the walls were made of stone with no decoration on them. The young nun placed her hand behind Brida's lower back, causing her to tense from the gentle touch.

"Sit at the head of the table," said the younger nun. "It's been a long time since we've had visitors and we want to make sure you feel welcome."

Brida was taken back by the flattering comment. "No visitors these days?" She wondered, glancing at the younger nun, and raising an eyebrow. "I was told the church wasn't always open."

"We maintain the purity of this place, and as such we don't accept many visitors."

"Either way, I can see why this place is so revered despite not accepting visitors," said Brida.

The young nun smiled in response.

"When was the last time the church had visitors?"

"The last time we saw someone was at the last ceremony."

Brida wanted to let out a sigh at the evasive response, but didn't do so out of respect for the religious women beside her. She rested her hand on the head of the chair. "I think I'm having a little trouble understanding how it works here."

"You'll understand soon. Please, have a seat now," said the older nun.

Brida sat in the chair that was pointed out to her. The nuns began to set the table, decorating it first with a detailed white tablecloth, silver cutlery, porcelain plates, crystal cups... It was like witnessing a sacred ritual. One in which she no longer participated since she gradually became lonelier. Since her grandparents had passed away, it became rare to eat at tables decorated this way unless she was eating with Thomas or with her former captain. Absently absorbed in their movements, her grandfather's voice came unexpectedly within her memories, calling her '*Mi azalea*', playfully folding her ear. His voice reprimanded her to not be so serious, to smile once in a while so she wouldn't become like her father, to avoid carrying the heavy blood of the family. But then the old man would eventually smile sadly at her, lamenting what she had inherited. She snapped out of it as the sound of the porcelain clicked against the wood. Brida caught another peculiarity of the sisters: As they richly set the table, and perhaps even before Brida had taken conscious note, each of the sisters mirrored the movements of the other. As the delicate, youthful hands lay down a clear crystal glass, a pair of mature but equally delicate hands lay down a lit silver candle in the same motion.

"The table is ready. I'll keep you company while my companion brings the food."

The younger sister passed through a doorway, appearing to head for the kitchen. The older nun took a seat to Brida's left, resting her hands in her lap, waiting for her companion. Brida had her legs crossed and rested her arms on the old handles of the chair. She clasped her hands together, wondering if it was right to inquire about the disappearance of that young girl. She decided to give it a try, otherwise, she was certain if the nun didn't want to talk about these issues, she would respect it. "Have either of you heard of disappearances in town?"

"No," said the older nun. "Has something happened?"

Brida glanced quizzically at the older nun. It seemed strange to her the nun knew nothing, although she rectified her initial thought, perhaps this congregation was reclusive. "A girl has been missing for three weeks, soon to be four. Her name was Elizabeth Montebrook."

"I remember a Montebrook. The girl from the Gallardo's often trailed behind her."

"Do you know Lisa?"

"Of course we know her. We know everyone who is born and lives in this town, even those who have died or are about to die. The only one we don't know is you," the older nun replied, giving Brida a suddenly appraising look.

Brida then realized she hadn't given her name to any of the sisters. Apparently she had forgotten common decency in her delusions with the paintings. Straightening up, she rectified her manners before the religious presence at her side. "I'm Brida Castillo. I come from Saint Elkan-"

"I didn't ask where you're from, or what your name was, it doesn't do us any good for us to know," said the older nun. "You have a familiar name, come to think of it, so familiar that it sticks in our minds. Have you ever been here before?"

"This is my first time in town."

The nun stared at Brida with a scrutinized expression before straightening up in her chair and lowering her gaze. "It looks like the food is ready, I can hear my companion coming back. I look forward to hearing your opinion at the end of dinner, we like to cook for welcomed visitors. If you need anything else, ask."

"Thank you."

The young sister arrived with a silver tray full of food and a wine bottle without a label. She began setting out the plates, one filled with meat, another with offal and roasted vegetables, one with lentils and beans and the last with an assortment of dried fruits and nuts. The elderly nun took the bottle and poured it first into Brida's glass, the liquid was intensely red and vibrant in the crystal glass. Finally the food was served. Brida looked at her plate full of meat, pomegranate seeds were scattered amongst a bow of dried fruit, pieces of kidney accompanied by lentils. It was a hearty meal.

"This all looks good."

"We're glad to hear that," said the younger nun. "Let's enjoy the food."

Brida took her cutlery and cut a small piece of the meat, noticing a scent that should be more familiar to her, like the meat of a cow but more pungent. When she tasted it, she felt a smooth texture as it touched her tongue, akin to that a heifer. The pomegranate seeds only made it taste richer and heartier, causing Brida to let a soft sound of delight, a sigh one could only hear if they paid excessive attention, lost in her sensations as her brief moment of surprise at the utterance was smoothed away by the meal. The nuns smiled at the new experience unfolding before them, and soon their gazes became sharp and scrutinizing, passing over Brida's body until they fixed on her lower stomach.

"What kind of meat is this?"

The mature nun tilted her head and folded her hands in her lap, causing the younger nun to mirror the movement. The younger sister smiled and quietly answered the question. "Bull."

"I've never tasted bull before."

"Eat the whole plate, it will do you good."

They ate in silence, enjoying their dinner. Soon Brida realized she had been served an extra portion, noticing her plate seemed fuller than her dinning companions. She picked up her glass and sipped the liquid, discerning a metallic flavor. Engrossed in the new sensations of the meal, she hadn't noticed their eyes staring at her, especially the attentive look of the younger nun. She finished her plate, feeling her stomach become heavy in a comforting, warm way.

"I can't remember the last time I had such a filling meal," Brida said.

The nuns were delighted, truly warming towards the detective. The older sister answered quickly. "That's good. As we said before, we love to cook for welcomed visitors. We don't always have company who appreciates our cuisine."

"Thank you for inviting me."

"We would love to have you join us again," said the younger sister.

Brida bowed her head slightly, appreciative for their eagerness to have her again. She lingered with the nuns a while longer, indulging in the serene company till she fixed her gaze on her wristwatch. "I should be getting back now. I don't want to take up any more of your time," said Brida, feeling embarrassed in some way. She had eaten so well and now she felt she had been a bad guest for not staying until the nuns were ready to conclude their mealtime conversation. She knew religious women had their own routines and didn't want to impose herself on their activities. The young nun looked solemn but quickly smiled at the detective. It didn't reach her eyes.

"On the contrary, we enjoyed this meal with you," said the older nun.

"Please visit us soon, our doors are open for you," said the younger.

"Will the church be open again this week?"

"Come by the end of the week. We will have our doors open at the same time you came in today. It has been a long time since we had guests, we've forgotten how special it can be to have them with us," answered the younger nun, continuing smiling at the detective. Brida couldn't believe they didn't have visitors inside this prodigious place. The nuns escorted her to the entrance and stopped halfway down the hallway to watch Brida pass through the green doors, returning to the static world of the town.

X

You need to grow up, Elizabeth had once said. Lisa set aside the pitcher of lemonade she had made to wipe the counter clean of the juice left by the lemons after slicing them. Lisa grimaced, her eyes burning. She rubbed her eyes against one of her palms, sniffing, feeling that hole in her heart expand. She hadn't been at ease since she got home, not even when she kept hugging her father to the point where he chuckled at how mellow she was being. Wiping her tears, she blew her nose and headed to the office waiting for Brida. Suddenly, she spotted a tall figure walking past the office and, in a burst of courage, called out to Brida, who turned her head in her direction, blushing for having caught the detective's attention just like that.

"Sorry, um, have you eaten yet?"

"No, no yet."

Lisa perked up, revealing those adorable dimples as she smiled. "Would you like to have lunch with me? I cooked today and I'd really like for you to join me. It's not much, but I know it will taste fine. If you feel like it, of course… I wouldn't want to impose or anything." Without getting an answer, Lisa continued, "I just want to talk a little bit more."

"Alright."

Lisa, startled, believing Brida would refuse, grinned at the detective, and led her down the corridor of the office connecting to her house by opening the internal metal grille her father had installed years ago as protection. Once in the kitchen, they sat down at the round table, where the girl couldn't shake the excitement of being able to provide Brida with a little something, since Brida never let her pay for anything.

It was a simple meal since she didn't often manage the kitchen, her grandmother wouldn't allow her no matter how hard Lisa tried to take the initiative. "Let me pour you the lemonade," she said, grabbing the jug. "I hope you like everything. I don't have much experience in the kitchen, but I can make simple meals. My grandma won't let me near the fire because I once burned myself with the griddle. It was an accident, really, I thought it was off."

"Won't your family join us?"

"No, they already ate." She was unwilling to admit the whole plan to invite her to lunch, much less how she went out of her way to prepare everything. Her father could've been an excellent addition, but he had been indisposed. She would've enjoyed having her father meet the person who had helped her so much in the city. Perhaps some other time. Lisa ate sitting across from Brida while recounting how her morning had gone, pausing for short breaks to eat pieces of her meal. Lisa stopped eating, gently wiping her mouth with the napkin she had crumpled in her hand. Every time she spoke, she stopped herself when she was about to touch on topics she really wanted to talk about, making even the detective notice how she restrained herself. As much as she felt safe at home, she didn't want to talk about those topics there. She swallowed saliva nervously, feeling a lump in her throat. She cast a worried glance at Brida. Brida was pale looking, paler than she was used to seeing her, and her dark clothes contrasted with her complexion, lending her a sick appearance, her opaque eyes were staring at the food she was eating. Her excitement about inviting Brida to have lunch with her may have been too much for the detective.

"Are you feeling sick?"

Brida smiled tiredly. "No, I just feel heavy."

"Maybe something didn't sit well in your stomach."

"Most likely. I had a hearty meal yesterday."

"Are you sure you're feeling okay?"

"I'm sure, don't worry."

Lisa remained silent, wanting to ask again if she was okay, pecking the pieces of chicken on her plate with her fork, still watching Brida with concern. She didn't know what else to say, maybe she could make a cup of chamomile tea for the two of them, so she could soothe her nerves as well. She pinched the edges of her fingernails as she watched Brida taste the lemonade, cringing when the detective raised her eyes and gave her a small smile.

"It's too sweet."

"I don't like it when it's so sour," Lisa admitted. "Next time I can make it sourer for you."

Brida offered the same smile, and in that instant Lisa saw verdant eyes come alive. "Thank you for inviting me. Would you like to go to the park with me?" asked Brida, taking a napkin, wiping her hands. "I'd like to get a better look at that Elkan statue, but I haven't had the chance. Besides, didn't you want to show me all the good places in town before?"

"Ah, yes, that's right!" exclaimed Lisa, smiling at the reminder. "You're going to love the park, it's one of my favorite places. Let me put the dishes in the sink, don't worry about it, I also have to get my sweater. I don't want to catch a cold."

"Alright, I'll wait for you outside."

Lisa nodded, putting the food away and leaving the plates in the sink. She went to her room to grab one of her wool sweaters, exchanged her slippers for sturdy boots and headed to where Brida was outside. Lisa took the keys of the office and smiled when she realized the table had been cleaned, there was no trace of food. She locked the door while Brida was lighting a cigarette, smoke curling up in the cold and floated over to Lisa with the breeze. She stared as Lisa approached, who made a face when she smelled the smoke.

"I don't like the smell of cigarettes, and you smoke like a chimney."

Brida huffed at the comment with a playful glare, taking into account how Lisa's sweater was badly adjusted in the neck area. "Here, let me fix your sweater."

Lisa complied with the order, feeling how Brida's hands took the collar of her sweater and adjusted it to fit her better, feeling just slightly more protected against the cold. Lisa began to realize that it felt pretty good to have someone like Brida looking out for her in some way. She knew Brida had no need to come to town, much less help her return. She was aware the detective was going through something she may not fully understand, but she could see she was carrying a lot of burdens. Lisa looked up, observing the older woman with a new outlook. Her father had told her there were people out there who just made you feel better and she thought that Brida might be one of them. Her thoughts were cut off when she felt the last touches on her sweater. For some strange reason she felt warmer and safer. She thanked her, suddenly becoming timid, clenching the keys in her hands.

The two walked towards the park leisurely, Brida keeping in with Lisa's short pace. The gate at the entrance of the park was always open, the rusty iron seemingly unwilling to move even with the strong wind.

The small park gardens were neglected, with weeds left unchecked and spilling onto the stone path. Their footsteps were loud against the pavement, alerting Brida to how noisy they were and instinctually quieted her step. The trees all had cracked, aged bark where enough insects visibly buzzed and swelled and ebbed in number as they crawled along its length that the detective decided to stay away and follow the stone path.

"It's not like it used to be, but it's still a nice place," Lisa began, quickening her step to get in front of Brida and guide her to the statue of the founder. "The park always brings back good memories of when I used to come here by myself to play with other kids. I don't visit it like I used to, but sometimes I come here to spend the afternoon."

"Alone?"

"My dad was always busy, so I usually got free reign to roam at that age. He had to work a lot to support the family. The good thing is that he only had me, I think it would've been worse for him if he had another child," said Lisa, with a small smile, shrugging her shoulders. "At that time my grandma was also busy taking care of my grandpa, who became ill, and so I was by myself a lot of the time. In the city, did you also go to the park when you were a kid?"

"I used to play with the stray dogs that were on my street."

"They never bit you?"

"No, they were good dogs."

"I can't imagine you playing with dogs."

Brida let out a bitter chuckle in response and her eyes fell on the town's founder. Elkan was mounted on a horse, raised on two legs with its mouth heroically agape and the eyes wide open. The statue of Elkan painted him as a strong man with a spear in his hand, dressed in an antique colonial manner. His features were mature, his faced adorned with a bushy beard and a grim expression forever plastered on him.

Sir Elkan Raleigh. 1573 – 1662. The founding father of Dameborne. Elkan Damerei Raleigh was born in England. He will be remembered as a man of great virtues who managed to protect this island from invaders, leaving it free and sovereign from the Spanish conquerors. It could be read on the metal plaque located in front of the pedestal. This statue was different from the one they had in the city. Here he looked livelier, full of the heavy weight of duty, observing the town as a conqueror, meanwhile in the city he had a more depressive expression, one of complete desolation. She remembered once asking her partner why the artists seemed to depict him that way. She recalled him laughing and replying that perhaps the man had committed atrocities that he himself didn't forgive and as such the artists wouldn't allow them to go unremembered.

Lisa observed the older woman and then the statue. "So..." she began flustered, feeling Brida's gaze on her, making her anxiously tighten the laces of her sweater. "We'll have a small festival next week. It's the grandest community event we have as the radio called it... if you wanted to stay a little longer, I'd like to show it to you too. I know the town festivals are no big deal, but I've always had a great time. If you want to."

"Maybe I'll stay a little longer."

Lisa felt reassured, stopping stretching the laces of her sweater. "You will?"

"I did tell my landlord I'd stay here for two weeks."

"You didn't tell me that."

"Well, I'm renting a room of yours, you'd eventually realize I'm staying an extra week," said Brida, tilting her head at Lisa. "Like a detective."

Lisa laughed, blushing, glad that the detective was staying in town longer. She knew Brida wanted to make an attempt at humor to make her feel better, and just for that reason alone she liked it. "Ah, you're trying!" she pointed out, making Brida smile.

Lisa really wanted to show her the quiet life they had, compared to how erratic the city was. Observing how Brida was concentrated once again on studying the statue of the founder, she began to think she'd started feeling better these past few days with the older woman with her. She hadn't realized she hadn't thought about Elizabeth the entire time she had been with the detective. The thought alone was enough to make her feel terrible. Suddenly she wanted to cry, feeling her throat close up. She kept silent as Brida finished her own observations with the statue. She didn't want to begin to accept she wouldn't see Elizabeth anymore, that little by little she would forget about her, leaving her in the past. For some strange reason, she no longer remembered her voice.

"The truth is..." Lisa began with a cracked voice, having to clear her throat to speak better, putting her hand over her mouth. "These days have been hard for me. Sometimes I think that all this is a dream and that soon I'll wake up and see my friend with me. Since she left I haven't been able to stop thinking about her. But today was different, I think I feel guilty about everything."

Brida glanced at Lisa, understanding what she was through at that moment. Forgetting even the little things, like the sound of one's voice or how the person smiled, or even speech patterns and how one could express oneself was enough to make one feel guilty for letting these facets of an important friend slip away. "Guilty about what?"

"The way it all turned out in the end. My grandma says she left with a man like they used to do in her youth. You know, the old days when those ugly men would kidnap a girl they liked best just because and the family had to accept it? Those times," said Lisa, frowning. Anytime she remembered those stories, nausea and fear would come over her. "I try not to explode when my dad or Rhys talk about Elizabeth, and I don't even know what to say because nobody knows anything! No one says anything, they don't even seem to care!" Lisa collapsed, staring at the floor wiping away her treacherous tears, feeling like a little girl trying to control her emotions without success. Her throat ached from how tight it felt. She tried not to make a sound as she cried without managing to stop her tears, wiping her face with the sleeves of her sweater. Brida looked at the girl who had broken down from stress.

"I'm sure your friend Collin cares that she's missing as much as you do."

"I know, but Elizabeth was special in a way. She was my first friend and I loved spending time with her, even if we sometimes had a lot of arguments," Lisa sighed wearily. "I started connecting with Collin just a few months ago, and I'm happy to have him as a friend, don't get me wrong. Collin has helped me a lot and I'm grateful about that. I think I would've been worse off if he hadn't there for me. Collin sometimes acts like a big brother, he makes me feel safe, but I also know he isn't as connected in this."

Brida stared at her, sensing the same protectiveness she felt for Lisa days ago. "I know this is hard for you. I also know Elizabeth was an important person to you, but remember you aren't alone. I'm here for the moment for whatever you need. You're a smart girl, and with time and help you'll get through this episode."

Lisa gave the detective a shaky smile, wiping away her tears. "Do you say this in your job, too?"

"Sometimes, when people need it. But never in a personal way like I'm telling you now, I always keep my line of professionalism. Here, wipe your nose."

Lisa watched sheepishly as Brida pulled a folded tissue out of her jacket and handed it to her. She blew her nose, embarrassed, and smiled when she felt Brida's hand on her shoulder. The hand felt heavy, but it was a heaviness that grounded her, something she hadn't felt since she was a child. It was sad to think her father didn't have that same quality, but since her mother left them, her father was no longer the same. She kept thinking how Brida's presence made her feel secure and serene so quickly. It was an ugly thought that next week, the detective would be going back in the city.

"Why don't you tell me a good story about your misadventures?"

Lisa nodded. "Okay. You'll be bored."

"Try me. I decide if they bore me or not," Brida said, leaning on the bench.

Lisa took a beath and paused for a moment to think of a good story. "The first time Collin invited me to go fishing, I didn't know what to do. He prepared my fishing rod and told me to hold it tightly between my hands and that if I felt a little stretch, to tell him immediately. I was scared, I started imagining some bad what-if scenarios, like what if the fish pulled the rod out of my hands, or worse, what if I fell out of the boat!" The image of herself screaming when the rod had moved and Collin laughing at her came to her mind. "I had never caught a fish before and even though Collin told me it was a very small fish, he cooked it for me and I really liked it. It's safe to eat the fish we have in the lake, so it was okay."

"Sounds nice."

"It was nice, Collin promised to take me fishing again," said Lisa, shifting her position on the bench. "Between us... Collin used to be problematic, I don't know how to call it. He doesn't do what he used to do anymore and he's trying to leave that life behind and earn 'good' money, as he puts it. I believe he was just kidding when he told me that. Few people received him well when he returned to town, and I felt sorry for him, so I told him he could work for us. My grandma made a big problem out of it, but then Collin told her he knew how to fix pipes and even knew carpentry. That's the only reason my grandma let him stay. He has to come by tomorrow. He went out with some friends these past few days, that's why we haven't seen him. Otherwise I would've introduced him to you."

"Well, then I have to wait to meet him," said Brida playing along.

"Everyone in town knows about him and his family, because well, in the end we all know each other, and sooner or later any secret you have, your neighbor will know about it. Just like everyone knows what happened to my family and my dad. I eventually stopped caring what they said."

"What happened to your father?"

"He was in a car accident that left him paralyzed. He can move his arms, but if he doesn't move them for too long, they start to hurt. My grandma always said it was a miracle that he survived his crash. From there I left my studies and started to take care of the inn," she said, giving a small sad smile. "I'm not upset about leaving school. I think I help my family more when I go looking for outsiders who want to get to know the town. I can recommend the inn and we make more money, while school is just another expense. I do try to get my own books to continue reading and learning on my own, it made my dad happy to know I haven't stopped studying."

"Does your father know I'm staying at the inn?"

"Yes, he always tells me not to bother you," she laughed, hugging her sweater, and looked up to Brida with a smile. "I always tell him who rents the rooms and what they're like. From the first day we got here, he knew you were here."

Brida didn't think much about the last comment, turning her head as she heard a new noise in the park. Soon they noticed a group of young people walking through the park carrying a pack of beers, using the gazebo as a place of leisure. Two of them glanced at Lisa, who looked away as they moved along. Their stare still felt heavy on Lisa. Their eyes always seemed to follow her when she wanted to walk around town alone, which she hadn't done since Elizabeth went away. She was still scared from her last run-in with them and their simultaneously judgmental and distant stares.

"Those are…" Lisa winced. "Elizabeth's friends."

"The ones who ignore you?"

"I still can't talk to them, and they obviously don't want to talk to me. I don't want to get into more trouble than I'm already in. I know they aren't nice people and it seems that everything I do, no matter how small, they always see it wrong."

"They get you in trouble?"

"A little, but no. I don't think I've told you this before, but the last time I went to ask the police here if there was any news about Elizabeth, her mother was also there and when she saw me she got really angry and wanted to hit me for 'making her daughter disappear.' I ran away from her and I was scared to go back. I'm still a little scared of running into her."

"The police didn't tell her anything about her behavior?"

"I don't know. I didn't stay there to find that out."

"Has your grandmother or father made any comments about this lady?"

"Yes, a lot. My grandma says the most about it and won't let that lady near the inn. The last time Elizabeth's mother tried to approach, my grandma came out of the office and I only saw them arguing outside until the lady left. If you run into her on the street, don't tell her you know me, otherwise she'll hit you too!"

Brida chuckled at that. "I don't think it's in her best interest to hit me."

Lisa looked at Brida with uncertainty. She kept wiping her nose until it turned a subtle shade of red, ignoring the presence of the group at the park gazebo. "I'd like to think that lady is just grieving, even if she takes it out on me." Lisa turned her thoughts to Brida's friend. Thomas's name had come to her mind, and with a bit of embarrassment asked: "Can you tell me a story about your friend?"

Brida stared at her, changing her position to a more rigid and closed-off one on the bench, turning away from prying eyes. Lisa waited for Brida to think of a good anecdote, until the older woman folded her arms and tilted her head, lost in a memory. "Hm... Well, Thomas and I have many good and bad anecdotes, but I can tell you one that is at least funny to you. Thomas made an arrest on someone who was afraid of heights. He found him on the ledge of a house, clinging to the window frame. The window was well secured, so he was unable to enter the house and was left outside without knowing how to get down."

Lisa chuckled. "And what did he do next?"

"Thomas said something that made the man hyperventilate, asking him to hold on to the window for more minutes, that he was going to lower him down soon because he could break his neck if he fell in the wrong way. The man was having a panic attack and Thomas couldn't go to him since he didn't have a ladder and there wasn't one around in the house. He was trying to get the man to follow his instructions to come down, but the guy didn't want to move. It wasn't possible to open the window on the other side since the owners of the house weren't there to help. In the end, it was one of the neighbors who lent Thomas their ladder to assist him in the arrest. I have more stories, but they are all related to my work."

Lisa let out a small laugh, imagining the whole situation. "I think you liked that story for more reasons besides work," Lisa said with a wry smile. "I can't imagine what I would do in that situation if I were an officer."

Brida rolled her eyes and smirked without responding.

"Do you miss him?" Lisa suddenly asked.

Brida took a moment to respond, her chest constricting. "I've been thinking of calling him these past few days," she admitted with a twinge of shame. Of course she had thought about calling him, but she didn't even know what she was going to say.

"You should, I'm sure he'll be glad you called him. If you want to know, we have some booths near the police station. They're always open. I can also lend you the office phone if you want." Lisa felt the stares from Elizabeth's friends lingering in the park. She hugged herself, hunching a little. She scratched her palm in an attempt to calm herself. "It's getting windier and I'm cold, can we go back to the office? I don't want to get sick. We can play cards."

Brida followed her gaze, placing a hand on Lisa's shoulder and shaking her gently, making Lisa smile enjoying the gesture. "I'll stay here a little longer. You go ahead, then I'll swing by later."

"Okay, I'll be waiting."

Lisa walked towards the entrance of the park, feeling Brida's heavy gaze on the back of her neck. She turned slightly and green, fluorescent eyes were following her, making her feel safer, she smiled and ignored her jitteriness.

Brida was alone, still sitting on that rotten wooden bench, next to the statue of Elkan. She took her pack of cigarettes out of her jacket and lit one, listening to the insects hiding in the trees. She inhaled the smoke and relaxed in the now empty park. The young kids had already left since Lisa decided to leave the park. She remembered how hard it could be to have people obsess over every little thing you did. It seemed that Lisa was being bullied. She frowned at the idiotic situation the teenagers found themselves in. She didn't even feel like thinking about how immature it all was. She looked up, observing the black, veiny clouds still stalking the town, making Brida think it wouldn't be a normal storm. The clouds seemed to explode with lightning at their peaks, rolling swiftly across the sky as they did so. In all the time she had been in town, she hadn't seen a hint of rain. This time it was clear the storm was about to make its presence felt.

It was strange to no longer spend her free evenings at Gustavo's bar, wasting the night away, while she now slept at a good hours, enjoying the morning. She knew it would only be a short time before she went back to her dull routine. Brida adjusted herself on the bench, resting her arm on the backrest and leaning her head on her arm, staring at the statue. She had heard about Elkan since she was a child; the likenesses of Elkan was always full of insects in her elementary school, something that the cleaning staff never seemed to be able to resolve. The insects always seemed to come back and obscure the saint's face. She always thought it had been a dreadful image for the children. She remembered once trying to touch the mural of the saint, but an insect had bitten her hand. She had never understood why he seemed to have that phenomenon, but she assumed the bugs had simply made their nest in the mural. Apparently, the tradition that Elkan seems to attract vermin also takes place in town. Brida closed her eyes, feeling the wind comb through her hair. She sighed, taking another puff of smoke. Maybe she had to listen to Lisa and swallow some of her pride.

XI

The warbling noises and voices of the television weren't loud enough to distract her. Her mind was lost, stuck on reminiscing about everything she had told the detective these past few days. She didn't regret telling her that Elizabeth's mother wanted to beat her when she learned her daughter was simply gone, but telling her all this sensitive information that she barely had time to process herself left her with a premonition that she couldn't decide was good or bad. Lisa took the TV's remote and turned it off, listening to the static and the crackling of the television as it powered down.

She looked at her father, who lay on a low-lying bed with a headboard adorned with inlaid walnut flowers. He looked small, lost in the heavy sheets that hid his thin body from her eyes. All she could see was part of his reddened face, his neck looking even paler than usual. Sometimes she thought her father's skin was made of paper, easy to tear and transparent in daylight. His dark gray hair formed little rivulets on the silk pillow, creating a peaceful image. She remembered when her father used to look pristine and clean cut before the car accident. Her father maintained his personal cleanliness, however, she recognized there was a great difference between personal hygiene for health and taking care of your image out of self-respect. Lisa ran her hand through his hair, feeling the incredible softness all the way down to the rough ends. Lisa didn't notice he was awake, with his gaze on the painting of a hare they had on the side wall of the bedroom. The hare never deigned to look at him. Lisa scrutinized her father's room. There were medicine boxes with writing on them scattered all over the furniture, books pilled on the floor, and a plate of food with its accompanying tumbler glass on the bureau. The room was illuminated by the soft light of the morning, creating long shadows stretched over the room.

"There are mornings when I think that my time is coming…" he said, his voice hoarse. Still observing the painting of the hare that accompanied him in his sedentary life. "But it's better not to think about it. It doesn't do me any good to think these things, though death is a natural thing. Your grandmother told me that yesterday you spent a lot of time with the detective you tell me so much about."

Lisa tried to not flinch, feeling physically shocked at her father's sudden down-turn in health. She didn't want to startle her father in turn. Had he sounded quite so weak before? Lisa whimpered, trying to speak through a tight throat. "Yeah… I like spending time with her. She's kind of helping me understand some thoughts, I guess."

"Understand about…"

"About what happened."

"Elizabeth."

"Yes."

Her father made a sound of affirmation and then huffed. "Your grandmother has made some comments about that," he said, looking at his daughter, who remained silent. He didn't even know what to say in the face of this situation. "Lisa, I know what happened with this friend affected you a lot and I hope you can get over it soon. I don't like seeing you like this. Have you ever thought about the possibility that maybe she just left? It wouldn't be the first time she's done that to spite her mother, remember?"

"No, Elizabeth always told me where she was going."

Always, he thought wistfully. "We never stop getting to know people, maybe Elizabeth didn't tell you everything like you want to believe. Sometimes people are like that, they prefer to keep secrets and be left well alone. I'm not saying this to make you feel bad, just to make you think."

Lisa remained silent, playing with the silk sheet that covered her father. Her father was looking at her with a kind, passive face as if he knew what she was thinking. "I don't want to think like that," she said.

"It's okay. I just wanted you to not worry so much about her. She might be okay, just like the last time she went away. Please don't get in trouble with your grandma anymore. I get tired that every time she barges in here it's only to complain, whether it's about you or something else. Most of the time I don't even know what she's talking about. I don't know how your grandmother manages to have such a heavy energy. She makes the whole house change if her mood swings."

"I'm sorry," Lisa whispered, feeling responsible.

"At least try not to get into so much trouble this time." he said, smiling softly. He felt so sorry for his little girl taking care of the inn alone, he should be there. He hated his lifestyle and his decisions on the day which robbed him of most of his mobility. He was only asking for a little more health, so he could at least be in the office. He was grateful to have Lisa in his life. He was also worried for her. "We'll talk more later. I'm feeling down again. Your grandmother will be here soon, don't worry about me. This medicine always makes me tired. Hm. Almost forgot, if you see Collin, tell him that your grandmother has been looking for him since yesterday."

"He has to come to the office, I'll tell him," Lisa said, staring at her father. She decided to open her heart to him and say the words that always made everything better between them. "I love you."

"I love you too."

Lisa gave her father a feather-light kiss on the cheek and ran her hand across his forehead, brushing his eyebrows in the process, making him smile. Her father took her hand and gave it a loving squeeze, closing his eyes and letting out a heavy sigh. She couldn't remember the last time she had seen her father healthy. She didn't want to leave the room, but she had to take the afternoon shift, since she didn't want her grandmother to be angry again because of her tardiness. Her grandmother would call it laziness. Lisa got up from the bed, leaving her father behind, walking down the dark hallway to get to her office. Fortunately, her grandmother was nowhere in sight. She sat herself down, rubbing her hands together in a nervous gesture as she looked at the panorama of the town. She didn't want to think that Elizabeth might have kept secrets from her, that she never had that infinite trust they supposedly had for each other; she didn't want to think that, at the end of the day, Elizabeth never thought of her as her confidant.

With a sigh, she grabbed her notebook and began scribbling to pass the time. She didn't even notice the shadows were shifting, indicating that time had passed her by. She heard a whistle and someone knocking on the door before, not waiting for an answer, the door opened and a man of average height stepped through, with faint freckles scattered across his face and a big smile that showed his slightly crooked canines. It wasn't a bad image; in fact, all told, his features gave an endearing touch to his appearance. His wavy, auburn hair was tousled from the wind, and he passed his hand back through his hair to comb it after he closed the door, carrying a box of chocolates with his free hand.

"Hey," he greeted her.

"At least this time you aren't caked with dirt. You don't know how much my grandma scolded me when you filled the entrance mat with mud," she said, smiling. It was a bad moment, but she would never had it against Collin. Her grandmother made him work a lot around the inn, a mat filled with mud was just a matter of time.

Collin barked a laugh, throwing his head back. "I already said I was sorry about that. You can't hold it against me all the time. I saw your grandma in the morning, she was with Rhys. She also told me you got back a few days ago, so I got you some chocolates. They were a little hard to find."

"You didn't have to get me anything," Lisa said with a small smile, accepting the box, setting it beside her books. "It's been an interesting week so far. I think you'd like to know about it."

"Did something good happen?"

"You can say that. I found the help I was searching for."

Collin tensed at what she said, nodding, unsure how to respond to such a revelation. He let the silence linger and then shrugged his shoulders defeatedly, putting his hands in his pants pockets and tilted his head to one side. "Ah."

"You don't look happy."

"No. No, I'm not very happy. Listen, Lisa, I don't think I have to repeat myself, but the fact that you went to the city, looking for this kind of help you didn't even know you could afford, is enough to make anyone concerned. Yes, you may have been accompanied by your aunt Maureen, but even so, if you hadn't gotten that idea in your head, you never would have gone to the city in the first place. What you did was stupidest thing you've ever done, and maybe you already know that."

Lisa pressed her lips together and lowered her eyes. She felt ashamed, but at the same time it bothered her to be scolded. She had enough of that with her grandmother and herself. Doesn't anyone care to know what happened to Elizabeth? She knew no one would understand her. The only one who understood her was the courteous man in the park who consoled her until he gave her direction, a path to follow. Still, knowing the detective wasn't going to help her like she wanted, the fact that she hadn't ignored her when she found her, already gave her a peace of mind in her soul that no one else in town could've given her. She didn't know how to reply without sounding rude, lowering her eyes.

Collin sighed. "I care about you, Lisa. I know I don't have a nicer way of saying things, but you know I mean them from my heart. So, this person will help you with that Elizabeth?"

"Don't talk about her like that."

"We don't know exactly where she is or who she's with. I think everyone understands how bad the situation is right now. I don't wish this kind of trouble on anyone, but Lisa, you have to stop making decisions that will end up biting you back in the long run. Do you understand what I mean?"

"A little bit, yes," Lisa said, defeated.

"Is this person going to help you?"

"No, not really. I mean, at least not with Elizabeth's case, since she told me she wasn't working right now, but she's being nice to me. She explained to me that the case would be taken to the city, so a full team would come here for the investigation, that it wouldn't necessarily be her on the case. She's actually a detective and she's on vacation here. I, well, I also told her all about Elizabeth, her mother, all her stupid friends and even about my family. I told her about you and how we met," she said, turning her glance in a sheepish way. "I didn't say anything about your past or your problems. I didn't want to share that. She's staying here at the inn if you want to know. I think she'll come back soon. You can stay here if you don't have anything to do, so I can introduce you to her."

Collin rolled his eyes then let out a short snicker. "I wish, your grandma already got me on a leak in one of the rooms and I plan on checking it out now. When I was on my way here the sky almost looked purple."

"It hasn't even drizzled since I got here."

"Who knows," he said squinting toward Lisa. "You look better than the last time I saw you."

"I'm feeling better and worse at the same time, but it's at least a change."

Collin scratched the side of his face with his thumb. "Yeah, I know what's happening isn't good for anyone, but at least you have more color in your face than before. I have to go now. I don't want your grandmother to yell at me like last time. I'll come visit you later to talk about whatever you want to talk about, okay?"

Lisa smiled, sheepishly. "Thank you, really."

Collin left the office to go the storeroom and grab his tool kit. Since he started working at the inn, he was more than grateful to the Gallardo family for bringing him into their business and giving him a chance where few others in town would. He ran his tongue over his chapped lips and began to whistle a song that had gotten stuck in his head recently. He fumbled with his keys and opened the storeroom door, barely about to touch the light switch when he heard other footsteps. He noticed a woman walking past the inn entrance with her back to him. She seemed to be looking in the direction of the church. Collin abruptly stopped whistling, taking note of the stranger who had stopped right in the middle of the entrance. Deciding to close the door of the storeroom and talk to the new visitor, the stranger turned her attention towards him in response to the sound. She was an attractive woman, in that instant he knew her eyes were her most alluring quality, the color moved as a stream trapping him in a wave, each second intensifying its color. Collin stared into those eyes before speaking. "Good afternoon. Are you the detective?"

Brida kept her gaze fixed on the image of the man before her. To Brida, it seemed the man harbored within him his own devoted light, alighting his skin with a warmth that she hadn't experienced in so long. Her mind could barely understand the image before her. The wind blew, carrying with it an aroma of living plants, of fresh, humid pine that seemed to emanate from this man. At first she felt apprehensive and wanted to move away, but soon enough, she calmed her mind, taking a long breath. "I'm *a* detective," she said.

Collin snorted amusedly, offering his hand in greeting, "I'm Collin."

Brida, seeing the outstretched hand waiting to be grasped, felt her own hand tremble slightly at the prospect of touch. Brida clasped the hand in a tight grip, feeling the warmth emanating from it. "Hm, Lisa told me a lot about you."

"I know she told you a little about me. It's all behind me now. I don't want to get in trouble with the law again," he said, playfully. Observing how the detective responded by raising her eyebrows. Evidently the woman hadn't taken his comment seriously which was good. Soon he became serious, licking his lips as a nervous tic. "Look, I don't mean to be rude, but I don't like you being here. Not with what I know."

Brida frowned, rubbing the palm of her hand. "And what is it you know?"

"Let's just say I think your presence here causes some problems for a certain someone."

Brida studied the man in front of her: he was no older than her, possibly younger, and his jovial nature seemed self-evident in how he carried himself. She couldn't contain the thought that he had a lovely voice, not so deep, and with a soft timbre to his words as he spoke. Prolonging the silence longer than she should have, she realized she hadn't said anything. "We seem to start out with strong opinions."

"I'm not that closed-minded, and if I were, I don't think I'd be talking to you," he said with a shrug, shoving his hands in his pockets. "People here are quieter and at the same time they want to know everything about everyone."

Brida assented at the tidbit of information, recalling Lisa's grandmother, but then the stoic and oddly welcoming image of the nuns came to mind. She never had any particular experience in small towns, but inferred that Collin's observation came from personal knowledge. "I must say I've had good impressions since I've been here."

"First I've heard of that, the way the town's been acting up lately."

"I've heard about it, but I haven't seen much myself."

"You just have to wait. Well, I guess being a detective is better received than being a troublemaker anywhere, right?" he said with a small hint of amusement. "I still can't believe Lisa really found someone like you. Rhys and I thought she was losing it. She never stopped talking about a person who could help her in the city, in the end I wasn't even recognizing her by the way she was acting…" Collin frowned, looking away. "At least she's back to normal now."

Brida stared at him.

"I mean, I didn't believe Lisa when she said she could get help. She told Rhys -a friend of the family- about it too, but neither of us took it seriously. Then, when I told her I was going to visit a friend for a while, she decided to take advantage of her time to go to the city with that aunt of hers, rather recklessly if you ask me."

"Yes, she was. Loss can make you behave recklessly."

"Glad we think the same. Imagine my surprise when Lisa told me about you today," he said, dryly. Collin shifted, a little awkward with the woman's hard stare, maybe he was being too blunt. "I'm not referring specifically of *you*, but your profession. I guess she met you and dragged you into town to do something about Elizabeth's disappearance and told you all about it. Lisa told me you're not working right now. That's at least good news for me, and her family."

"I know you're worried about Lisa," Brida said. She found it intriguing how a person could open up in such a way with a stranger. Seeing herself already embroiled in the conversation, it was better to continue on until she found a polite way out. "She lost a friendship she considers precious to her. Lisa has told me what happened, most of which made me think it was a one-way relationship on Lisa's part," she said, looking closely at the man's expressions. She knew Collin somehow didn't seem to hold Elizabeth on a pedestal like Lisa does. Just as her father used to say, the bell rings twice. "I'm sure you think the same thing."

Collin nodded, pleased to know someone thought like him. "Yes, I do. I don't want for her to put any more energy into this. I'm worried."

"She has told me you've been helping her. I know my presence is unwelcome to some, but as I told Lisa earlier; I'm not here in any official capacity to help with Elizabeth's case. The only way I can help is to make her comprehend the situation. I'm here for personal reasons."

"Which are?"

"Personal."

Collin shrugs. "Sure, everyone has their reasons for coming here."

"Seems like it."

Collin smiled and shook his head at the detective's curt replies. Maybe her being in town won't be so bad if she wasn't going to be hunting for Elizabeth and giving Lisa high hopes. He was sure nothing good would come of it. He ran his hand through his hair and let out a heavy sigh. "I'm sorry. I guess I jumped to conclusions too fast. I never caught your name."

"Because I didn't give it."

Collin smirked, laughing under his breath. "So, are you going to tell me your name?"

"Brida."

"That's a nice name."

"Thank you. I'll think about what you told me."

"Think about what?"

"About my presence here."

With that Brida walked away leaving Collin with a sour taste in his mouth. Maybe he was being too harsh, but it doesn't hurt to be careful with a stranger in uncertain times. It was ironic, he was vetting the detective when he used to lie and rob people as soon as they had their back turned. He felt weighed down as he walked to the storeroom to pick up his tool box again. He wanted to know what her personal reasons were for coming here, but that would be hypocritical of him when he arrived in town under even more questionable personal conditions. He could only wait and see what would happen next. He resumed his whistling, unable to keep those green eyes out of his thoughts. He entered the room reported to have a water leak and indeed, when he opened the door, he observed water pooling out of the bathroom and onto the carpeted floor of the bedroom. Collin sighed and continued whistling.

Time went by until eight o'clock in the evening. Lisa sighed and leaned her head against the desk, her eyes hurt from reading her book so intensely, continuing her self-taught studies but nothing was getting into her head any longer. She heard a knock on the door and raised her head to look at the visitor. Lisa smiled as she saw the older woman enter the office and tried not to show her emotion too much, clasping her hands together. Brida gave her a small smile as she watched those doe eyes widen with excitement.

"This town has a peaceful lake, I liked spending my time there."

"I'm glad you're liking the town," said Lisa, straightening her posture in the chair. She gave a little yelp when her back popped. "I used to go to the park a lot as I said before, but now that I spend more time with Collin, I go to the lake with him more often than going by myself. There's a part where all the fish go to hide and you can see them if you lean over, it's nice. The next time you want to go to the lake, tell me and I'll show you where it is."

"You're my guide, after all," said Brida, half smiling.

Lisa giggled and nodded.

"Already had dinner?"

"No, I was too focused on this," Lisa signaled her book and notebook. She checked the time and groaned, slumping on the chair. "It's already eight o'clock. I think I've already lost my plate. My family eats dinner earlier than I do, since six o'clock, by seven o'clock at the latest and they don't eat until the morning."

"Hm. Join me for dinner, then."

"Really? I wouldn't want to bother you."

"I'm inviting you."

"Then I'll let my grandma know I'm going to leave the office and change my clothes," said Lisa, secretly thrilled to spend more time with the older woman. It was nice to meet new people and she didn't have much of a chance in that social area. She didn't want to entertain any negative thought, so she gazed out the window at the sky and turned to the detective. "Do you think it's going to rain tonight?"

"It seems so."

"Then I'll grab my umbrella, I'll be right back!"

Brida took out a cigarette and tapped it lightly against the pack while she waited for Lisa to return. She thought back to what she had discussed with Collin, bringing up the same questions she had ever since she arrived in Dameborne: Why had she decided to come to town? Was she so lonely that she decided to bond with the first person who talked to her outside work? She stopped tapping her cigarette and focused her eyes on the ring on her finger. It was bizarre she found herself in that man's birthplace, sightseeing. She removed the ring, tucking it into her jacket. There were factors that didn't fit into her personal equation and were all the details she had been collecting, storing them, evaluating them, and making them stick to not forget them. For an unknown reason, the fact that Lisa had been talking for days with a strange man in the park had stuck in her head, knowing more of the young girl's personality, it was unlikely she would've felt comfortable being near a man even in an open area. *Perhaps Collin knows more about that man*, she thought, narrowing her eyes. He had been particularly concerned about her presence in town so she didn't think he would be opening up about it any time soon. It would have to wait. She frowned, suddenly going blank. No, it couldn't be *him*. It was statistically impossible, dismissing the notion as quickly as it came.

"I'm back!"

Brida loosened her expression when Lisa appeared with her sweater on and an umbrella in her hands. It had flowers woven into the pockets and widened out at the sleeves, hiding part of her hands. "Isn't that sweater a little big for you?"

Lisa laughed. "Yeah, I know, but I really like it."

Brida hummed quietly to herself as the young girl did her final preparations. Lisa tucked her umbrella under her arm, grabbed her keys and locked the office, listening to Brida light a cigarette and the smoke slithered out into the open air. They walked through the inn and Lisa saw Collin wiping off his hands, likely fresh from finishing up some repairs. His hair was sticking to his face and his pants were wet at the bottoms. She turned to Brida with a new idea. "I don't know if you've seen Collin but he's the one over there, I'd like you to meet him. Can I invite Collin to dine with us? So you can get to know who I'm talking about so much, you'll like him."

Brida glanced at Collin and wondered if it was a good idea to invite him, knowing she would eventually give in to Lisa's request. She had nothing against Collin, only that he had this faint aroma that reminded her of something important from her past. Something she didn't know she missed so much, no matter how grim the memory. "Sure."

Collin wiped the back of his neck with the same cloth he always used on the job and noticed Lisa walking over to him, with Brida waiting a short distance away. She was wearing this ugly sweater that got him chuckling internally. "Hey, you," he greeted.

"Hey, want to come with us?"

He glanced at the older woman. "You sure?"

"If you're worried about Brida not wanting you to be with us, she already said she's fine with you coming along. She looks serious, but has made me feel good ever since I met her. You'll like her," Lisa said confidently, smiling and raising her eyebrows conspiratorially at Collin. "Come with us, I really want you to meet her. C'mon, we'll wait for you to get ready!"

"Well, if you want my company so badly, I'll go get the sweat off of me," he said, smirking. "And if you want to know, I already talked to her a little."

Lisa stared at him questioningly until she nodded. "I'll ask you later how that went. Go take a bath, we'll wait for you at the park," she said and turned to wait with Brida who had stopped watching in the direction of the church, making Lisa her focus point once again. Collin noted that motion with interest, he grabbed his toolbox and headed for the storeroom. Fortunately, his apartment was close by, just a few blocks away. He followed them into the park and hurried to his apartment, assuring Lisa he wouldn't be long. He finally arrived at the old building, unlocking the metal gate to greet the lady who always lurked outside to gossip in case she caught a glimpse of something. Collin rolled his eyes wishing he too could have that kind of time, but he knew he was too active for that. He'd go crazy. He finished washing and changing quickly -not even turnings on the lights in his room in his hurry- and went out with his hair still damp, feeling the wind on the back of his neck. He shivered as he shoved his hands into the pockets of his old jacket.

He spotted them at the gazebo. "Hello."

"You'll get sick with that wet hair," said Lisa.

"I didn't want to keep you waiting."

"First, I'd like to introduce you two! Brida, this is Collin," she said, taking Collin's arm and pulling him closer to them. "He's the one who's been taking me fishing since we met. Collin told me that you had already talked a little with him, but I still wanted to introduce him to you."

Brida gave a soft smile to the girl. "Yes, we talked, but nice to meet you again."

"Yup, same here," came Collin's short, and one might even say embarrassed, response.

Collin walked alongside Lisa, listening as she told Brida one of her anecdotes about the town. He discretely turned his head to observe the detective's face and was surprised to see her watching Lisa with a gentle expression. He bit his lip, feeling the skin dry against his tongue. Maybe he had been too quick in his accusation, but if the detective didn't find him coming along to be an inconvenience, then maybe he hadn't thrown away her first impression of him. After a brief walk, they arrived at the dinner. Collin opened the door and held it for the other two to enter, smiling at Lisa who entered whispering a thank you. Brida stubbed out her cigarette before entering, looking at Collin who was still holding the door for her. He didn't know why he was so nervous now about having her attention.

"Thank you."

"Yeah, you're welcome."

Collin shook his head. He closed the door and sat down at the table Lisa had already found for them, which trembled when he rested his hands on the corners. He moved it a little noticing the unevenness. "Seems like Rhys hasn't fixed the table since the last time I was here!"

"You know he's waiting for you to do it," Lisa said.

"Yeah, but you know, no money, no fixed table."

"I know how you work by now," she said, turning to Brida. "Did you know Collin used to think money inexplicably came from mattresses? He saw his grandparents pulling money out of the bed, so he thought the money came from there. One time his parents told him there was no money to buy him candy, and he told them to check the bed so that would solve everything. He told me as much himself."

"Hey! That was when I was a little kid! Not that I'd be against the idea."

"A mattress full of money?"

"Yeah," he said. "It would solve a lot of problems."

Brida stopped paying attention to them and turned to the window, hearing the conversation the two friends were having as a filler sound. She noticed the same group of teenagers she saw yesterday with Lisa, drinking and smoking in one of the corners of the park. An officer was shouting at them from the police truck leaning against the window frame. The officer got inside by closing his window and drove away, when one of the teenagers threw a glass bottle at the moving vehicle crashing onto the pavement. The truck stopped, flashing red lights causing the teenagers to flee from their spot when they saw the vehicle backing up.

"Brida?"

Brida turned to Lisa, who gave her a worried look. Collin simply regarded her curiously. Still having the scene that just transpired in her head, she thought it best to privately ask Collin about that particular group for a chance to address the man in the park. Solely to satisfy her own curiosity. "Is something wrong?"

"I was trying to get your attention, but I think your attention was elsewhere," she said, pointing at the window with her eyes. "I just saw the police rushing by, did you see anything?"

"Nothing in particular."

"Talkative as ever," Lisa said, fondly. "Well, we were saying that maybe tomorrow we can go to the lake if it doesn't rain tonight. We can show you that part of the lake where all the fish go to eat. Collin knows where it is better than I do. Oh, and I think I need to go see if Rhys is okay. He hasn't come out of the kitchen, I'll be right back!"

Collin remained silent as he watched Lisa leave, feeling increasingly anxious as he was left alone with the detective. He was twenty-six years old, fidgeting like a teenager waiting for the last bell. He felt a glance at his side. He knew he couldn't ignore it, sitting so close to her. He was aware Brida was looking at him with a serious face out the corner of his eye, listening to the tap-tap-tap of her finger against the table. He didn't want to see those unbelievable eyes, he had never known a green as vivid as the ones this woman had. He sighed, knowing he couldn't ignore her and turned his gaze to Brida, who was observing him. For some reason she looked stiff. "So… You seem to be thinking really hard about something."

"The town doesn't seem to have the same problems as the city," Brida said, glancing at the window. The police truck and the teenagers long gone. "Saint Elkan isn't a place where one can leave the window unlocked. This girl's disappearance doesn't seem to have shocked the town."

"Well, this is a small place. It's not uncommon for your neighbor to know what you do and even what you don't do," Collin huffed. "The neighbor might even know if you've gone to the bathroom. Hard to keep a secret in a place like this and secrets spread. Elizabeth's secrets? They weren't that deep and she wasn't subtle about it. I think it's the same old with her at this point."

"Do you think she just ran away from home?"

"I don't know about that," he said, shaking his head. "You know, when you start to make shitty decisions, it leads to shitty consequences. So, I wouldn't know what type of pit she threw herself into."

A straightforward line of thought, one she also shared. "When I met Lisa, she told me something interesting. If I remember correctly, she mentioned a man," said Brida staring at Collin, gauging his expressions. His eyebrows rose then crossed his arms, looking down at the table. "A man who gave her the idea to hire help in the city for her friend's disappearance. Lisa doesn't remember what the man's name was or what he looked like, do you know anything about that?"

"I can believe you're a detective when you ask questions like that," he said with a smirk, then turned serious, recalling all those times he saw Lisa talking to that strange man and how it made his hair stand up on end. He glanced at Brida apprehensively. "I know what you're talking about, but I don't think it's good if we talk about it right now. You know…" he said, pointing to the kitchen with his eyes. "Lisa could be back at any minute and I don't want to have any problems with her."

"Alright, we'll talk later."

"So, what were you looking at before?"

"A group of teenagers bothering the local police."

Collin gave a huff. "I know who you're talking about."

"Right."

Collin leaned against the table, crossing his arms on top of it. It had been an interesting interaction so far, he didn't understand why he felt the need to open up to the detective, but he wasn't going to downplay it. He sensed the detective wasn't the type to judge on the first impression. "I was like them when I was younger. I have a loving mum and a good dad, but I guess I had some pretty fucked up friendships. You know, being dropped off in a strange place with a bloody nose, beaten face and empty pockets changes you for better or worse."

Brida stared at him, leaning against the back of the chair. "Looks like you've pissed someone off to get to that point."

"Yeah, well, I ripped some people off, ran with the money and I didn't give a shit about it. I knew they would've done the same thing if they'd had the chance," he said, feeling the need to explain himself better. He licked his lips and sighed. "I mean, I left some, a little bit of money. But now I'm clean. No trouble at all. And I don't need much. I don't want a family, surprisingly enough, but maybe a nice little house by the lake, where I can go fishing whenever I want. That's my dream."

"Are you local?"

"Something like that. My mum is from here, she traveled to Ireland and met my dad. Then they moved back here to have a good life, I guess. They had a quiet life, sometimes I think they got unlucky with a son like me. They are in Ireland now, near my dad's family. I was a pretty hedonistic guy back then, but not anymore. What about you?"

"I've lived my whole life in the city, never had the need to leave."

"Not even once?"

"No."

"What about your parents?"

"My mother died, so my father and his family took care of me."

"Ha, you sure are dry." Collin gazed out the window, thinking about his parents. He didn't always dwell on them because it only made him beat himself up for his own stupid decisions. He turned his gaze to Brida and contemplated asking something he knew could be a touchy subject, but it would ease his mind to do so. "Did you make him proud?"

"He was glad I was a cop."

"That's really good," he said, licking his lips as a nervous tic. He only had one memory of when his dad told him he had done well. It was the first time he caught a fish bigger than his dad's. It was also a point just before a big shift in his life. Soon after, everything went down the drain when he met a bunch of assholes he considered friends for a long time. "Never made my parents proud of me. Sometimes seeing them reminds me of all the shitty decisions I made. At least I can say I made them a little happy that I didn't give myself long-term addictions. Now, I'm here, trying to find whatever my mum loved about this town so much. But every time I glance around I see those idiots shooting themselves up with heroin in the park, smoking whatever they were able to get their hands on. Sometimes I think it's only a matter of time before I stumble back myself."

"You've been doing fine, it seems."

"Thank you. I hope it stays that way. I guess now, you understand why my apprehension with this Elizabeth business. Lisa has those rose-tinted glasses only because that girl gave a little bit of attention to her when they were younger. What a fucking joke that girl was."

"I got the idea Elizabeth may had several personal struggles."

Collin shrugged. "Everyone has problems. I've never been one to care about others, not in this way. If someone wants to tell me something, they're free to do it and that's it. I couldn't tell you in what shit she was into, but Lisa is sensitive about this issue and doesn't want to see Elizabeth's bad side. I mean, now that I think about it I might be a bad person for wanting Lisa to understand that Elizabeth wasn't a good friend as she wanted to believe. My mum said not to speak ill of the troubled, but I can't help it. It made me angry every time I heard her talk shit about Lisa when she was with that group," he said, shifting his position in the chair. "It's really none my business to recount all of Elizabeth's problems, but that girl was into the one thing I painted the line at."

"Hm," Brida said, frowning. "Was she addicted to something?"

"She was, she had mood swings."

"I'm guessing Lisa didn't know about it."

"No, she didn't. It would break her heart if she knew her 'friend' had more little secrets swiped under the rug," he said rubbing his temples. "That's why I was often around when that girl was in the office or around Lisa, it was never a coincidence. Her grandma once told me that I was right to shoo that girl away from time to time, it was a weird experience."

Brida agreed, now understanding Collin's point of view. "Do you feel protective of Lisa?"

"Yeah, she's like a little sister. She's very mature, you know, but sometimes she views people with a lot of positivity and all that. It's not bad, I think. But not all people are good, and that's why leeches like Elizabeth can sink their teeth into those people and hurt them. I guess because Lisa and her family gave me a job I try to pay my debt by being good. Seeing her being treated like, well, like those people I used to take advantage of didn't sit well with me."

"You think Elizabeth was all bad with Lisa?"

Collin sighed in exasperation and looked towards the unopened kitchen door. This conversation was getting on his nerves. He disliked giving that girl so much attention. "No, I guess they talked and laughed. I saw them being all friendly in the park, but I thought it was all bullshit. Even with the shittiest person in the world you can be happy for a few seconds. Knowing Lisa, she didn't tell you that Elizabeth came to her many times asking for money. Lisa, of course, didn't want to give her any. All the money goes to her dad and the inn. Elizabeth got angry about it and at first she started screaming, then it got to the point that Elizabeth wanted to hit Lisa. I was close, so I overhead part of it, and I entered the office just as Lisa was taking cover from the blow," he said, glancing at the kitchen door that as of yet remained closed. "We'd better talk about this later. I'm kind of getting ticked off about this."

Brida nodded, letting Collin enjoy the silence that formed. She heard a squeak and glanced at the kitchen door as Lisa emerged with two plates of food followed by Rhys, who had another plate in his hands. Brida greeted Rhys cordially while Collin patted Rhys' back amiably, causing the old man to smile and return the greeting. Brida observed Rhys, noting the exhaustion that lay just under his friendly expression before he returned to the kitchen. They ate, chatting amongst themselves. Brida had no choice but to open up a bit in conversation, sharing her own grim stories from work. Lisa winced at the tales while Collin was completely invested in her dry storytelling. A loud thunderclap that rattled the windows heralded the arrival of a storm, and soon they began to hear droplets hit the pavement and the roof of the dinner. A veil fell over the town that could be easily seen from the window. The clouds were black, spreading rapidly, twisting with lighting and flashes of light.

"Good thing I grabbed my umbrella," said Lisa, turning her head to the window and then back to the two adults. The wind whistled loudly, making Lisa tense up as she finished her meal, watching the settling fog obscure the park from the restaurant's window. The three of them were enraptured by the harsh weather. The lights flickered when the next clap of thunder rang through the dinner.

"We'd better go now," Brida said.

Everyone seemed to be on board with the idea. Brida gave Lisa the money and she went to go pay the bill before they left, wanting to say goodbye to Rhys personally. Brida grabbed Lisa's umbrella on her way out, opening it and listened as the raindrops hit the thin fabric hard. Lisa returned and closed the entrance door, hugging herself, bringing the collar of her sweater up to protect her neck from the rain and cold, and clung to Brida unabashedly, shivering slightly. Brida then looked over at Collin, who hanged back.

"What are you waiting for?" asked Brida.

Collin laughed. "We won't fit."

"C'mon, Collin. I don't want to get sick," said Lisa, squinting at her friend. She leaned against Brida for support, who seemed unfazed by the weather. "Come with us to the inn and then I'll lend you my umbrella, don't think you're going to walk in the rain."

"Alright, alright. Make some space."

Brida averted her eyes and hugged Lisa's shoulders, leaving Collin glued to her other side. She was tense from so much physical contact, exhaling all the air from her lungs discreetly, feeling Lisa's trembling. Every time she rubbed shoulders with the young man she had to keep herself focused on the road. Even with the strong smell of rain, she could still perceive the scent of pine she had been so fond of. Sharp, warm with a hint of sweetness. His scent wasn't piercing to the nose, it only brought to mind an unforgettable comfort she once had. When they finally arrived at the inn, they left Lisa by the office, which she quickly opened, dashing inside for warmth. Collin walked in shortly afterwards, feeling a part of his shoulder and arm wet from the rain and let out a nasally laugh. Brida stood outside watching the sky, the lightning turning the sky white, as if someone was taking photos of the sky with a flash. She closed the umbrella and shook it off, leaving it in the corner as she entered the office.

"Don't know why my mum loved this place," said Collin, taking off his jacket.

"It's making the lights flicker too. I'll go and get some candles for you both. I don't think we'll have power tonight," said Lisa amongst the flickering lights along the ceiling. "I'll be right back. I won't take long."

The lights gave up on them, leaving them with an eerie silence that spread throughout the town. Winds rattled the doors and windows as they battered the office. Each crack of thunder was so loud it felt as if it could rumble the earth, making Collin feel the soles of his feet tingle. Collin ran his hand through his hair as he often did in a flustered gesture and looked at the woman next to him, surprised to see luminous eyes scrutinizing the dark hallway. Brida's gaze shifted to look at Collin, who could only manage an awkward smile.

"Tomorrow we'll talk," she said. "Right?"

"Ah, yes… That's right. It's been a long time since I've had any visitors. How about I invite you to my place for lunch? You can come over at one o'clock. I'm not the best cook, but I want to thank you for paying for my meal today," he said, passing his hand over the back of his neck. Sometimes he had some manners because his mum had inculcated them in him. Deep inside, he thought it would make his mum smile at his politeness, especially to a woman like Brida. The thought surprised him internally. He took Lisa's notebook, tore a piece of paper from the back and wrote down his address. "It's two blocks past the park, you'll have no problem locating the building."

"Thank you. At one o'clock I'm there."

Collin felt a strange thrill in his chest.

Lisa returned with two flashlights clutched against her chest with one arm and a lit flashlight in the other hand. She handed them one to each of them and smiled at Brida. "If you need anything else, you can come to the office."

"Aren't you going to sleep?"

"I have to take care of my dad, he's awake. He sends his regards and also says to be careful with this type of storm. It looks like a thick fog is coming, it's best not to use the car at all. A lot of times people can't see each other in the fog," she said, chuckling a little bit. "By the way, thank you for the dinner."

"Don't worry about it. I'll take my leave," said Brida. "It was nice meeting you, Collin. Good night, Lisa, and to your father and grandmother too."

Brida left the office, the strong, chilly winds took the opportunity to enter the office and sent shivers down Lisa's spine. She looked at Collin who watched the detective walk under the harsh rain to get to her room. He saw she was staying in the third room of the inn. Lisa cleared her throat, grabbing Collin's arm, pulling his attention. "Something on your mind?"

"Lots of things. You looked happy with that woman."

"She's nice. Just yesterday she made me feel better and I couldn't stop thinking about why I felt so comfortable with her. I've only know her for a week..." she trailed off, deep in thought. "When I first met her, she was very patient with me and I can tell she's fighting her own issues, so I'm grateful she's helping me while she does. I know she can't help with Elizabeth's case, I'm trying to accept it, but it seems I'm still gaining more from her presence here."

"Well, she said she has her own reasons for being here."

Lisa titled her head and smiled a little. "She's sad, you know?"

"How do you know?"

Lisa shrugged her shoulders. "Sometimes when she talks about her friend, she gets distant. Maybe that's why we connected so much. Don't give her any trouble, she seems like she's warming up to the town and that's for the best. I have to go, I told my dad I wouldn't take long. I'll see you tomorrow, be careful with the rain. Don't forget to take my umbrella, don't worry about it, I have another one."

"Do you want me to lock the office for you?"

"Yes, please. See you tomorrow, Collin!"

"Okay, good night," he said, watching Lisa leave with a quick step past the dark hallway. Collin got out of the office, locking the door, watching the sky twisting above him. He couldn't see the outside of the inn just a short distance away, the fog was too dense. He couldn't see the park across the street either. He felt the urge to turn around and look at the third room of the inn. His eyes drifted to the room. The heavy, green curtains didn't allow him to observe the woman inside and then caught himself, chastising his own impulses. At least he would see her soon. He made his way to his apartment, fumbling for his keys, feeling the frigid air creep into his clothes. Tomorrow he'll have his own answers.

XII

The new presence in town had gotten his head turning enough to keep him from sleeping well. He remembered the first time he had seen Lisa walking to the park with a forlorn face, sunken eyes, and slumped shoulders. He wanted to follow her, but Lisa's grandmother was a woman who would get him into serious trouble if he didn't do what she said at the exact moment she wanted it done, and he wasn't in the mood to be yelled at by the old crone again. It was enough he had to endure that heavy presence of the old woman.

Time had passed as he finished his duties for the day and Lisa still hadn't returned from the park. He had taken advantage of that absence to check on her and found her talking to a man near the statue of Elkan. He had observed how Lisa fixed her gaze on that man with a look full of devotion, as if she had met a saint. Collin clearly remembered the hairs on the back of his neck stood up and how, with each step taking him closer and closer, bile rose in his throat. He knew the man had a face, but for some reason, he couldn't see it in his memories.

Still, he knew his eyes. He had seen flashes of maroon eyes, tinged with red.

Lisa turned to look at him with a small smile, hugging herself clutching her light sweater in her hands. She said something about that man helping her find Elizabeth. He frowned as he tried to get a better look at the man, but he couldn't get his face in his head. The image didn't etched in his mind. He could only clearly see Lisa as he glanced over, who was thanking the stranger. He didn't have perfect memory, and sometimes his mind played cruel tricks when he was alone, but this was in plain sight. They were in the middle of the park, with the sun as its highest point in the sky. He said to Lisa, "Your father is asking for you." Collin didn't know why he lied at first. Something told him to grab Lisa and protect her from this stranger. His hands itched, feeling a gaze in the back of his head.

It was always like that. Every time he saw Lisa in the park, blood rushed to his ears, ringing unpleasantly and he could hear his own heart thumping in his chest. He didn't know why he reacted that way. He watched them talk from his position in the inn. He couldn't see their faces, but he could see their bodies. Lisa gestured and then listened to everything the man told her, still as a statue. Watching how this man spoke to Lisa, keeping her transfixed and rapt, as if his words were that of a trusted guide and mentor, yet elusive of identification and those eyes, glowing. Collin had grown wary of him. The last time he had seen them, he had been quite upset. Collin didn't remember why he was so pissed off that day, but no, he wasn't angry. He was tired of hearing about the man, of seeing him in the park. He recalled having a headache, his eyes hurting as if someone was pushing them against his eyes sockets. It was cloudy that day, so cloudy that some parts of town were naturally drafty. He didn't know why he felt his heart pounding and his skin perspiring as he passed the entrance to the park. He knew they were sitting near the statue of Elkan, as usual.

The man had a clawed grip on one of Lisa's shoulders, speaking slowly, voice keeping a consistently low tone. He tried to concentrate on what the man was saying, trying not to let his thoughts get the best of him. He wouldn't call what he felt at the time senseless fear; it was more like a coiled spring of defensive caution and mistrust. Collin didn't want to admit he had started to fear how this stranger's image couldn't stick in his mind, even as he had been staring at him. He's still sure of it now; he did see him. He remembers those flashes of deep maroon eyes, like those of an owl. That day, every time he closed his eyes, he saw flashes of red. He interrupted the conversation, making Lisa frustrated with his intrusion.

The man wasn't pleased either.

He had stood motionless then, listening as the insects began to make their presence known amongst the trees, sounding as if they were breaking through bark in the process. The trees shook in the wind and brought Collin out of his shock. He had reluctantly told Lisa her grandmother was furious with her and looking for her to get Lisa to leave. Lisa had protested about it, but the stranger calmed her down. Collin watched Lisa leave and, as he turned to look at the man, he heard the fluttering of a bird. Collin had warned him not to speak to Lisa again, but the man didn't pay him any attention, continuing to walk away. Collin tried to get his attention, but soon he was alone in the park. The insects went quiet.

Collin sighed, running his hands over his face, brushing away the guck accumulated on his eyes in the process. He stirred in bed, stretched his body, and stood up. The clock on his bureau already read eleven in the morning. The rain was still pounding against his window, but at least it wasn't thundering like before. He passed his hand through his messy hair and went into the bathroom to wash his face. He had never felt the need to see a person's eyes like Brida's again. They drew him back to the darker parts of the lake, where moss gathered between the creaks of the large rocks on the edge. As a child he loved to stand still, close to it, staring at the birds nibbling at the moss in search of insects. They were fond memories and those eyes gripped him in a swift glance. He snorted at his thoughts, he was already out of his mind.

Brida was reading a financial magazine she had found on one of the drawers in the room, turning the pages in boredom without bothering to reread the paragraphs that didn't stick with her. She held a cigarette in her left hand, letting the ashes fall to the floor in her distraction. A distant rumble of thunder made her raise her head and check the time. It was close to one o'clock in the afternoon. She could've shown up earlier with Collin, instead decided not to, knowing maximum punctuality wasn't necessary.

She finished her cigarette by stubbing it in the ashtray she had placed on the bed and prepared to leave the room. She felt a distinct stare on the back of her head. She turned around and saw the mountain hare, somehow looking more alive than before, as if suddenly details the artist hadn't originally included had appeared, focused solely on the hare. A light in the eyes, the body seeming ready to leap and flee. With a new urge to distance herself from the piece, she adjusted her jacket and stepped out of the darkness of her room, locking the door. The rain was falling with less force than it had during the night, being able to walk calmly to Collin's apartment without bothering to protect her head. She arrived at the old building and rang the bell, waiting for the young man's appearance. Soon Collin peeked out of his apartment door in casual clothes and mussed hair, striking a comfortable and comforting picture. Brida felt the need to look elsewhere, not because she disliked it, far from it.

"I had a feeling you'd come at just the right time," he said, stepping aside to let Brida enter through the iron gate. Again, the detective had that look on her face that he didn't know how to interpret. Locking the gate, he guided her to his place. "Come on in. I don't know how to cook much, but I made something simple to eat."

"Thank you."

Collin went in first and held the door open. The room was in stark contrast with all the grey of the town just outside of it. As she entered and Collin closed the door behind her, she was astonished at the flood of light the room cast upon her. She perceived the smell of the food Collin had mentioned, but there was also that vivid aroma she had smelled from him before when they first met, only stronger. As if it permeated every object in the room. It reminded her of her old home in its humid greenery and dim warmth, like the other side of a coin. It was intoxicating.

Collin had rushed to the small kitchen to put out the fire on the griddle. Brida, for her part, inspected the place. The walls were a yellow ochre color, the furniture generally a mahogany brown, often sporting old, black iron handles. There was a work table with small statues of calves and bulls attached to a wooden cross. On the walls were family photos. One of them pictured a young Collin holding his parents' hands near the lake. Collin was his father's carbon copy, only his face was narrower with his mother's fine features showing through. She gave a faint smile looking at the photo. Collin returned and looked at the detective and smirked, holding a casserole in his hands. "Did you like the pictures?" he said, setting the food down on the table.

"Lisa told me you go to the lake to fish."

"Yup, the lake was always my favorite place. My dad was the one who taught me to fish ever since I was little. My mum didn't like me getting in the boat with him, but eventually she stopped saying no to him. She knew my dad was going to take me anyway. It brings back good memories."

Brida glanced once more at the photos. She allowed herself to reminisce her own father and the brief moments they spent together, eventually becoming just like him. Soon her grandfather's solemn expression flashed in her mind. "I've never gone fishing myself. In all my life I've never felt the need to get out and see new places. Only this time I felt the need to go elsewhere."

"You really never cared to travel?"

"No, work kept me too busy."

"You can sit down, you know. The food is ready," he said, heading back into the kitchen, thinking over his next words. "Lisa said you were liking the town, that's good. It may not be as pretty as it used to be. I remember the lake used to be a bit more populated, but at least traditions are still well preserved."

Brida took a seat at the small table, and took a deep breath, trying to loosen up. It had been so long since she had had a gathering like this. Yes, she knew Thomas often went out of his way to invite her to eat with him, but this was different. There was nothing at the moment to link her to Collin. A beginning without the other person being connected to her past. "What kind of traditions?"

Collin returned with two glasses full of water and handed the other to Brida, who murmured a thank you. "Oh, you know. The little celebrations we have as a small town. Every year, in the middle of November, the town gets together and holds a ceremony. We're supposed to be celebrating the founding of the town, but it's more of a party to get drunk and skip work. Although, around that time every year my mum would tell me strange stories about Elkan and an overlooked villainous life, but I never paid attention to it. I remember her telling them to me when I was little."

"I think I heard a similar story," she said. "It's normal to know after the fact many historical figures weren't virtuous people. Elkan got the same treatment."

"Yes, well, other figures have stories of strange love affairs, bad political campaigns, even stories about their crazy sexual relationships. But Elkan, I think, is worse than all of those. I remember quite well my mum used to say Elkan had killed certain women in town for something he took as disrespect, or something of the like, but my dad told her not to say that anymore when I was around. I don't know where she heard it."

"Do you like history?"

"I'm not a fan of it. It's always the same."

"It is," she said distantly.

Brida took a bite of the food, privately enjoying the flavor.

Collin inspected Brida, who finally looked comfortable, and he was pleased that she was able to ease herself in his presence. He tried unsuccessfully not to think so hard about how he wanted to see those eyes and their deep greens, which carried an intensity akin to a hazy memory from not so long ago of a man on a park bench. So, he kept his eyes on the food, noting all too harshly the silence of their meal. He was certain the detective was one of those people who didn't talk while eating. "How's life as a detective?" he asked, trying to sound casual.

"Tiring, busy, fulfilling."

"Really?"

Brida glanced at him, leaving the fork on the plate. "I can say since I was promoted to detective, the humidity doesn't affect me as much anymore. The wool uniform I used to wear always made me sweat on humid days." Brida paused, sipping the glass of water lost in a memory. She tapped the glass with one finger. "Sometimes I miss patrolling in winter."

"Was there something special about it?"

"I had a patrol partner, and I admit what I liked the most was the atmosphere of the time."

"And now?"

"Now, I'm more cooped up in the office than I used to be."

"And do you like your job?"

"It's the only thing that keeps me going."

Collin continued to stare at the detective and tensed his lips into a tight line. It didn't seem like a good enough gig to him, but what would he know, he once worked in an office and hated it with all his being. He wasn't a deadbeat who didn't want to accomplish anything with his life. Since he turned fifteen he had already been working here and there. He liked to work, but he also liked his time. Collin decided to change the subject, feeling flustered. "Did you like the food?"

"It was good, thank you."

"I'm not good in the kitchen, but I've kept some of my mum's recipes."

"I was never good in the kitchen either. There was a time when I ate together with my friend when we were at the academy and he would only let me make coffee for fear of my cooking. Thanks to him I learned how to season properly and manage salt better when cooking."

"Wouldn't he want to give me lessons too?"

"I could ask him."

Collin chuckled, shaking his head. "I was joking."

"I could still ask him," she said with a small smile. Thomas wouldn't have no problem teaching someone in his kitchen; on the contrary, the man loves to keep his grandfather's authentic cooking afloat. She well remembered how Thomas would get inwardly exasperated when his grandfather wouldn't stop talking about food. "Do you only work at the inn or do you have another job?"

"Uh, yes, I work for others. I'm a good plumber and I'm pretty handy. I help repair walls, maintain old people's gardens, clean roads, a lot of things that not many bat an eye to. Small things that for them is already a burden. I even get to bathe dogs."

"So you do everything."

"A little bit of everything. Next week we'll have the festival and I'll have to help a lot of the old people set up their stalls, along with the nuns and their ceremony. I'm just going to help them move some things around outside, the church will be open for the mass only."

"I met the nuns days ago, they were very accommodating."

"Really?" Collin inquired quizzically. "The church wasn't open this week. But who knows, only they know who they invite to their church. Maybe they let you in because you were coming from out of town, although that doesn't make much sense."

"Why is that?"

"Outsiders aren't allowed to enter, they can only enter when it's open mass. Only the people from town are allowed in and even we have to wait for them to allow it. I rarely go to help them prepare their ceremonies, and they don't even let me go beyond the main part of the church either. I've never felt the need to go deeper and I don't know how that um… congregation -I think it's called like that- even works."

"I was told they do it to maintain the purity of the place."

"Yeah, so they say," he said, letting out a long sigh. He didn't have the head to go around wondering why their church was so peculiar. He never questioned exactly why they behaved the way they did or what kind of congregation they had in town. He never had the need and still does not. "Let me prepare the tea and take out some biscuits I brought with me. Give a me a moment."

"Yes, of course."

Collin got up from the table to go prepare a robust black tea. He pulled out a package of shortbread cookies and another package of chocolate chip cookies and placed their contents on a small plate. He waited for the tea to be ready, sensing a stare on his back. "You have some heavy eyes," Collin said, turning his head smiling.

Brida gave no reaction and averted her gaze. "Sorry."

His fingers twitched, inexplicably chilled. "Oh, no, don't worry. I guess I'm a little nervous, it's been a long time since I've had visitors. Hardly ever have any. The decisions I made when I was younger didn't leave me with many connections, you know."

"You *are* young."

"I don't feel young." Collin returned with two cups of tea and placed them on the table. He went back for the plate of cookies and took one, while Brida picked up her cup. He sat down and reached for his cup, attempting to rid of the sensation in his hands with the warmth of the tea.

Brida gently blew out the tea smoke and took a small sip. Then she sighed heavily, setting the cup aside. She needed to be sure. "Yesterday, I asked you about the man Lisa had talked to in the park. I've been thinking about that person ever since she mentioned it. I know you may have more information on this."

Collin raised his eyebrows. "You sure cut to the chase. Yeah, I remember we agreed to talk about it. Lisa didn't tell you what he looked like?"

"She couldn't really tell me much. All she said was that she only remembered his demeanor."

"You seem to want to look into this."

"Not quite. I'm only assessing a concern of mine."

"Ah," Collin said, frowning. "Well, I guess I should start from the beginning if you're really not going to look into this. I remember the first time I saw Lisa in the park with that man and I thought it was weird. I don't know if Lisa has told you that she's afraid of strangers, especially men. Seeing her alone with a man gave me a bad feeling. Whenever she would come back to the inn, she would be talking about this man as if he was someone important. I tried to ask the neighbors if they knew anything about him, but I could never really describe him well, and the things I remembered seemed too weird to say out loud, so the neighbors thought I was going crazy or on drugs."

"You didn't see his face?"

Collin licked his lips. "No, I did. I know I did, but I can't remember it."

"Lisa had the same problem."

"That's strange to me. She was the one who spent the most time with that man," he said, passing his hand down his neck. "The only thing I remember are his eyes, and now that we're alone… I can say with certainty that your eyes sometimes remind me of that man's. A light… But they look normal. I really don't even know what I'm saying." Collin considered what he was saying and twisted his mouth. He remained silent as Brida watched him with a sudden change in expression and intensity, with different eyes. At the moment, he didn't know if it was a good look or if she thought he was crazy.

Brida caught the exact moment Collin withdrew from the conversation. She became aware of that warm light in the room again, but this time dimming, becoming weaker. For some reason, that made her tense. She squeezed the cup's handle and cleared her throat in an attempt to get his attention. Thankfully, it worked, and the light seemed to return just slightly. "If you remember anything else, you can come to my room anytime."

"Sorry, I didn't know this would take so much out of me."

"Don't worry about it. What do my eyes have to do with the man in the park? You said my eyes reminded you of that man's. A light, you said."

"When I saw his face, at first I only saw a brown color in his eyes, but I know I also saw flashes of red. I thought I was just having some incredibly bad eyesight, but it happened every time I tried to look at his face. When I first saw you, your eyes had that same glint. I don't know how to describe it, they were like the eyes of an animal."

Brida fell silent.

Collin put on a strained smile. He wondered internally if anyone had ever made that comment to her, thinking again on what he said. It wasn't exactly a normal thing to say someone had a light in their eyes. Of course, people have metaphors and sayings about these things, like the glow of a pregnant woman, or the loss of light in one's eyes from shock or trauma. But not in such a literal way. "You don't seem to be very surprised to hear about this," he said.

"No, I'm not."

Collin took a sip of his tea, letting his mind wander over what the detective had understood from what he had said. He didn't have the energy to explain himself further and hoped the detective wouldn't ask him any more questions about it. "Going back to the man in the park, I never asked his name. I don't know why it didn't occur to me. I guess I was more worried about making Lisa stop going to the park. I know it's annoying, but I don't remember his face. I only remember the way he spoke and his eyes, but he had some strange mannerisms. For example, he put his hand for a long time on Lisa's shoulder… you know how birds hold their talons around their prey? It reminded me of that."

Brida huffed and sketched a tired smile. "Alright, at least, your perspective gave me a better understanding of things. I've already taken up too much of your time. Thank you for the food, next time I'll make sure to repay it."

"No, don't worry about it. Are you…" He stopped himself before finishing the question; he knew the detective wouldn't stay long. He glanced at the clock and was surprised that time had passed them. He tried to smile and walk with her to the entrance. "You know, don't take this the wrong way, but I didn't think I was going to enjoy your presence very much. I'm glad it was otherwise."

"Thank you for sharing your time with me. See you soon, Collin."

"Yeah, yeah. Be careful out there."

"I will, thank you."

Brida took a deep breath, taking in the last pieces of sweet light and aromas that permeated the room, the aroma now richer with Collin beside her. She opened the door and stepped out, hearing the church bells ringing just as she shut the door. She reached into her jacket pocket and felt the ring, pressed her teeth together and scowled, pressing the cursed object into her hand. The church bells vibrated in her skull.

XIII

Thomas Cipriani finished his paperwork and squeezed his eyes shut, feeling them water and ache from being so focused on the fine print of the report. His shift had already ended one hour ago, but first he had to finish what was asked of him. It was his job at the end of the day. He wasn't too worried about getting home late. He bit the tail of his pen. where it had already been gnawed on many a time before. Brida had warned him that one day the pen would explode in his mouth. And how funny that just at the moment he felt the taste of ink in his mouth. He grimaced and took one of the napkins he had in his jacket pocket. It was already late, and there was little movement at the station. He wondered if maybe he needed a break too. Away from the city, away from his problems with Alina, away from his own worries. He knew he wasn't going to do it. He was never one to run from his problems for long. It was always worse if he didn't confront them.

Thomas looked around at all his colleagues and saw there were only two others in the department doing the same as him, apart from the new captain who was locked in his office, probably preparing statistics as Ortiz always used to do. His colleagues looked as tired as him, being a little annoyed that they had more worked piled onto them. At least this time no one was getting bitten by some lunatic like the last time he had to arrest a man for drug possession. His patrol partner was getting those stitches removed soon. That would've been a story Brida would've loved and laughed at with him in the break room. He felt his eyes heavy and ran his hand over them, trying to wake himself up to no avail. He got up from his desk and went to make coffee in the break room. He was alone in there. Thomas turned on the coffee machine, leaning against the counter of the small kitchen they had. He checked to see if they had at least some of the leftover sweet bread from the morning and to his good fortune, there were still several homemade breads and cookies in the cardboard box. He heard footsteps and saw the new captain, Samuel Cano, who had a weathered look behind the square glasses he wore. The man struck a stark contrast from Former Captain Ortiz. Though the man hadn't been there long, Thomas found himself missing Ortiz's style as his higher-up in comparison. It was understandable, considering Ortiz served as captain for many years. Cano was too staid for the time being, staid in the sense that you knew he carried the old-fashioned ways. Hopefully in time that would change.

"Is there any bread left?"

"Yes," Thomas said, grabbing one of the small loaves out of the box and passing it to him by placing it on a napkin. The captain took it and sat down at the small table, seemingly waiting for the coffee as well. Noticing this, he took another cardboard cup, placing it next to his own.

"Wasn't your shift already over, Cipriani?"

"Yes, but I still have some things to finish, so I think I'll stay here for another hour," he said, grabbing the jar of sugar and a plastic spoon. Ortiz had never been a man with a sweet palate, he didn't think his new captain had the same bitter inclination. "Would you like your coffee without sugar, sir?"

"Put two spoonfuls in it," he said taking off his glasses and cleaning them with his tie. "I was thinking about Castillo these days. We're investigating a case downtown, and I've heard rumors about a rash of cases coming from Dameborne. Do you know if Castillo finally did something with her time?"

Thomas stopped preparing the coffees to think about his next response. That was exactly what Brida had said the last time he had seen her. Apparently, Brida was aware of the rumors more than he was. "Brida's in town, looks like she finally wanted to find out where all our history comes from."

"So she's on a sightseeing tour?"

"Something like that."

"Well, at least she's done something with her time." Cano leaned back in the chair and put his glasses back on. He didn't seem to like the cleanliness of his glasses and went back to wiping them with his tie. "Ortiz mentioned something to me about her particular case and how it affected her. If you see her these days, tell her she'll have a full desk.

I believe she has some days left, hopefully she'll enjoy them because we're going to have double the work here."

Thomas stared at his captain silently, contemplating his words. Of course, many in the station knew the facts of Brida's case, but not the details of said facts. In major part, that was due to Ortiz keeping a tight lid on media coverage and closing the file on the incident himself. Ortiz followed the case personally, and now Cano is the one who holds authority over it. Although, to be honest, it wasn't a priority to look for that man. The city's police force was already overburdened, and Thomas wasn't sure they could divert even a portion of their resources for the incident Brida had suffered without being stretched paper-thin. He knows Ortiz had pursued all possible routes for the case and the file had been put on hold. Brida hardly commented on the matter, remaining sharply focused on healing, restarting her routine, and getting back to work as soon as possible. He didn't know whether to be grateful or worried about Brida's reserved nature. "Yes, I'll tell her," he said, pouring the coffee into Cano's cup, who thanked him and placed it beside his sweet bread. Thomas blew out the coffee smoke, pondering something he hadn't paid much attention to until now. His thoughts centered on whether it would be such a bad decision if he also went to town. "Captain, I've been thinking of taking some days off."

Cano sighed heavily, which made Thomas inwardly cringe, thinking the captain hadn't taken kindly to the idea. He knew he was asking a lot during a time of low manpower, but he also knew he wouldn't be denied his days. Cano looked at Thomas with tired eyes, resting his hands on the table. "When were you looking to take those days off?"

"Actually, I'd like to know if I can take them next week."

Cano nodded, still regarding Thomas with weary eyes, then shrugged his shoulders, adjusting his glasses in the process. "Think it through because we're short on patrols, alright? Let me know the following Monday if you really want to go," he said, grabbing his coffee and carefully placing the bread Thomas handed him on top of the cup. "Don't stay too late."

"Yes, sir. Thank you." Thomas waited for his captain to leave and shrugged, taking his own coffee and bread back over to his desk. At least it hadn't been too much trouble to mention he wanted a vacation with the new captain. He planned to take two, at most, three days off. He set the food aside and went back to work. Staring again at the fine print of his report, he thought even Alina could be calm without his presence for a few days. His report lost its importance as he delved deeper into his thoughts. He had to talk to Alina.

When he finished his paperwork and said goodbye to his colleagues, he went to his patrol car, which for many was a normal occurrence to take back home as of late. Thomas arrived home and parked the patrol car in the garage. He made sure he had everything organized and operating properly. With his once-over of the vehicle done, he was able to enter his house, relaxing his posture as he did. Thomas was grateful that, at least tonight, the city was quiet for a change. He took off his jacket, hung it on the coat rack, and headed for the kitchen, where Alina was on the phone, having a small conversation with someone he assumed he'd rather ignore. Thomas remained quiet until something caught his attention, something Alina was saying.

"- you to this house, you have no right to be calling here. Goodbye and don't call again," she said, slamming the phone down onto its receiver with finality. Thomas stared at the scene, not knowing what to think. Alina didn't seem aware of his presence, so he knocked on the door frame, making her jump and shoot Thomas a withering look.

"Who called?"

"No one important," she replied with a hint of irritation. "I didn't hear you come in."

"No, you were too focused on the phone."

"Well, I'll leave you alone. I'm going to take a bath."

Thomas watched as Alina left the kitchen without another word. He approached the phone curiously, wanting to know why she had been so abrupt on the phone. Call it a sense of intuition or foresight, but something told him it was important to see what she was trying to hide. He didn't think it was any of Alina's friends, let alone the guy who was always trying to send her flowers. At least, he hoped not. That would only lengthen the time it would take for Alina to deign herself to sign the divorce papers, and Thomas didn't feel like waiting for a signature his whole life. There were several people Alina didn't like, but Thomas couldn't think of many of his own friends who could call him that Alina would take such issue with. He left the phone alone for the moment. Later he would have the courage to ask her who it was again. He began to prepare a small, simple dinner. Now that he had some time alone before Alina returned, he wondered if he really wanted those days off. On the one hand, he didn't care if the captain got mad at him for taking some time off. On the other, it would leave him more time of his own. Now that he thought about it, a person who didn't want Alina to call the house and he himself had asked her to call at all it would have to be Brida. Thomas paused, setting aside the cooking for the moment. Of course it made sense, the only person that could've gotten that kind of reaction from Alina had to be Brida. Thomas frowned, his mouth tightening. He was fed up with Alina's behavior. He listened for sounds coming from upstairs until Alina came down, changed into an evening gown. "Tell me who called."

Alina stared at him, unwilling to answer, and moved to grab her purse from the living room. Thomas folded his arms, already knowing the answer. "Brida called, right?"

"Hmm."

"Alina."

"So what, yes, she just called and even asked for you, but I told her not to call this house anymore. Happy? Yes? Well, I'm leaving now," she said gripping her purse in annoyance and towards the front door. She heard Thomas' footsteps and turned around, she was taken aback to see his expression, not annoyed as it was usually, but exhausted. It made her angrier to see him like that. "Why do you always treat me like I'm the bad guy?"

"You're the one who put yourself into that role."

"I hate you."

Thomas wanted to sigh. He thought of his grandfather who rested in peace, asking him to please send him patience for what he was about to request of Alina. He gazed at her glumly and cocked his head to one side. "We need to talk."

"About what?"

"About us."

Suddenly Alina felt uneasy, she didn't want to talk to Thomas about anything, even holding his gaze made her uneasy. In the back of her mind ran the thought that Thomas was going to finally tell her the truth, that he was going to tell her what she had always suspected. She hung her purse on the rack. "Let's talk then."

Sitting on the living room couch, Thomas reflected on everything he loved about Alina, starting with the pretty cupid's bow on her lips. He cared for her, but he didn't love her like he used to. He didn't know how to begin. He smiled at her, going back to those fond memories they had had before, bringing his hand closer to her, who looked at him gravely. He felt victorious when she rested her hand on his. How many feelings this beautiful woman hadn't provoked in him. Holding hands, for an instant, he considered they could move on, but it was clear they no longer felt the same. They had hurt each other in a way that created more discontent. He turned away from those thoughts, wondering how many times they would be so cowardly as to have this talk again. "Do you really hate me?"

The silence which accompanied the question caused Thomas to look at Alina's face, he gently stroked her hand, softer than his own, until he felt a squeeze on his hand. Alina took a deep breath and then shakily released it. "No, I don't hate you, but I resent you."

"I know."

Alina felt remorseful at the tone of voice used by her soon-to-be ex-husband, she felt like a little girl who wanted to give all the excuses to her parents. She wanted to take her hand away and yet at the same time she longed to embrace this damned man who had made her fall in love with him. "Thomas, I don't know what else we can talk about. I know you love-"

"Can you stop assuming about my friendship with Brida?" He had expected this. He'd had enough. "Why do you do the same with all my friends or any woman I talk to? Don't think I haven't noticed. I would have to be blind not to. Right now it's Brida you're taking it out on because I know I've been keeping an eye on her after the incident she suffered. But before that, the problem were my coworkers. You even asked me if I liked a woman just because she said hello to me. I don't think this is fair, Alina." He waited for his wife to say something, but only received silence, taking the opportunity to continue his speech. "I know you have your insecurities, Alina, but this no longer falls on me. What I wanted to talk to you about has nothing to do with anyone, it has to do with us. Alina, please, I want you to be honest with me because I'm tired of waking up every day and knowing you sleep in another room. We can't even stand to be in the same room without having a real conversation. I'm tired, Alina. Doesn't it tire you out?"

Unwilling to accept Thomas' words, she withdrew her hand. She hated him again. "Why do you always want me to be the problem?"

"What's that got to do with this?"

"You always have something to say about me, as if you've done nothing wrong. I'm always the bad guy and you're always nothing. I'm sick of this, of you. When you first mentioned divorce, I couldn't understand why you wanted to get away from me. Thomas, tell me the truth, do you love her?"

"Alina," he began wearily.

"Don't lie to me!"

Thomas clasped his hands together, suddenly embarrassed for the both of them. "I don't know how many times I have to repeat it to you. I need you to listen to me, really listen to me. I know you blame me for a lot of things and I accept that. I know how much you wish you had never met me, but none of this helps us because you are the one who doesn't want to talk to anyone. It's been weeks since the petition and you know it. We can't save this marriage the way you want us to."

"Thomas-"

"I'm not finished. Do you know what your way of solving things is? It's to ignore them until you can't because the problem has gotten so big that you can't control it anymore. That's your way of pretending to work things out. All the times I tried to talk to you, make amends, something, I don't know, you completely ignore me. I can do nine things right out of ten, but you only see that one wrong thing and the other nine don't matter to you! It doesn't seem fair to me, Alina!"

"And you don't do the same with me?" she said heatedly, jumping to her feet. "You can say all you want about me, but I know that to you I'm the one who's wrong, the one who always looks stupid in front of everyone. Don't think I haven't seen the faces you make or the comments you do when you think I don't hear you. Go ahead, tell everyone I'm the one always causes a scene, that'll make you feel good about yourself!"

"I've never said anything about you to anyone."

"Right, I'm crazy then."

It's always the same with her, Thomas thought. He consulted the clock on the wall and reclined on the couch, noticing how his back ached. "I haven't talked to anyone about our problems, Alina. I don't even know what to say to you anymore without you taking it the wrong way," he said, looking at her. "I did love you Alina, but we can't go on like this."

"You really want to leave me."

He didn't deny it. "Yes."

"My mother told me you wouldn't be a good man for me and I stood up for you. I defended you because I loved you and I wanted to prove to everyone that you weren't what they said!"

"Defended me from your mother?" he scoffed, letting his frustration grow. "Your mother always wanted to see the worst in me, even on our wedding day. Don't think you're the only one in this house who hears shitty comments towards his person either. You're not the only one. Your mother definitely played a role."

"Don't bring my mother into this."

"You brought her into this!"

Alina couldn't bear to look at Thomas and turned her face away, running her hands over and over through the end of her hair. She hated him, how much she hated him. She wanted him gone. "I'm always the problem in this damn house. If it's not me, it's my family. It's always the same with you, I could never be happy with you. Everyone was right."

"Who's everyone?"

"Everyone!"

"Your mother, you mean."

"Why do you want to leave me?"

"Because I don't love you anymore."

"No. Why do you want to leave me?"

"Because *I don't love you*," he said, emphasizing his words with the resentment of their long-lived tension. "You think I'm going to tell you that I love someone else like I did with you, but let me tell you one thing and I hope it sticks in that little head of yours. Compared to you, no other woman has ever interested me in this exact way. In our entire marriage, no woman ever made me feel this way, but you let another man do just that. You want to present yourself as the victim, but let me tell you another thing, the one who got cheated on was me! You are no victim."

"You have no evidence of that."

"I loved you, Alina, I really did. I knew you had some strange attitudes and I forgave you for them. I know at the time you were trying to make me jealous, to see that I was 'losing' you, but I also know you want to be with that man. I know that because your sister did told me you have accepted what he gives you. I'm not going to lower myself to 'fight' for you because these are some bullshit attitudes. You'll never be happy like that. You'll never be happy with anyone if you continue like this. Sometimes I think you only used me."

"I didn't use you."

"No?"

"I didn't."

"Doesn't seem that way. I know most of the time work consumes me, that I'm not there for you. I know I haven't been the most sensitive person in things that matter to you, but Alina, you have to understand that we can't have it all in life. How often I wish I had even more time for myself, but I can't! Sometimes I just can't! I like my job, I like being a cop. I like patrolling and even filling out all my reports. I wouldn't change a thing. You've always asked too much of me, Alina."

"Was what I was asking too much of you?" she laughed tauntingly, wiping her eyes. "I only wanted you to be with me. You blame me for all these things when our whole marriage was miserable. I was miserable with you. I asked enough of you!"

"Did you love me?"

"You know I did."

"I don't think so."

"You're such an asshole!" Alina exploded. "There were nights I wished you'd never come back to his house! That something would happen to you so I wouldn't have to put up with you anymore! I hate you! I hate you so fucking much!" she screamed at him, bursting into tears and covered her face. "I'm so fucking stupid. My mother was right, you're horrible."

"Yeah, sure," he said, rolling his eyes. He stood up, heading towards the kitchen, disregarding Alina, who stood with her hands clenched tightly, staring at the back of Thomas' head, momentarily considering throwing something heavy at him. She genuinely wanted to hurt him, however she knew the consequences it would bring. She grabbed her keys and left the house, causing Thomas to take a breath and slumped his shoulders. The whole atmosphere of the house changed with her exist. He stood there in the kitchen doing nothing, mind blank, breathing deeply, until a sound brought him out of his reverie. It had been the knife that had fallen off the cutting board, where it had been sitting precariously when he paused dinner. He picked it up and resumed cooking. He barely gave the potato a cut and lowered his head. He didn't feel like doing anything. He wasn't even hungry. Without a second thought, he picked up the phone and dialed a number from memory. He waited for it to ring and heard the voice that brought him comfort when he felt he was taking many missteps in his life.

"*Pronto?*"

"*Ciao nonna.* Sorry for calling so late."

"What happened? Tomasso? What happened?"

Thomas hesitated, believing now he had made a mistake in calling her. The mistake had already been made. His nonna wasn't going to leave him like a dog with a bone in its mouth. "I don't know what to do."

"What happened to you?"

"I'm a moron, nonna."

"You aren't."

"I don't know about that. Sorry to call you-"

"No, nothing of that. You know I like to hear from you. Something happened. Something happened, and I'm sure that woman had something to do with it. Ah, I hate to hear you like this. Tell me what happened. Tell nonna what happened. No, no, better yet, come to the house. Come on, I'll make you dinner," she said with finality.

"Are you sure, nonna?"

"When have I not been sure? I invite whoever I want to my house. Now come here and I'll prepare you something good. I'm sure you haven't even eaten. Come, come, I haven't seen you in a while. Make your nonna happy. I'll leave you to get ready." She hung up and Thomas felt numb. He ran his hand over his chin, feeling like the world's biggest moron. He thought about past decisions and why many of those choices were strangely ending his marriage. He knows he was wrong to marry so soon to someone he hadn't finished getting to know, that had been his mistake. And Alina had always been insecure about her own friendships as well as his own. At first he tried to understand it, but this whole issue was already out of his limits.

Thomas changed into casual clothes and washed his face. The feeling of shame never leaving him, not even when he reached his nonna's house. He stared at the entrance of the house, bereft. Alina always suspected the most bewildering things, none of it true. It puzzled him that his friendship with Brida had never been as much of a problem with Alina as with his other friends or coworkers, but after the 'incident' everything changed. Thomas didn't know if it was paranoia combined with jealousy, he didn't know. He and Brida knew each other since they were quite young, seeing each other as siblings from different families. Brida was a comfort zone for him, a constant and a source of solace. An anchor. He wouldn't change a thing, not even the moment they drifted apart. He was certain they would reconnect as they always had, and eventually they would talk. As he listened to the sounds of the city from his car, Thomas reminisced his connection with his closest friend. For as long as he could remember, they had always communicated openly about what they wanted from the other, till Thomas realized he had the sibling bond he had always wanted to have. From the first moment he knew he didn't have to put up any pretenses in front of her, that he could be himself. Brida was reserved and he was patient. His patience gave him one of the best friendships he'd ever had in his life. One that made him grow as a person. Now that he reflected on it, maybe that's why he was afraid. Maybe that's why he was so intent on it because he was afraid of losing someone so valuable. He didn't want to call it dependency because he didn't think it was. Brida was simply a pillar in his life he couldn't see himself without, like family.

"Tomasso."

He heard tapping on the window and saw his nonna hugging her sweater with one hand, while with the other kept tapping on the car window. He was quick to get out of the car, watching as his nonna clutched her sweater and Thomas hugged her, as if protecting her from the damp cold of the city. "You shouldn't have gone out in just a sweater, nonna! You'll get sick."

"Bah, you worry about nothing," she smiled, grabbing his hands, squeezing them lovingly. Soon, she placed her hand on Thomas' face, the grandson she loved so dearly. The first grandson she was given and the one who was always behind her and her late husband. His handsome face looked so droopy at that moment, almost bringing tears to her eyes from emotion. "You look down."

"I don't feel very well."

"Come to the house. I'm preparing the pasta you like so much."

His nonna took him by the arm. Memories greeted him as he entered from the narrow white door. The walls were pale yellow with dark green leaf patterns. Upon stepping into the kitchen, he saw the pots set out; one where the water was boiling and the other where the tomato sauce was. Thomas smiled when he saw what kind of sauce it was, it had meat rolls with ham. "I missed your cooking, nonna."

"You should visit me more often," she said adjusting her round glasses. "So, tell me. What happened over there? I got worried when I saw your call at this hour. What happened?"

"I wouldn't know where to start."

"I have all night."

Thomas laughed and folded his arms, leaning his hips against the kitchen counter. He didn't even know where to begin. He didn't have enough energy to even talk about it. "I had another argument today. It wasn't the worst, but it doesn't feel good when someone wishes you dead. Maybe she didn't meant it, but she said it, nonetheless. Alina has always said things she later regrets saying, but I don't think this is one of them."

"*Cretina,*" his nonna replied, indignant at what she had heard. "What's going on in her head? Wishing death to my grandson. Bah, I don't understand that woman. I'll never understand. I've always believed one can control oneself even in arguments, to wish death is already too much."

"Maybe."

"Not maybe, not maybe me."

"I said things to her too."

"In arguments we all say things, that's where it shows who's immature and who's not. Don't beat your chest too hard, it doesn't do much good. I hope you can settle this soon. I don't care much about you getting divorced, I even pray that you can finally get rid of that girl. You shouldn't go home in such an environment, full of anger and all those negative emotions," she said, patting Thomas' cheek causing him to let out a chuckle. His nonna always saw him in such a positive light.

"I hope so too, nonna. I don't want to live like this."

"No one would want to live like that. Now, tell me about your work, how has it been going? How has your friend been doing? I haven't seen Brida for a time now, you should invite her to lunch. I can't imagine what she feels, after what happened."

"She's on vacation, nonna."

"That's good, that's good," she repeated. "I hope she enjoys her time off. Who would have thought something like that would happen. You never stop getting to know people. We never know what's in their hearts. The world is getting crazier every day." His nonna shook her head and clicked her tongue, patting Thomas' hand. "You should take a vacation too, look how pale you are."

"I plan to take a few days off."

"That's good, you should."

The night with his nonna was helping him clear his mind. Dinning with his nonna in that square table he used to share with his grandparents when he was younger, he felt comforted. He had always preferred to be with his grandparents than with his parents for this exact reason. He thanked her when he finished and helped clean up the kitchen. But he had to return home, promising his nonna everything would be resolved soon. Once he arrived at his house, he let out a breath of relief knowing Alina wasn't present. Alina could keep the house, he just wanted the divorce and to walk away completely. He turned on the television and heard that the storm had already started in town and would soon reach the city. He turned it off and went to bed, feeling his back pop as he lay down. It was decided. He was going to take some time off. He closed his eyes, trying to fall asleep, yet strange sounds kept him awake, sounds much like the fluttering of a bird's wings.

XIV

Brida strolled through town with an umbrella in hand. The benefit of having an umbrella stored in the trunk of the car was that if it rained it wouldn't catch her off guard. It was best to be prepared at all times. The stone streets were old and cleverly done, with parts of the sidewalk displaying plaques in the ground indicating some old streets that had been renamed or otherwise modified. The rain pounded on the umbrella, causing Brida to concentrate solely on that noise. Her footsteps couldn't be heard clearly, as it rained heavily, drowning out other sounds usually ambiently present. She took a breath and noticed how it fogged up in the chill air. The town was almost empty, except for the occasional passerby. There wasn't much reason to go out in this storm.

Her mind was occupied with yesterday's call. Upon hearing Alina's voice, she had remained silent as she considered hanging up and calling another time, instead, she asked for Thomas, remembering the shift he had, presumably he would be home at the time she called. Alina began a string of questions causing Brida to withdraw into herself, staring at a fixed point, when there was a tentative pause, Brida had the bright idea to ask again if Thomas was at home. Alina repeated the same questions. Brida leaned against the booth, pinching the bridge of her nose. For some reason, she had been glued to the phone as she listened to Alina's accusations. Initially she was paying attention to Alina, disinterestedly listening while her eyes drifted to the church tower, buried recollections of her former partner's smooth voice crept in. Her thoughts had begun to distract her to the point she didn't even realize Alina had hung up.

She turned down a street, catching sight of the church. Looming above the fog, the tower bell was easily visible even from where she stood. She headed for the church, already knowing her way around without having to look at the old street plaques. As she arrived, she left the umbrella outside, not wanting to get the floor wet and offend the nuns. She took a breath and admired the engravings of on the doors, passing her hand over them, feeling the lines against her digits. So much detail for a simple door. She pushed the door open and, to her surprise, the darkness of the interior didn't strain her eyes at all, unlike the first time. Everything around her had quieted down, even the rain seeming unwilling to disturb the sacredness of the church. She walked through the center of the chamber, feeling a soft mat on the soles of her shoes, a verdant carpet connected to the altar. She stopped when she heard whispers and soon saw the elderly nun kneeling with her head bowed before the central painting of the altar. Not knowing what to do, she determined to move away from the old nun so as to not disturb her while trying to understand the prayers, maintaining her focus on the painting that had captivated her on her previous visit.

"You're back."

Brida turned sharply and spotted the young nun behind her. Her black eyes regarded Brida with an emotion she couldn't quite discern. The older nun continued her prayers undisturbed by her companion, nor by Brida. Experiencing once again the damp smell that brought an instinctual tension to her muscles. "Yes, I was a bit apprehensive about coming back here."

"Why is that?"

Brida turned her head to the old nun and then to the younger one. She didn't want to upset the old nun with the chatter and murmured, "I wouldn't know myself."

The young nun had seen the head movement, trailing it with her eyes. She moved her arm to rest her cold hand on Brida's lower back, causing the detective to tense even more at the contact. Brida turned to the young nun, who smiled at her, tilting her head slightly. "Come with me," she whispered, beckoning Brida to walk with her without removing her hand from her back.

They walked back down the hallway connecting to the dining room and the kitchen, rendering Brida, through the smell of plants and the hand that refused to leave her back, to be unnerved for a moment. The nun dropped her hand on Brida's back to indicate the same seat the detective had occupied the first time, the main chair at the table. The table was already set for visitors, with porcelain cups in their respective sets and a silver coffee set beside the central floral vase, two plates of baked sweets placed on each side. The centerpiece was decorated with live and wilted flowers emitting a bizarre aroma of stale blossoms mixed with the coffee. White lilies fell from their arrangement accompanied by ears of wheat. It all seemed to have been prepared for three people in mind, and considering their infrequent allowance of visitors, it was as if they had only organized for the visit they had agreed upon before. The young nun watched as Brida took her seat, picked up the coffee pot and poured some of its contents into each cup.

"From the first time I saw your eyes I loved them, and now they shine," said the nun smiling, peering at the detective.

Brida was a bit taken aback by the nun's bold comment, leaving her unsure how to react to such appreciation, opting to respond with a slight smile and a polite thank you. The young nun nodded, liking her courteous gesture.

"Are you enjoying our home?"

"Yes, the town has a lot of history, more than the city."

"There's a lot of hidden history here," said the young nun. "We often like to tell a little secret or two. What have you learned here that is so different from the city?"

"We don't have any festival connected to the founder."

The young nun stopped pouring at Brida's comment, then nodded and continued the action in silence. Brida kept observing the nun and noted how the hand that had been tenderly holding the handle of the coffee pot now grasped it with a clenched grip. The nun's face appeared to be relaxed, yet her shoulders had tightened into a straight line. The young nun picked up on the silence as she handed Brida her cup of coffee, who accepted it, thanking her with a nod. She set aside the silver pot and didn't take a seat, opting to stand near the detective. "I'm sorry, I'm not being a good hostess. What else have you learned?"

Brida took a sip, appreciating that the coffee had a spicy flavor. It had been a while since she'd had a spiced coffee. "Nothing much. I already knew some facts about the founder. It's always the same with historical figures," she said, setting the cup down on the small plate. "Now that I remember, I was told a strange story about the founder."

"What kind of story?"

"That he killed women."

The nun didn't react at first, her gaze fixed on the detective without blinking. Brida couldn't discern her pupil, those eyes were swallowing her. What small light was in the dining room from the candles was reflected in those eyes like sparks, keeping a grip on Brida. The young nun lowered her gaze, clasping her ringed hands. "It's a tragic story indeed. They had welcomed him and invited him into their home. But he decided in the end to betray the love she had for him." Here, the nun fell silent and remained so before she finally lifted her head. Upon seeing her eyes, Brida froze where she sat. The pain in those eyes had reminded her of what she wanted to leave in the past, inadvertently touching the scar on her lower abdomen. The young nun followed the movement. "His betrayal was unforgivable," she murmured, positioning herself behind Brida, who tensed, the hairs on the back of her neck bristled as she felt the nun closer than she appeared to be. The nun ran her hand over the wooden chair.

"Why did he kill those women?"

"Elkan was a fervent believer with great loyalty to the king, or so they said. We know the history books of this place say Elkan and his men accused them of witchcraft, threatening the church they built with the mere existence of those women and had them tortured in the most sadistic ways possible. They thought the devil was at work in this land, close to the hearts of the women who lived here. They believed these women to be witches. Several men helped Elkan in his mission to make this land holy as their king commanded. Elkan was ruthless with all of them, leaving no one unmarked."

"Were they burned at the stake?"

"No. Elkan was creative and so were his men."

Brida remained quiet, aware of the younger nun's presence behind her. The room became damp and cold. The corners of the dining room darkened. The presence grew larger and larger, sensing it as if it were a shapeless giant on her back. She had the impulse to turn around and see the nun with her own eyes, but she restrained herself. She heard rustling in the distance, and guessed the old nun was still concentrating on her prayers.

"Have you been marked?"

Brida furrowed her eyebrows. "I don't understand the question."

"You are touching your stomach."

She hadn't even realized she still had her hand on top of the scar. Brida stopped touching her stomach and rested her hand on the table. Could she call the scar a mark? It could be if she thought about all the lingering terrors that had crept into her mind since her former partner left her almost dead under the skylight of her house. Perhaps worst of all, she still remembered how he had gently laid his hand on her cheek and soon a pang and scolding warmth was felt in her stomach, forcing her to take an abrupt breath. Her gaze fixed on his eyes, red flecks of light visible in the glare of the skylight. How she wanted to strangle him and tried to. He whispered tender words in her ear and Brida took his face in her hands, bringing their gazes together, the sound of something splashing on the floor deafened her.

"You don't have to answer," said the young nun, running her hand over the wooden chair once more, without daring to touch the detective. "So many people have come to heal in this place with us. It would make me feel terrible if I were to make you uncomfortable or worse, make you run out of here."

"I was injured."

"Not just any injury, I might infer."

"I don't notice when I pass my hand over it."

Brida listened as the young nun moved and slowly felt her hands come to rest on her shoulders. Slender fingers gently advanced until her hands were fully supported. "I wasn't lying when I said people have come here to heal old wounds," the young nun said, moving her thumbs subtly, feeling the detective's muscles tighten to eventually loosen under her administrations. Brida frowned as she felt her body let go as if it had a mind of its own. "Do you have dreams?"

"I don't dream so often now."

"Do you like to dream?"

"Not particularly."

"I, on the contrary, loved to dream. I used to live in my dreams, now, I simply cannot anymore. There are no more dreams for me. They elude me," she murmured, a finger close to the detective's jugular. "I must leave you. My companion has finished her prayers, I'll be right back."

Brida felt those warm hands abandon her shoulders. The dining room took on a different air as the young nun merged into the shadows of the hallway. In her boredom, she touched one of the cookies and to her wonder the sweet crumbled under her finger, perchance the nuns hadn't noticed their cookies had gone stale beyond what Brida ever thought possible. The sound of footsteps and the slight movement of the door caused her to look up. The old nun had entered the dining room, closing the door behind her, and smiled at Brida, clasping her ringed hands together in front of her.

"I am sorry I didn't receive you, I was finishing reciting my prayers. My companion told me she found you in a better state than the last time you came here. We are glad to hear it. This site has always been a place to heal." The nun's tone became kinder, casting an intimate spell within them. "Apparently my companion wasn't lying. Your eyes are livelier than last time, your posture more even, I can even see more color in your cheeks." The old nun paused, taking her time to take in all the good changes in the detective. "Ah, forgive my bad manners, we are just glad to see you better."

Brida gave a small nod of her head in acknowledgement. "Thank you." She didn't know what to make of the fact the nuns were paying careful consideration to her appearance and health. She wasn't used to this kind of treatment. In fact, the only ones who paid attention even to how she sat in her office were Thomas and Ortiz. Not even her father -when he was alive- had ever noticed her as much, not in that way. It had been her grandfather who often kept an eye on her. She could reminisce about a nine-year-old Brida, listening to her grandfather play the acoustic guitar in his rocking chair. Her grandfather smothered a sorrowful smile, cupping a hand to her cheek. *Qué mal augurio tienes en esos ojos.* She had become so deep in thought she almost didn't hear the nun's question which made her conscious of where she was.

"Did you enjoy the coffee?"

"Ah, yes, thank you."

The old nun had the same expression of delightfulness the young nun had shown. Their cups were still just as full. "My companion has also told me you have been liking the town, tell me, what did you find most interesting about in this old place?"

"I've just been enjoying the sights, although I think my favorite is the lake," she said, with a small smile, musing on how Lisa and Collin enjoyed the lake in their respective ways. Collin because he wanted to reconnect with his old self and Lisa because it had become a safe place for her due to the healthy friendship she formed with Collin.

"I can see why the lake," the old nun answered, sitting down close to Brida. "The lake is as old as this place, it has no treasures inside, only old memories. It all belong to the past now. We loved to wander, explore, play, to show our reverence in this forest that surrounds us, some of us went to the lake to purify ourselves. This place is full of our memories, no one can erase that. Not even the hand of a simple man." The old nun closed her eyes, resting her hands on her legs. Brida stayed silent, respecting the old nun in her reminiscences. The nun soon opened her eyes. "Surely you already know about the festivity we will have here. We will have a ceremony for those who wish to participate in the sacred ritual."

"I was told the congregation doesn't allow many to enter into your church, but you let me in without any problem and even invited me back. I wonder why is that."

"Yes, we don't allow entry to many who have come here. Those we deny only come here to satisfy a morbid curiosity, and while we love that they think they can understand us, we resent their presence. This is a place of healing and will be respected as one." The older nun smiled tenderly, placing her hands on the table smoothing the table cloth. "We must be strict in who enters and who does not."

Brida tapped her finger on the table. The nun took a sip from her cup, satisfied with the conversation. Brida averted her gaze to the empty seat on her right side, expecting the young nun to come soon. Just like her first stay, she enjoyed her afternoon with the old sister until she took note of the time by checking her wristwatch. "Thank you for the coffee and your invitation. I would like to explore your church and learn about it."

"You are free to do so."

Thanking the old nun, Brida stepped out of the dining room, sliding into the darkness of the corridor seeming to have a permanent smell of damp than other sections of the church. The sweet humidity of the perfume of plants forced her to take a deep breath. Approaching one of the walls, the numbing smell grew stronger. Now she could recognize its sweetness, pine. There were painting frames hung along the hallway with no animal or image portrayed, vacant in brown and black colors, appearing with each step she took. She passed her hand across her forehead, breaking out in a sweat for a second, whishing she could take off her jacket to regulate her temperature. She heard the faint whispers of the young nun praying and pictured her in the same place the old nun took when she prayed, running her hand across her neck, now hearing the tinkling of a small bell. Ignoring how she felt, she walked into the church chamber, listening to that small bell for guidance till she saw the young nun kneeled in front of the altar, ringing a small bell in tune with her prayers. Brida focused her mind to the imposing painting of the angels and the people falling from cliffs, their lances tingled with their own devout light.

"You are curious."

Brida was startled by the interruption of the mutterings and turned to the young nun who remained kneeling, her dark eyes focused on her from her spot. She thought ruefully perhaps she had interrupted the nun's religious session. "I believe anyone could be in a place like this."

"There are many memories here, only we remember them."

Her lips hadn't move. Brida observed the nun's face, almost like a sculpture nestled in the shadows of the church chamber. The verdant gems on the necklace connected to the medallion on the nuns chest twinkled with every breath drawn.

"Will you stay?"

"It would be best not to impose on you."

"Then come soon to us, before the festival. We want to prepare another meal for you," she said, rising gracefully from her kneeled position. The young nun glided towards the detective, unblinking, her eyes absorbing the light, immense in its vastness. Extending her hand, hearing the fluttering of wings, the young nun rested her hand on Brida's lower back. "I will accompany you to the entrance. My payers can wait, in the end, we have the time to simply wait."

They headed for the entrance without looking behind them. Brida avoided seeing any paintings that would bring back memories. She thanked the young nun for inviting her again and exited the church, closing the cooper green doors, the rain intensifying, muffling her ears. She had grown accustomed to the stillness of the church, feeling the difference in temperature hit her face. The umbrella remained in the same place she had left it.

XV

Her favorite sweater was starting to fray. Lisa frowned at the threads that had slipped out of place. She laid it on her bed and picked another with white daisies knitted on the arms. She whipped her nose with a handkerchief, feeling it stuffy, fearing she was already getting sick from the weather. From her room she could hear the faint music her dad had put on alongside the rustling of paper as it moved. Martin Oliver Gallardo was seated in the chair near his bed, reading a book under the hare's gaze. Lisa peeked over to see her dad engrossed in his reading, her heart swelling at the peaceful image he casted. His hair fell over his shoulders, neatly combed, causing some natural curls to form. The room had been cleaned and tidied, the medicines arranged on his bureau next to a pile of books. Martin suddenly turned as he sensed his daughter's presence in the doorway and smiled.

"Ready to go with Collin?"

"Yeah, I'm waiting for him to finish what Grandma made him do and then I'll go for a walk with him at the park. He'll come to the office later. Wouldn't you like to go with us to the park? I can prepare the wheelchair, it's no bother."

"Maybe some other day."

"It's okay, we can organize it better," she said, reaching over to her father and grabbed his hand. He appeared better than on other days, even having a blush on his cheeks. Inwardly, she knew she will soon see his pale face, to which she had unfortunately become accustomed to. "I love you."

"I love you too," he replied, squeezing her small hand. Martin reflected on Collin, that young man, who kept Lisa company and understood her sensitivities. He was aware that Lisa wasn't well emotionally yet, little time had passed since Elizabeth had decided to leave. His daughter was intelligent -it was impossible not to see how hard she was working on her own studies- so, it would be a mistake to force her to understand her pain. Everything had its own time, he was sure she would soon understand. "We haven't talked. How have you been feeling these days?"

"I don't know. Sometimes I feel good, then I feel bad. I don't know how to explain it, I don't even know what I feel at times. It's like a, I don't know, like an emptiness and I don't know how to react to that kind of feeling," Lisa fumbled at the end, pinching her nails. "I don't like it."

"That's okay, it'll pass soon."

"I don't know."

"It will pass."

"Do you think she'll return?"

"I don't know," he said, putting his book down on his lap. Martin stared at their hands, wondering if he should confide his thoughts to her. A parent's thoughts always differ from their own child's. Lisa had always been a sensitive child. Martin was grateful his daughter had grown up and continued to love him. He could envision the pain Laura felt every day since she had lost her daughter, but in a selfish thought he was grateful it was Elizabeth who was gone and not Lisa. Laura had always been a woman of complicated emotions and, unfortunately, her daughter was her equal in many ways. There had been worries about their friendship, believing this girl would put dark thoughts into his daughter's head. Martin knew it was wrong to reason this way, but he was only a father. "That girl always struck me as volatile. She had somewhat irrational behaviors."

"Irrational?"

"I know her mother has been in constant pain since she left, but neither you, nor I know what kind of relationship she had with her mother. Sometimes people leave and never tell the reasons. We may never know why Elizabeth always wants to leave. Your friend, Elizabeth, had certain thoughts that seemed to me too…" He couldn't tell the truth. "Bizarre."

Lisa nodded. "I'm trying to understand."

"With friends it's difficult to know everything completely. All I ask of you, for now, is that you understand the situation and leave all this Elizabeth business aside for the time being. Figure what you feel and simply accept it. Do you understand what I'm asking of you?"

"I think so."

"You know you're not alone, as long as I'm here." He wouldn't know what would have become of him if he didn't have his daughter in his life. Ever since the car accident that left him without his mobility, a great guilt took hold of him. They heard the metal gate of the corridor leading to the office open. "I think Collin is searching for you," Martin smiled, patting the hand that still clutched his.

"Do you want him to come in?"

"It's okay." His daughter called Collin to his room, till the young man was seen entering, knocking on the door frame even though it was open. Martin noted Collin's weathered face, sporting bags under his eyes. "How did the piping go?"

"There was a broken pipe, but it's fixed now."

"Only one? That's good news," Martin said, letting go of Lisa's hand. He hoped what they had talked about would soon bring his daughter to her senses. "Go enjoy your walk."

Lisa pecked her dad's cheek, promising to come back home early, and grabbed Collin's arm, who waved a polite goodbye to Martin. They passed through the metal gate, locking it, as the office would only have one lock on out of the three it had. The faint music was no longer audible, Lisa looked back and bit her lips, wanting to preserve the warm feeling in her chest. Collin picked up his umbrella from the desk along with his jacket, waiting for Lisa to grab her keys and the scarf she had left on the chair. Lisa was in the process of shutting the office door when she felt a playful tug on her ear.

"You won't be cold?"

"No, I'm well tucked in," she said adjusting her scarf, folding the end of it into her sweater. Lisa was excited to spend time with Collin at the park, even though it was no longer a place where she felt safe, if she was with Collin it was like a protective blanket was covering her. She had loved the park for all the good memories, but now she wasn't so sure. Lisa remembered Elizabeth's words, starting with the good ones, where they could both laugh at a silly joke, share gossip, giggle when the other said a private quip only the other understood, but then the bad ones always crashed into her good memories. The damp air made her cough, moving closer to Collin, who held the umbrella above them.

"What are you thinking so hard about?" Collin asked, nudging her gently.

"About everything, I guess." Lisa rubbed her hands together, looking down with a puzzled frown. Her mouth stayed in a tight line, making her appear frustrated, but her rosy cheeks betrayed how she really felt. To Collin it seemed that Lisa was mulling over her behavior, continuing to stare at her, reflecting on how interesting it was to see Lisa thinking so openly. "I've been thinking a lot these days. There are things I still don't understand, things Elizabeth used to say to me when she was angry. Before you arrived, that's what I was taking to my dad about. One time I saw her arguing with her ex and- I didn't like seeing her argue with anyone like that, it made me nervous to think that someone might hurt her."

She contemplated the drizzle, strolling with Collin to the gazebo where they could better enjoy the foggy scenery. Lisa spotted tiny yellow flowers climbing over the metal railing, she picked one and pinched the petals, seeing her fingernail mark on the petal. She didn't know how to explain everything she had seen with Elizabeth. She didn't know if Collin could understand it all when she couldn't herself. Elizabeth and herself had been good friends, that much she knew. They had leaned on each other at times and listened when the other demoralized. She knew Elizabeth had a temper. One in which her own grandmother had told her that soon that girl was going to get in trouble with her long mouth. Lisa sighed, leaving the flower on the ground. She knew that a friendship didn't always have good moments, but the fights they had, sometimes were too much. Too much for her to handle. Afterwards she had to deal with the results of those fights: the long stares, the silence, the discomfort, the passive aggressive comments, how she was shushed out of the group. The hitting.

She never thought Elizabeth would one day hit her, open hand against her face. *One day you'll realize what a shitty world you live in. You think you're so innocent, but you're just like everyone else*, she had said. Lisa hugged herself, running her hands through the knitted flowers of her sweater. She missed her even if it was wrong. "I guess there's still a lot of things I don't know about her, but at least what I knew was enough to see that she wasn't well."

"We're never done getting to know people."

"That's what my dad also said."

"You should listen to him."

Lisa turned her attention to the park. She picked another yellow flower, this time simply twirling it between two fingers. She sagged her shoulders, sensing the tension emanating from Collin, anxious to really know what it was that had put him in that mood. "I've also thought about why I feel so comfortable with Brida and sometimes I think I get it, but then I don't know what to think. I feel like it all started when I met her that night, I don't think I've told you about that."

"No, you haven't," he said perfunctory.

"Okay, I'll be quick," Lisa murmured, lowering her eyes. She twirled the flower several times nervously, seeing how the petals created a visual effect, almost like a yellow circle. "I got lost and before you say anything, I was aware of the people around me. On that night I accidentally bumped into Brida and that's when it all started, you could say. I knew she had drank, so I invited her for a coffee and she listened to me. She *listened* to me. Nobody had made me feel listened for a long time, well, except for the man."

Collin turned serious when he heard her mention that man in the park, red images flashed in his mind and he closed his eyes, taking a deep breath. He wanted to reproach Lisa for so many things, especially why she had gone to the city, why even her grandmother had given her permission when even that damned woman was overprotective of her only granddaughter. What he most wanted to reproach her for was how her attitude had changed upon her return, as if the Lisa of the past -when Elizabeth was still with them- had come back with strength. He was thankful for Brida's presence had that effect with her, yet it seemed too extreme, although thinking about it, when he was younger he also took on a lot of attitudes that didn't help him for the future, maybe Lisa experienced one of those rebel episodes everyone has in their life. Collin shrugged. "It's okay you feel that way about her, she seems like a good person. We had a nice time when I invited her to eat. From what I saw in her, she's a person with a lot of problems on her shoulders and I knew several people like that out of town, most of the time it was better to stay away and turn a deaf ear."

"She isn't like those people."

"I'm not saying that she is."

Lisa gazed back at Collin. He stood with his arms crossed, eyeing the overgrown weeds. Lisa blinked repeatedly, controlling the urge to cry. "Collin?"

"What?"

"Are you angry at me?"

Collin hesitated in his answer. "A little."

"Why?"

"I think it's pretty easy to understand that I was upset to learn you went to the city when I wasn't here," he paused. "I was even more upset to know you spent all your savings to look for help you knew you couldn't afford. Now I can't tell you anything else because you've done everything on your own without thinking about others. I know we haven't known each other long, but Lisa, you can't be making these kinds of decisions alone. Lately you do actions that I don't know if you actually think about them. I only hope you never do it again."

"I won't, I promise."

"It's a promise now and you know those can't be broken, right?"

Lisa tried to smile at Collin, knowing he was trying to cheer the mood between them. "I know," she coughed, covering her mouth with her sleeve. She understood why Collin was angry, noticeable by the way he couldn't look at her in the eye, reminding her of when her dad would get upset with her. There were only so many times her father had been angry -more like disappointed in her- and seeing Collin have the same mannerism brought tears to her eyes. She knew it would take Collin a while to fully forgive her, but she had to admit she felt no guilt for seeking help to try to find Elizabeth. Her heart ached again, contracting in her chest. She wiped her eyes covertly. "I would never do it again. I don't think something like this would ever happen again."

"Who knows."

How long they stood there, contemplating the rain, only they know. The main sounds were Lisa's coughing and sniffling -which she was trying to control- and the rain pattering on the vegetation. Lisa leaned against the metal railing, and sighed shakily, she couldn't stand the silence any longer.

"Will you forgive me?"

Silence.

Lisa wiped her eyes again, she knew Collin couldn't forgive her. She was unrepentant and at the same time she felt terrible. She felt her shoulders being embraced, making her whimper, turning to Collin to hide in his chest. She couldn't control her weeping, feeling her hair being combed, calloused fingers running over her temples. She felt small.

"I'll forgive you, Lisa, you know I will, but not now."

"I know," she sniffled.

"But that doesn't mean I'm going to ignore you like some certain people would. Learn from this. And I sincerely hope you don't do this again." Collin slightly rocked her, watching as Lisa nodded and wiped away her tears. "You'll see soon you'll have good friends. I know I don't count much because you see me as a big brother, but for the time being I'm here for whatever you want."

Lisa smiled, still sensitive from the conversation. "Thank you."

Collin huffed playfully and smiled. "You cry a lot."

She gave him a little slap on his arm, but kept hugging him until she calmed down completely. She felt calmer knowing Collin wasn't going to leave her. She knew Collin wasn't like most people she knew. Although Collin came to town because of his wrongdoings, she was glad everything happened the way it did because thanks to that she was able to meet him. What a weird thought, to be grateful for his missteps.

XVI

It was barely four in the morning and he couldn't sleep a wink. He shifted into a fetal position, eyes unfocused on a spot in his room where the shadows danced with the light filtering through his half-open curtains, listening to the continuous tapping on his window. Black dots jumped and others bumped into each other, varying in sizes. The vibration of the insects rattled against his ears. Collin Fay took an abrupt breath, the pressure on his chest intensifying. He lowered a hand to his ankle, feeling only his skin, no ropes, realizing there never was one to begin with.

He had dreamt again. He saw a woman, next to him, shedding tears at their condemnation. They were bound with ropes, arms pinned to the sides, legs clamped together, face up on the ground. Lights flickered around the corners of the place, rendering him nauseated by the burnt odor. The walls reflected the lights. He moved his head, realizing the walls were adorned with various religious objects, iron crosses, ornaments, paintings, glass jars and candles, too many candles. A man in black regarded them with contempt, as if he was disappointed in them, placing a board over their bodies. He asked questions. Each time he answered, the men around them loaded the board with heavy stones. Collin wheezed under the pressure. The woman next to him screamed and spat at the man who asked the questions. Collin witnessed how they began to hit her head. The man in black left them under the pressure of the stones. He could only hear his own labored breathing. Collin jolted out of his reverie, willing himself to forget the content of his dream. He rubbed his arms harshly, gripping them until his hands imprinted on his skin.

As a child, he would wake up at night, weeping, screaming for his mum, other times too shocked to emit a sound and his poor mum wouldn't know what to do with him. His mum would comb his hair, hugging him to her breast, until one night he lay with fear in his chest: *You've seen it*, she had murmured against his forehead, kissing him tenderly. He had been silent, not knowing what to say. His dad believed he had a too lively imagination.

He struggled to concentrate on sleeping again, closing his eyes, ignoring the chittering of the insects. Suddenly he felt heat in his lower abdomen. A numbing perfume wafted to his nose, the humidity mingling with the dying sweetness of plants. His eyes fluttered open as he felt liquid gushing from his stomach, a metallic screech echoed throughout the room. His mouth salivated, a wet sensation on his cheek, his throat closed as the pounding in his chest made him gasp for breath. Then, in an instant, Collin stood up. His bed was clean. His stomach was closed.

Collin ran his hands over his face, tired of having another nightmare. His heart was still pounding uncomfortably, rubbing his chest, trying to calm it. *Still, be still*, he chanted in his head, in his mum's voice. The tapping on the window went on and on, and eventually he turned to see the insects gathered at the bottom frame of his window. Collin crept out of his room and sat at his workbench, staring at his unfinished fishing lure. He couldn't hear the tapping, good. *Still, be still.* His mum's voice chanted in his mind, waiting for his nerves to settle down, until all was quiet. He began to relax, slumping his posture. He turned on the lamp on his workbench and began working on his fishing lure. Choosing different feathers, picking up the thread and began to wind the feathers together to simulate a fish's tail. When he was done, he ran his hand through the feathers, smoothing them out.

He recalled the first time his dad tried to take him fishing.

His mum had stood with a frown on her face grasping a five-year-old Collin by the arm. His mum had always been a pretty woman, with her brown hair held in a clip, dressed in a pale-yellow dress contrasting with her tan skin. Collin glanced at her and then at his dad, knowing there was a rift between them. "I don't want you to take Collin to the lake."

"Why not?" His dad had cocked his head to one side, confused by his wife's reaction. "If you're worried something bad is going to happen, it's not going to happen. The lake is calm, I checked this morning."

"The lake is not calm."

Collin looked up to his mum and clutched her dress in his fist.

"What do you mean by that?" had asked his dad.

"That lake is not calm. Don't take Collin there today."

"Nothing will happen."

His mum scooped him up in her arms, leaving his dad in the doorway of the first house they had as a family. She had lingered in the living room, regarding her son with an expression he couldn't understand. For the first time, Collin felt a dreadful sensation take over his mind nestled in his mum's arms. Before long, his mum fully embraced him, putting his head in the crook of her neck and gently patted his back. He didn't know why his mum didn't want him to go to the lake with his dad, it seemed unfair that his dad could go to the lake and he could not. He had been envious. He could only see the lake from afar, imagining all the secrets that could be there, asking his mum if there were any boats lost underwater. His mum only chuckled at his innocent question.

"Every lake has its secrets."

He remembered that same night he had another one of his nightmares, which alarmed his parents when they heard his cries. He had wrapped his arms around his mother, shivering from the cold even though it had been the middle of summer. He couldn't stop gasping for breath, coughing, wheezing and then he vomited on the floor, scaring his parents. The stabbing sensation in his chest had persisted for a long time. Collin didn't go near the lake until he was eight years old and his mum wasn't happy.

"Nothing will happen, Eydie," his dad had said.

"You don't know that."

Even so, the two men of the house went fishing, leaving his mum behind with a grim expression on her face. His dad never fully understood why his mum was afraid of the lake. It wasn't fear, it was *respect*. His mum respected the lake too much. They had spent their morning and afternoon sitting in the boat, fishing in the lake that reflected the sunlight in stunningly patterns. A body of water everyone in town adored. Collin peered into the waters, staring in the murky depths of the lake. He felt he was seen. He controlled his impulse to look away. When they returned, his mum gave him a hug, threading her hands through his hair.

"Did you like it?"

Collin turned his head, looking at his mum, puzzled at the question since she never liked him going to the lake with his dad, much less alone. He had expected to be reprimanded. "Yeah, I did," he answered, disciplining his face. Eventually he had to get used to the lake. "It was quiet."

"Not always," his mum murmured.

No, not always, he thought.

He had been dozing on his workbench. The morning daylight bothered his irritated eyes, feeling them droop with each blink. He checked the time and saw he had to go to the inn to check if the rooms had any more problems. He put away his fishing lure, heading to his room to change, ignoring the insects that kept piling up at the bottom of the window and grabbed his umbrella. When he came out of his apartment, he saw the old woman sitting in the doorway near the iron gate. The two ignored each other's presence. Collin trudged through the rain to the inn, passing his gaze over room three. The windows were obscured by dark greenish curtains. His imagination roared into full bloom and he felt mortified, jerking his gaze away. Collin took out his keys and opened the office, expecting to find Lisa's grandmother, yet no one was there.

"Mrs. Livia?"

"Come in," Lisa's grandmother's voice replied, trailing distantly down the dark hallway that connected to the house. "The gate is open. Come to the kitchen."

He found Mrs. Livia in the kitchen, preparing two cups of coffee. He greeted her properly by giving her a kiss on the cheek. The old lady wore a cream blouse with a dark skirt that came below her knees. Collin felt the urge to pass her a sweater and shield the lady from the cold. "I'll check the other rooms for next week. Hopefully, the festival will attract more people."

"Let's hope all rooms will be filled."

"How is everyone feeling today?"

The old woman regarded him coolly, turning off the stove. "Martin woke up with the typical pain in his extremities, the cold is bothering him, but you already know that. Lisa is sick and she's in her room if you want to go see her."

"Thank you."

"I'm going to deliver the coffee to Martin and from there I'll go to the office. You can go see Lisa first and then you get to work. If you want coffee, you can make it here." She grabbed the cups and exited the kitchen.

"Yes, thank you." He was used to the Mrs. Livia personality by now, so he didn't mind. He heard coughing, ears perking up. He heard the coughing again and knew it was Lisa. Collin felt apprehensive about entering Lisa's room without permission from the girl herself. "Lisa?" He knocked on the door.

No response.

Collin knocked again. "Lisa?"

"Come in."

Collin opened the door and found Lisa lying on the bed, above her several paintings of white rabbits in chiaroscuro. The rabbits seemed to be enjoying a valley with their gazes fixed on the viewer. The room was quiet, the only sounds were the girl's shallow breaths. Her face was pale, though her cheeks were flushed, making him suspect she had a fever. Collin placed a hand on her clammy forehead. "You have a fever."

"I didn't want to get sick."

"I know, I know."

Lisa looked at Collin, a slight frown formed on her face. "I really didn't want to get sick, it makes me feel sad. I don't want to be sick for the festival, I promised Brida I'd show her lots of things about the town," she coughed, covering her mouth with the blanket. "I don't feel good."

"You'll feel better tomorrow."

"I hope so, I really do."

Collin got up to make Lisa a cup of tea. He mixed the chamomile with honey the way Lisa preferred and went back into her room. From his place he witnessed how Lisa emanated light, the only light in the room together with the rabbits in the paintings. She looked so tiny, like a little girl lost in the expanse of the heavy covers. He left the cup on the bureau and removed the heavy covers, leaving her with the light sheets, not wishing her to overheat no matter how much she wanted to pull the covers over herself. A sweet smell hit his nose. Sickeningly sweet. Something that was blooming, something he shouldn't be smelling. Not making sense of his thoughts, he got out of the room, scrubbing his nose.

He went to check on Mrs. Livia who was already at the desk doing calculations in a large notebook, after informing her that he would come back later to check on Lisa, he left to take care of the remaining tasks at the inn. Collin spent his morning checking the rooms, keeping an eye out for possible repairs, until he came to a room where the entire window area was peeling. Beginning to remove the paint with a spade, he saw it was already eleven o'clock. He went back to check on Lisa, wiping his hands with a rag, putting it in one of his pants pockets. Passing the office until he reached Lisa's room, he knocked on the door. There was no response. "Lisa?" Nothing. He tried the knob. The room was locked. "Lisa, wake up," he called, knocking on the door. Why had she locked the room? He was getting nervous. "Lisa, open this door! Are you alright?" Nothing.

Collin searched for Lisa's room keys and found them hanging in the kitchen. When he returned, the door was ajar. Everything was pitch black inside and he ran his hand along the wall, looking for the switch, until he glimpsed a silhouette on the floor. Lisa was on the floor, leaning against the bed. "Lisa!" He grabbed her, easily carrying her and placing her on the bed. She was sweating profusely, shivering, hugging herself trying to dispel the cold. "Lisa, why did you lock yourself in?"

"Um… I didn't, I didn't lock myself," she slurred tiredly.

"The door was locked."

"I didn't lock it."

"Don't ever do that again."

"I didn't do it."

Collin clicked his tongue and pulled the sheets back over her. Lisa fell asleep immediately and Collin sighed, irritated about the whole situation that had happened. He shook his head, letting his frustration go. He raised his eyes to the rabbits, whose fur glistened, distinctly noting every hair in their coats. A burning stench soon alerted him, looking down at Lisa. There was nothing, yet the smell persisted. Lisa's image was there, at the same time he wasn't seeing her. He saw another girl. A girl he had dreamed about when he was little. The girl was tied up with sturdy ropes, crying expressionlessly. Those black eyes were opened disproportionally, no pupils were visible. There was only black liquid until he soon saw Lisa's eyes open, staring at the ceiling. Collin breathed shakily and carried Lisa carefully out of her room. He couldn't leave her there. Not with that stench of charred flesh. "Lisa?"

Lisa hugged his neck, trembling, trying to make herself small. She coughed, closing her eyes. The dim light of a foggy day filtered through the living room making her hide her eyes, feeling them burning. "Why did you bring me here?"

"You need fresh air."

"Will it help me get better faster?"

"Yes, yes it will," Collin said, and tried to smile, patting her back. He settled her on the sofa, bringing blankets for her to lie down comfortably. It smelled good there, like rain. Alive. Collin felt his face tighten into a frown, no longer perceiving the burning stench. He ran his hand over Lisa's sweaty forehead. Collin felt a helpless exasperation as he went back to the kitchen to prepare another cup of tea. He put water on the stove to heat, grabbing everything he needed. Collin scented the chamomile, stilling himself, chanting in his mum's voice; *still, be still.* He took the kettle when it was ready, pouring in another cup that already had honey in it. He stepped out of the kitchen and glanced into Lisa's room. Peering into the darkened interior, the rabbits appeared to have their sights planted on the bed. A bloated body was on the bed, its extremities mummified as if they had been dipped in wax. The feet had a different aspect to the hands, blackened. The feet had been burned. He turned to the hallway, careful not to show any reaction when he reached Lisa. The tea was already tepid, but Lisa didn't comment on it.

"Will I feel better tomorrow?"

"Yes, and every following day."

Lisa smiled, trusting his words. Collin passed her another knitted blanket, observing her lay back on the small sofa pillows, reminding her not to cover up completely. Lisa whimpered, grimacing, hugging herself. "But I'm cold."

"You'll overheat."

She looked at him and smiled again, forming those adorable dimples. Lisa rubbed her eyes, wiping away the tears sleepily, breathing slow and rhythmically, falling asleep. He let her rest but not before checking her temperature one last time, heading to Mrs. Livia to know if he had to do anything in particular for the maintenance of the inn. The woman promptly instructed him to check everything was in working order. The ominous stillness of the day had him on edge, seemingly due to rain soon. He began to whistle, finding himself examining his own behavior concerning Lisa. He knew to some extent being protective of a person one cares about was natural. What puzzled him was viewing Lisa as someone who needed a guiding hand most of the time, in part he knew it was the way she grew up and in another he also knew it could be dangerous for someone like her to be left all alone. Girls like Lisa were the ones that other people hurt in the worst possible manner. From the time they met, he realized she was socially inept, which lightened his brusque personality with her.

His neck ached as he straightened up, continuing to inspect and clean the air filters in the available rooms. Collin went about his day, coming across a stray rooster wandering around the inn entrance. He stopped whistling and stared at the animal. The rooster had taken an interest in the new place, passing by him without much fuss, watching it entertained him enough. He'll certainty have good luck with the rooster accompanying him in his working hours. The image of the unknown girl lingered in the recesses of his mind, resurfacing in periods through the musty smell of the day. He cleared his throat as the odor grew pungent, turning to the rooster who explore what caught its attention around the neglected garden. Grimacing, he stopped what he was doing to check where the foul stench came from.

Collin searched through various parts for whatever reeked without success, considering he was only dawdling, growing annoyed, pressing his temples tightly, he returned to the storage room. The sharp pangs made his eyes sting. He endured his discomfort, not realizing that all the while he was gritting his teeth. When the rooster neared to where he was, the animal's vibrant brown hues distracted him enough to tolerate the smell.

He was glad for the company of that lost rooster.

He snorted at the rather peculiar thought, arranging the storage boxes. Collin whistled again, expecting the vivid images in his mind to dissipate like the foul scent assaulting his senses.

XVII

Brida reminisced about her family and the old, small apartment they'd lived in, with a rotten smell infusing the entire building. Many thought a cat had died somewhere to make the hallways reek and others thought it was just the way the building smelled, as it was old and dismantled. The people who lived below and above them had plenty of problems of their own, whenever she woke up at night hearing the neighbor weeping, she would lie awake wondering if listening to the pain of that unknown woman might keep her company. It made no difference. Her grandmother used to make comments about that woman, sealed to a miserable life in which everyone knew and yet preferred to look the other way and ignore her. Her grandfather, on the other hand, shook his head in pity. Sitting on the stairs waiting for her father to arrive from work, that unknown woman ran her hand through her hair, combing it. She remembered she felt the urge to hold that woman's hand, not knowing how to respond to the gentle caress. The Castillo's were never people who showed their feelings out in the open and she, as a Castillo, didn't know whether to remove the hand or let the woman comb her hair. She opted to quietly enjoy the unknown woman's treatment. Then one day she never saw that woman again and missed at various moments in her childhood the soft hands in her hair. She no longer enjoyed the same way sitting on the steps of the stairs, but there was no better and safer place to wait for her father at that age, all she could do was to look up in case that woman reappeared. That woman had resembled her own mother in that respect, as she had heard passing comments from people who knew her in life. A desolate woman who had been between a rock and a hard place. Brida never got the chance to meet her own mother to give an accurate opinion about her, but what she did know was that her mother broke her father.

She had many stories of that place.

Brida took a sip from her glass, savoring the taste of the alcohol. The only aspect she shared with the Gallagher's was their taste for whiskey. She couldn't stop thinking about her family and all those who had already passed away, pondering for a moment if that woman had died too or was still dealing with the same cycle of problems. She dropped her gaze to the pocket notebook she had left on the bed, where she had begun to write down information about the places she found interesting in town, cataloguing them. Reverting back to her memories, her grandfather had been the closest to her. He passed away too soon to become a pillar, but he had been in her life long enough to create an impact on her psyche. She supposed she had been fascinated by him, how sometimes she couldn't quite grasp him. At the end of his days, the poor man couldn't even get out of bed anymore. Always wanting to be given a glass of wine, denied every single time. One day, she had come to his room with a glass of wine for him. Her grandfather had looked so joyous by that simple gesture.

"Eres la única que en verdad me ama, ven aquí mi azalea."

Brida observed him sip his drink as he recounted his life, his cheeks reddening from the alcohol. Those eyes that always wandered, were now clear as he regarded her with such tenderness. Meanwhile, Brida thought that maybe she had done wrong, knowing her grandfather was on his way to die. Why not give him one of his pleasures and make him pass away content?

"Ay, mi azalea. Temo tanto por ti."

Brida stopped reflecting on that man and checked the time on her wristwatch. She left the room, opening her umbrella as she walked out. Crossing the park, bypassing the Elkan statue, she arrived at the entrance of the church already familiarized with the cooper door with canine doorknockers biting the hops. The door yielded to a slight push of her hand, letting her pass unhindered into the darkness of the temple. The humidity scent of the plants surrounded her senses as she kept passing the rows of pews, her footsteps muffled by the green carpet. She heard a door open, the groan echoed in the chamber as the image of the old nun emerged from the shadows.

"Welcome back," the old nun smiled.

"Good afternoon," Brida returned the greeting.

"We've already set the table, all you have to do is sit down."

Brida followed the nun into the dining room, recognizing how the table was set, just as it had been the first time she had been invited to eat. A detailed white tablecloth, silver cutlery, porcelain plates, crystal cups and the center candelabrum, unlit. The old nun made the detective take her reserved seat. Nothing had changed. As she took her seat, Brida heard a distant thump.

"Did something happen?"

"Nothing to worry about, my companion is finishing preparing our meal."

"Can I be of any assistance?"

The old nun kept silent, her ringed hands clasped under her low stomach. Shortly the nun moved, now resting her hands on the table. "I wouldn't want you to. You are our guest, but I know my companion would like to see you. You can go in, the kitchen is easy to locate."

Brida thanked the nun with a slight nod, leaving her seat to push open the door leading to the internal part of the church, entering the hallways of the monastery. The same thump echoed, reverberating throughout the corridor guiding her to the kitchen. Compared to the hallway that lead to the dining room, this one had a desolate layout. The walls were barren, with the only ornamentation being the iron chandeliers hanging from the ceiling. Advancing cautiously to the door, scenting the warm smell of food emanating behind the old wooden door, and knocked. The thumping stopped. Brida waited for permission to enter the kitchen, not receiving one, she took the liberty of pushing the door, squinting at scattered lights placed around the room. The dim light illuminated only certain contours, causing her to stop, adjusting her eyes to the scene awaiting her, inhaling a coppery scent. The young nun stood in front of a butchered male goat. The animal lay open on a rectangular table, staining the table with its blood. The young nun stared at Brida, setting the knife aside and wiped her bloody hands across the apron she was wearing.

"*Mi azalea.*"

Brida jerked her gaze from the butchered animal to the nun. "What?"

"I said, welcome back."

Brida gave a court nod, hearing droplets hit the stone tiles. A small puddle had formed. She kept her eyes fixed on the scene, believing she had interrupted the young nun skinning the goat. A smell of roots tickled her nostrils, raising her eyes to the nun now standing beside her. She hadn't even heard the rustle of the heavy attire the nun wore. "Can I be of any," she paused. "...assistance?"

"Are you well?"

"Yes, just more tired than I'm used to."

"Are you sure?"

"Yes, don't worry about me."

The young nun smiled at her. "Then our meal will be ready soon. For now, help me leave this on the table. We wanted to make another special meal for you, we had forgotten how exuberant it was to cook like this," she said, passing a bread basket to the detective. The young nun took one greenish bottle from the cupboard. They crossed the barren corridor to the dining room, where the old nun awaited for them seated on the left side of the table.

Brida set down the basket on the table, wistful at that simple notion. She settled back at the head of the table, taking in the time passing until the young nun returned with a large casserole, setting it close to the detective. The sharp aroma of viscera filled the room. The nuns served the wine and food, bearing a faint smile reminiscent of the paintings of saintly women from her old school books.

"We hope you love the food."

"I'm sure I will."

They ate in a peaceful stillness, listening to the sounds of the cutlery and the clicking of the candles as they poured the wax on the tablecloth. Drinking the wine, a taste of cloves filled her mouth, perceiving the dining room dimming. A metallic sound clanked in a remote part of the church. The young nun's gaze fixed on the detective, expressionless, even as she wore that characteristic smile of theirs. The movements of the candle fires were lethargic, hazy, their faces blurred. Brida slumped in the chair.

She arose in an unfamiliar place, her body numb. Her eyes noticed the twilight pouring in through the skylight enlightening only half of the room she was in. The mattress was soft, contrasting with the stiffness of her muscles. Her fingers twitched as they touched the silkiness of the sheets. The room was heavily furnished: a large wool rug, wallpapered walls with walnut patterns, an old sturdy table cluttered with objects she couldn't entirely identify, statues and decorated ceramic plates hidden in a glass case, several bookshelves strewn about the walls. On the dresser next to the bed, was a green tablecloth protecting the wood from the heavy lamp. Above the headboard hung the largest painting, depicting a nest of snakes. The striking detail awakening her awareness was the chair with velvet pillows next to the bed. She didn't have time to dwell on her current situation, hearing the door open, the image of the young nun appearing.

"You gave us a fright."

Brida forced herself to answer. "I'm sorry."

"Don't apologize," the young nun smiled, crossing the room. "We noticed the moment you lost consciousness and we brought you to this room. I hope you weren't frightened by it. Do you feel comfortable here?" The young nun sat down, her black eyes reflecting the twilight.

"Hm. Yes."

"Good. We arranged this room if you wished to stay with us. I'm glad you liked it despite what happened over dinner. It is late and it's better for you to rest here. Don't worry about anything, we'll be attentive to everything you may and will need."

"You shouldn't trouble yourself like this."

"Get some rest, we'll be right here."

Brida felt her eyes close without her consent, opening them every time they closed. A dizziness overcame her, her body collapsing like a rope snapping from too much tension. She let out a shaky breath, staring at the young nun. The ringing of a bell resounded all around, vibrating inside her skull. The young nun kept her hand in her lap. Brida strained to stay awake. Her eyes closed as the bell rang again.

Not for the first time she dreamt of her house. The grand house she locked after the *betrayal* she suffered. She woke up with a jolt, *knowing* her stomach was open, her arms were grabbed. Hands were holding her. She was sweating, feeling her hair cling to her neck. The same hands caressed her face, passing to her hair, combing it, pulling strands away from her face. Brida gasped in pain. Her stomach contracted, liquid wetting her nether region, sticking her shirt against her skin. A voice murmured against her temple, comforting her in her pain, asking to let go. Brida gritted her teeth, grasping one of the hands, soon feeling them envelop her, asking her again to let go. One of the hands went down to her stomach, coming barely a centimeter from the open wound. An intense heat was felt. The hand grazed the wound, experiencing the pain of thousands needles embedding themselves in her body. She couldn't see in the darkness of the room, but she could smell the aroma of the freshest plants, of recently cut roots, the coolest moisture one could scent on a rainy day. As the hand parted from the wound, the voice murmured again against her temple:

"*No tengas miedo.*"

Brida let out an agitated breath, feeling again something approach her gaping wound, a figure leaning over her. A kiss pressed against her temple, another kiss brushed her stomach, the last kiss made her groan as it planted itself on the wound. Inside. When the kisses ceased, Brida felt drained from the embrace, hearing the murmur of that voice again. Brida nodded to what was told, closing her eyes. The heat in her stomach subsided, allowing herself to be lulled by the whispers.

Awakened by the sound of the door opening, the young nun settled again in the chair next to the bed. Brida didn't know why she had so much trouble moving her body, numb from neck to toe. The young nun set the silver tray on the bed, carefully picking up a porcelain cup, bringing it to Brida.

"How do you feel?"

"Better, thank you," she murmured hoarsely. Brida forced her body to move, leaning against the pillows. The taste of herbs was strong. The headache in her head throbbed against her skull, observing the dark liquid in her cup. Simply drinking tea had tired her out. "Thank you for taking care of me."

"You don't have to thank us," the young nun smiled, pleased.

"How can I repay this favor?"

"We do not seek favors."

"You've taken care of me."

"We do not seek favors," the nun repeated steadily. After a pause, the nun filled the other cup. "I took the liberty of hanging up your clothes and a ring fell out. Don't worry, the ring is over there." She merely glanced at the dresser.

Brida stiffened and examined the ring lying on top of the green tablecloth, contrasting in color. She didn't grab it, mumbled a thank you and directed her attention back to the tea. There was no need for her to wear that item, since coming to town her hands had been bare. Strikingly, the idea of that ring getting lost in this place didn't displease her.

"You are attached to this ring."

"Not to the ring itself."

"Does it have a meaning?"

"A ring is a simple ring," Brida said, placing the cup on the tray.

"Hm." The nun poured the tea and handed the cup back to the detective. "An object coming from a loved one, carrying their love, their concept of self into you." The nun took the ring, passing the item between her fingers. Shortly she left the ring where it was. "Rest, it is still early."

Hearing the rustle of robes moving followed by the soft clock of the door closing, Brida leaned against the pillow supporting her back.

Her dream perplexed her, fixing her eyes on the ceiling, pressing a hand on the place the scar was located. She passed saliva tasting the tea in her mouth. She questioned why she had lost consciousness so suddenly, she could theorize a possible answer, but none would settle her doubts. The door moved, turning her attention to the presence of the young nun. Her silhouette, draped in shadows, lingering at the door, then with slow movements closed the door with that same soft click. The young nun approached Brida. Blinking, she couldn't discern the face of the young nun, squinting, pushing the cobwebs away from her mind.

"How do you feel?"

"Better, thank you."

"Why don't you rest more?" she asked, sitting down in that chair next to the bed. Ringed hands rested in her lap. "It will do you good. We'll be pleased if you get more rest."

Brida was aware of being observed, she also knew the longer she stared at the young nun the less she was able to perceive her. Her dream flashed through her mind, face tense as she lowered her gaze to the soft sheets and the heavy bedspread. The ring rested beside her. Vexing herself for not throwing that object away, taunting her whole process with the fact it was there. The dream remained vivid, wondering if she might be conjuring it all up.

"Did you have a dream?"

"I don't know whether it was a dream."

"Sometimes dreams helps us."

Silent, motionless in their respective places, the brightness of the room diminished with each blink of an eye. The shadows gradually dominated the surroundings. The young nun's gaze never wavered. She sighed, the calming heartbeat soothing her senses, before closing her eyes. Slowly the fuzziness of the day gave way to a blank mind. Upon awakening, she was all alone. Within the hour, Brida had risen out of bed, grabbing her jacket that hung on the handle of one of the furnishings. She reached for the ring and hid it in her pocket. The silence of the morning accompanied her till the clanging of the church bells shattered the stillness by staggering her step. Her head throbbing with each chime. What kind of person she had become, losing consciousness in front of the nuns forcing them to take care of her. Shame overpowered any other emotion, tensing her mandible. Wandering through the monastery corridors, she overheard fluttering wings to discover the young nun holding azalea blossoms in her hands by the central courtyard. Seated on the border of the neglected fountain, Brida approached the young nun, sitting next to her, looking down at the flowers.

"Thank you for looking after me."

"Don't be ashamed, it was a pleasure for us." The nun smiled, caressing the petals of those nostalgic flowers for the detective. The edges were white transitioning to a deep crimson at the center. Strangely enough, there were no azaleas planted in the garden.

"How could I return the favor?"

"We don't need any favor."

Brida clenched her teeth, tensing her expression. The nun ignored her companion's discomfort, running her fingers over the flowers, finding them pleasant to the touch. A light chuckle echoed, instinctively easing Brida's body.

"Do you love these flowers?" asked the nun.

"My grandfather loved them."

"They're lovely."

Brida concurred quietly. Her grandfather had always cherished those flowers, reminding him of his birthplace and his family. The young nun had left long ago to continue her routine, but not before telling the detective she was free to leave whenever she desired. Brida remained seated contemplating the memories linked to those flowers. It wasn't necessary to trace back her family's recollections to acknowledge her loneliness, longing for her father's muted presence in the house. They may not have conversed as much, but they would always share their company daily until that fateful evening when he went to take a light nap. Her father had always been one for small details, often leaving her certain types of sweet bread to accompany her morning coffee. And she always accepted the thoughtful gestures and returned them by making sure nothing lacked in the house.

"*Sometimes you make me worry too much.*"

Her father had every reason to be concerned for her. Her job wasn't exactly easy. Although her station may not have as many sexual assault claims as other stations in the country, there would always be that one colleague who crossed the line. Unfortunately, this could be said for other fields as well. There were many kinds of dangers in her life simply because she was a woman. She was aware her father constantly kept up with the news, bought the weekly newspaper without fail and turned on the television on news channels most of time. There were so many things for him to worry about. Work, money, the future, life as a whole. Already in her uniform, Brida turned to her father, who almost always accompanied her in the early morning, serenely sipping their coffee.

The enjoyment of such occasions ensured her discipline in her daily routine. His pale eyes, fluid and transforming in waves, identical to her own, conveyed a sentiment Brida often ignored to ease her conscience.

"*I'll be fine.*"

Her father had stared blankly at her and promptly looked away. Deciding the conversation was over, reaching for her jacket hanging at the entrance, her father's voice made her turn around again. His sunken visage, averting his eyes, uncomfortable to open up in that way.

"*When I die, you'll be all alone.*"

Brida hung her jacket and, with slow steps, approached her father until she embraced him with absolute force, startling them both. Apparently, her father wasn't the only one with regrets. In moments like those, Brida could never find the right words to let this man full of flaws know she loved him so deeply, holding all her admiration, so she made sure through her actions he never lacked anything, just as she never lacked anything because of him. Although they had struggled financially through her childhood, she always had a plate of food on the table.

"*I'll have you.*"

Her father had been silent, knowing she wouldn't have him for long. Life had to take its course. He had exhausted his life with all the jobs he had taken, breaking his heart by overworking himself. Ever since her father had the first heart attack at work, they knew he wasn't going to live a long life, and if he did, it would be a wonder. Brida sighed, leaving the monastery garden, unwilling to delve into more old memories. She missed her father, and yet nothing could be done. Visiting a grave wouldn't alleviate the longing to see him again. She entered the church chamber, where the old nun kneeled before the large painting behind the altar. Without wanting to disturb the sister in her prayers, Brida made her way to the entrance, the green carpet muffling her footsteps, laying a hand on the coppery door, heaving with the feeling she was forsaking her cave to enter the world of the first time. Her stomach felt full, which made her nauseous. Controlling the sensation, she left the protection the place had offered to her.

XVIII

Thomas parked the car in the garage, letting the engine die, staring blankly into nothingness. He hadn't been sleeping well and was suffering the effects of a strained mind. He was gravely pondering whether his nonna was right in saying that he needed a vacation as well. These days he had been pensive. Even when he had to fill out his reports, his mind wandered, having to double-check what he wrote. He no longer questioned why he was in his situation, aware it was partly his fault and had no choice but to wait for Alina to deign to grant him the divorce. The actual problem was that he was fed up with waiting and didn't want to waste years of his life. They had been like this for almost a year now, him waiting and her wanting to sweep it all under the rug. Had they understood each other to begin with? He had believed they had, but apparently Alina would come up with any little thing that made him wonder if maybe he never got to know her. Thomas rested his hands on his thighs, noting his fingers tremble as he stretched out his hands. Had he ever felt confident he could tell Alina his thoughts? He had tried once and it had backfired. He reminisced how Alina's face changed from a pleasant smile to a wide-eyed grimace. How ironic, he felt alone in his own marriage.

He got out of the car to start his routine. When he finished checking everything was in working order, he entered the house, leaving his wool jacket hanging at the entrance. There was no sound inside, only the electrical humming characteristic of any house. Thomas continued with his routine, heading to his bedroom to change and try to be comfortable in his own house. After taking a bath and changing, he went to the kitchen, turning on the small TV to watch whatever movie was playing on a random channel until the phone rang. Without hesitation, he picked up. "Hello?"

"Thomas," Brida's voice sounded on the other end. "'Good thing you answered."

"Brida!" he exclaimed in pleasant surprise. "How are you?"

"Better. I've been enjoying the sights here."

"I'm happy to hear that. That's good, very good." He heard his friend laugh and felt the moment his muscles eased, leaning on the kitchen counter. He admitted he had sounded a bit awkward. How can he not be when he's been arguing about everything these days with his soon-to-be ex-wife. Even at work he had been asked if he was feeling well, making him uncomfortable because the fatigue was evident on his face. "I've heard the town has a lot of greenery. It would be nice to walk along the edges of the forest and breathe in that fresh air."

"You'd like it here. There'll be a festival if you want to come."

"I've been thinking about what I told you."

"You told me a lot of things."

Thomas snorted. "About taking some days off."

"It would do you good."

"I guess it would help me."

"Hm. How have you been?"

He hesitated in his response, shifting the phone to his other ear. He didn't want to bring up his whole situation to Brida -one she already personally knew-, but not talking about it was stressing him out. He disliked mortifying himself at the prospect of sharing his thoughts, not because it embarrassed him, rather because he valued his privacy too much, believing in not having to share everything all the time. Although he admitted that, deep down, he wasn't comfortable talking with just anyone either. "I'm tired," he conceded. "I'm really tired about everything that's been happening here.."

"I can imagine."

"Anyways, I visited my nonna the other day, she asked-"

"How are you feeling?"

There was a moment of silence, Thomas felt his heart beat erratically, finally letting out a small laugh. He clutched the phone in his hand and in a low voice he told the truth: "I'm not well, but I don't want to throw my problems at you. I want you to enjoy your trip."

"I can listen to you *and* enjoy my trip."

Thomas was fortunate to have a friend like Brida, but he didn't want to discuss it over the phone, it was preferable to talk about it face to face. With the simple reassurance Brida wanted to listen to him, soothed his heart. "I know you can't be on the phone for long. I'm happy you are enjoying yourself over there. Who knows, maybe I'll be in town for the festival."

"I'll see you soon then."

"If all goes well, yes."

"Alright. Rest, Thomas. I can hear your tiredness."

Thomas chuckled. "I will, don't worry. Thank you for calling."

"I'm looking forward to seeing you. If you come, I'm staying at an inn downtown. It's called Gallardo's Inn, near the church here."

"I'll write it down."

"Rest, Thomas. Have a good night."

Before he could answer, the line had been cut off and Thomas smiled as he put the phone back in its place. He returned to his routine with a light heart, preparing his dinner. A year ago he couldn't have imagined he'd end up in a situation like the one he was in, but that was life. Rebuilding friendships, awaiting for divorce and unable to hold a normal conversation with Alina without the help of a marriage counselor. There had been some arguments here and there between them, arguments any couple had, but everything got worse since the 'incident'. Something that made him reconsider their relationship was the quarrel they had in the hospital when he had taken care of Brida. A dispute he hadn't wanted to have right there, but Alina wouldn't leave him alone, attracting the attention of the nurses. Thomas had never felt so mortified in his life until that moment, dreadful as he caught the gaze of one of the nurses who regarded them with disdain for disturbing the tranquility of the hospital. At the time he had tried to talk to Alina about how that made him feel, but it all feel on deaf ears, in the end he had comforted her. He didn't try to open up for a while.

In his most agitated state, he thought to himself: *I don't want to live like this.* The thought had come to him in a fit of inward panic while caring for Brida one night at the hospital. Lying on the uncomfortable couch, listening to the sounds of the machine simulating her heartbeat, he couldn't calm down almost bringing himself to tears. He forced himself to calm down, he didn't want the nurses to see him create *another* disturbance. When Brida jolted awake one night from active nightmares, he was quick to be at her side and reassure she was safe. Thomas had been ready to comfort her, but Brida had a certain type of character. He sometimes disliked how stoic his friend could be, even after she almost died, almost as- no, he knows how Brida thinks of things. He remembered Brida had taken his arm and soon released it, putting the nightmare aside. The doctor had insisted it was the shock from what she had experienced, turns out Brida had accepted her present situation and let it go. In Brida's words, in that nonchalant tone as if the doctor was the madman in the room, she told him clearly: *I chose my own emotions.* He admired her fortitude, it made him confident Brida wouldn't let herself fall. That doctor didn't insist anymore, it even made him relax to no longer hear the same thing.

There were mornings when Thomas couldn't believe Brida was alive, staring at the beeping monitor. He wanted that sound to be with him always, no matter how artificial it was. The beeps were good. He had cried once as he took Brida's hand in his. Mourning all he had built in life knowing that all of his foundations had crumbled. *I don't want to live like this.* That thought hadn't left him since it arrived, it had shook all his foundations. It had accidentally slipped out.

"What do you mean?" Brida had asked.

"It's nothing, it's really nothing."

"Thomas."

"It's nothing, I promise."

Brida stared at him, unnerving him. He felt her hand on his arm, pulling him into an embrace. The position was awkward for his back, but Thomas couldn't have been more content. Happiness turned into self-deprecation as tears escaped him. In that moment he stopped pretending. Here he was, being consoled by one of the most important people in his life when it should've been the other way around. It wasn't him lying in a hospital bed. It wasn't him that was found on the verge of death in his own house. He couldn't help glancing down at her stomach. He had seen-

Thomas shook his head, dispelling the memory. His dinner was almost ready, preparing the colander to drain the pasta. It crossed his mind that after that point he had one of the harshest disputes with Alina. Apparently, Alina saw *something* between Brida and him. He never understood it, because every time he cared for Brida at that time, his eyes strayed to her stomach, hands trembling, wanting to check for himself that it was really closed. He had tried to close-

Thomas frowned.

He tried to push the flesh-

His hand had been inside.

The plate slipped out of his hands, falling to the floor. Sighing at the mess he had made, he bent down to pick up the pieces of the broken plate. What he did was stare at the pieces of ceramic on his knees. He knew all of this had affected him. He knew he wasn't doing well. He didn't have a wound deep enough to have been in the operating room for hours. He was just struggling with his choices in life. Clearing his throat, picking up the pieces, he wondered when it would all change.

XIX

It was the middle of November. The festival was coming together, the streets continued their activity, taking advantage of the fact there was no rain that day. It was seven in the morning, and the fair would open officially to the public at ten o'clock. Locals were setting up their booths to sell food, handicrafts, objects, jewelry, and other goods that would be seen throughout the week. Collin was setting up a stall for an elderly lady who kept arranging her pottery crafts. He appreciated helping with these types of events, witnessing how creative people could be if they put their minds to it. The old woman thanked him when he finished setting up the booth, receiving little money in return, but he didn't mind at all. He just thanked her and wished her luck in selling everything. Collin entered the park, finding Lisa seated on one of the benches. Her ginger hair combed in a half ponytail with a turquoise ribbon adorning it. On her lap rested another ribbon of the same color.

"I thought you'd gone home."

"No, I'm waiting for Brida."

Collin sat next to her, peering at the ribbon. He adjusted the high collar of his shirt, shaking off the discomfort he'd been feeling since he got up. He felt a hand brush against his Aran jumper, as if stroking the soft wool. Collin looked at Lisa questioningly. Lisa had a better face, calmer although tired, almost sad. It seemed like good news. After the pain, there was sadness and finally acceptance. "What are you thinking about this time?"

"About the same thing."

"You shouldn't overthink it."

"I know, I try not to."

"It's okay, don't overexert yourself."

Cautiously, Lisa shared her thoughts: "You know I've always struggled to make friends and if I had them, I would lose them easily. No one from school stayed with me, but Elizabeth did. I thought it was fine, that it was better than being all alone, although there were times when it was all too much for me," she shrugged. "I know that maybe it wasn't all good with her, but I don't, um, I still don't like it when I hear people call her bad things. I get why she was so angry most of the time, but still."

"Who is this 'people'?"

"You know," she began again, with the same caution, muttering to him. "Like that… that jerk. You know who I'm talking about." She folded her arms, looking at Collin who was entertained by her display of emotions. "I was listening to him while waiting here. He was telling *that* group that Elizabeth went mad, telling lies about her and everyone in that group, that she couldn't stand her own truths and that's why she left. I wanted to shut him up, to shut them up because I know things about them, things Elizabeth told me were hurting her. Have you heard them?"

Collin nodded. Of course he had heard of it. Personally, he did agree with that moron in certain points. Individuals like Elizabeth always have a hard time accepting the consequences of their actions, preferring to blame others and think that they are the poor victims. Clearly, he wasn't going to tell Lisa that and ruin her good mood. "I've heard a thing or two. Don't listen to them. Most of the things they say are very ironic coming from them. And what would that cun- ah, guy know? Any girl would go crazy if they had that guy in a close radius," he nudged her, making her chuckle. He disliked speaking so brusquely in front of Lisa. Feeling better at getting her to laugh, he tugged on her ear playfully. "Maybe I need to put cotton in your ears.

"No, please no," she laughed, covering her ears.

"Then stop listening. You already have big ears, they'll only grow bigger if you continue."

"They're not big."

"No? I could see them from over there," he signaled over his shoulder, causing Lisa to roll her eyes and burst out laughing. Her cheeks were rosy, looking more animated. Soon he had a sobering thought. Collin sharpened his gaze. "This guy didn't come near you, did he?"

"No," she said, smiling at him. "No, we just saw each other, he didn't approach me. I would've walked away if he had come near me. If he gets close, the whole group gets close and I'm afraid of being in a situation like that. Besides, I think he knew you were here..."

"He'd better."

Lisa smiled at him and hugged his arm, resting her head on his shoulder. Collin recognized himself calmer seeing how Lisa behaved since she returned from the city. He still had a twinge of anger, -knowing it was indignation-, but soon, everything was going to pass. They must've had these kinds of talks before, and he admitted to himself it was partly his fault. He wanted to shield Lisa from situations that he knew could escalate, yet he also knew he had to let her learn. Grab the bull's horns, as his mum might've said. Collin slowly loosened up, blinking into the cold air. Before long he saw a pair of eyes that always caught him unprepared in their vibrancy. Lisa straightened up as soon as Brida joined them. Brida turned to Lisa and smiled at her in a way that made the young girl feel a surge of excitement. Collin witnessed Lisa revel in the detective's presence.

"Hi, I got you this for the festival," said Lisa, passing the ribbon to the detective.

"Should I put it on?"

"If you want I can tie it in a part of your hair."

"Alright," said Brida, returning the ribbon to the young girl and sat on the other side, leaving Lisa in the middle. "Does it have any special meaning?"

"It can mean a lot of things, It depends on the person," replied Lisa, turning to Brida. Even with the detective's permission to touch her hair, she felt shy to get so close to the older woman. Upon touching it, she was slightly amazed to feel the smooth texture of the hair. She took an under-side lock and braided it with the ribbon, tying a knot with a small rubber band, arranging the last part of the ribbon into a small bow. Lisa smiled as she watched the strands of the ribbon fall out of the braid. "I don't think I measured it right."

"It's fine. How do I look?"

"You look good!"

Collin contemplated the scene with a wistful sentiment in his heart. It was a unique emotion for him that, in a way, made him feel vulnerable. He licked his lips, looking away. "We can go to the lake now if you both want. I'm sure it's calm today."

"Yes, we can go now," said Brida.

Collin turned his attention to the streets in comfortable silence. Having the detective's presence at his side made him nervous, even more so if they came close to each other at any point. He sensed a breath on his side, and soon the most pleasant odor he had ever experienced reached his nose. With great discretion, he took a deep breath, filling his lungs with the warm scent. Brida was close to him, not making much noise as she walked with Lisa in tow, listening to all the girl's stories. He wondered why he felt the need to breathe in her scent again, as if it was wiped from his mind every time he exhaled. He had dated many women and many of them had a good scent due to the perfumes they wore, yet he knew this particular scent was natural, bewildering him. He vaguely remembered in his childhood he loved to smell his mum's wrists.

"Are you okay?"

Collin felt that aroma hit his nose again, and when he looked up to Brida, a green ocean intercepted him. Her eyes broke into waves, then calmed down and then broke again. Collin blinked, reasoning it had been a nonsense thought. "Yeah, I think I'm distracted today."

Brida considered him. "If you say so."

Lisa stared at him, and he merely offered her a small smile. "Well, anyway, I don't know when the festival started, but the balls are held in the casino which is connected to the only hotel we have. My dad used to participate in those dances. I don't know exactly when it all started, but Collin can tell you it's been around a long time."

"It has," he agreed. "It started with a politician, but I don't remember if it was a mayor or a businessman. What I do know is that customs have changed a lot over the years, but I think that happens to all festivals. At least the government hasn't prevented the people from continuing to celebrate. You know there's always issues with that."

"I thought you didn't like history," remarked Brida.

"I don't, it's always the same," he smirked at the comment. "Everyone knows the festival is old, my mum even has pictures of her parents participating in the events. Yes, several elements were changed, but it's still celebrated the same way," he shrugged, letting Lisa lead the conversation, turning to the lake.

The lake sign needed a fresh coat of paint, bearing the name of the body of water: Tonalia Lake. The surface was smooth and reflected the light of a cloudy day. The forest bordering the other side of the shore was dense, obscuring much of the landscape. The mountainside wasn't high enough to have layers of snow all year round, already beginning to powder. Collin soon felt forlorn, reflecting on his life. Letting out a sigh, grateful to Lisa that she was still chatting about their customs, he gave himself permission to be quiet and reflect.

So far, since he had returned to this town, it had been good days. He had enjoyed living with his dad's family, had loved listening to his grandfather's stories when he took him into the forest to forage for mushrooms. His nightmares hadn't diminished with the change, reluctantly becoming part of him. His mum had taught him ways to calm himself and had given him a sachet of cloves to hang by his bedside. He had liked that sachet, until one day it ripped. He had struggled to connect with the other children. His mum had worried the move affected him, while his dad hadn't given it any thought. Then he grew up. Oftentimes Collin reminisced about how miserable it was to mingle with his old 'friends'. Some were good, some were bad. In the words of those friends; Collin was too 'good' sometimes. He remembers a guy who loved to get into fights, loved to put people on the spot. Collin had suspected the guy was addicted to the adrenaline of the moment more than the fight itself. Who knows. First this guy would start arguing with the people around him about a particular topic, and if he didn't like something, he would take the discussion into the fray. Collin witnessed many times as the fights escalated, smoking a cigarette, watching from his side as people moved and threw punches. It was fucking stupid. He never had the rush to go into a fight, not like that. The irony of it all was that there had been good times, he had laughed and enjoyed some days with them. He hasn't told Lisa anything about it, she could get an idea, she was smart like that, even if she didn't have it all figured it out, unlike him at that age. He learned the hard way. How could he explain all the things that happened to him and those around him when he had been in that shithole? There were still a variety of unpleasant emotions when recalling that young Collin.

He never took drugs. He'd been fucking stupid, but not that stupid. He recalled how one girl repeatedly patted another girl's arm and then injected her, being euphoric for that a brief space of time. He'd seen worse, but he didn't feel like remembering it all. Collin knew why they did it, never had the need to experience that kind of 'pleasure.' At least that had reassured his mum. He had hated it. He had despised it when one of those good friends died of an overdose, alone, in a seedy part of the city. The funeral had been short and sober. The casket had been closed. One could image the state of the body to have the casket closed. Collin had went to pay his condolences to the poor lady, who couldn't stop crying for her only son. Many from that circle didn't come from dysfunctional families, quite the contrary, some had been the perfect example of the academic. Like his good friend in that casket, they were just kids who had experimented with something that slowly pigeonholed them into an addiction. Then, he had seen how the girlfriend of this friend arrived late, clearly high. Collin, out of anger, wanted to grab her and throw her out from the chapel. He didn't, because in the end he didn't care. He didn't even approach her, knowing the girl wouldn't even remember the funeral. Collin was aware he wasn't a good person, because he could understand it was a shitty situation for the addict, but also for the people around them, so yes, he judged them. The lady's cries made him think of his own mum.

His mum always worried for him.

Running a hand over one of his bare arms, as if searching for something. He disliked the times when his mum distrusted him, but over the years he learned he wouldn't have trusted himself at those time either. One false step and all would go to shit. He had lost two good friends to heroin. His mum had every right to worry. If it wasn't the drugs, it was something else; accidents, loneliness, problems with money and life and ultimately resorting to suicide. It wasn't something that was talked about, but it was known and, consequently, ignored. Some of his friends left the world far too young. The one fact he knew was that personality and mindset affects everything. But he had stalled.

He turned twenty-three and returned to town.

"...My dad never liked to go fishing. I always remember him working and traveling when he could," said Lisa, moving closer to the water. "The only thing we went to the lake for was to walk along the shores and find pretty rocks. I remember I had a favorite rock that I had drawn eyes on with a marker and kept it in my pocket until I forgot I had it and I never found it again. I think it just slipped out of my pocket and was lost forever."

Collin laughed. What a great timing he had to pay attention. "You didn't tell me that one."

"Well, of course not. You would've made fun of me," said Lisa.

"I might've given you a rock with eyes."

"No, thank you," she replied sheepishly. She turned to Brida, pinching her nails. "I forgot to tell you that my dad sends his regards and thanks you for, um, for helping me with this. I told him some things and he thinks I bother you every day. I told him it wasn't true because otherwise you would've said something to me and well, in the end he just told me to say hello."

"You don't bother me," said Brida. "I look forward to meeting him."

"I'd really like you to meet him. He's been feeling better these days. He wants to be present at the ceremony and might want to see the market. I hope he continues to feel well all this week, I would like to go with him to see the dances."

"We hope so," Brida replied courtly.

"I'd like to stay longer, but I have to return to the inn and I don't want to get scolded again. I'll tell my dad you said hello," she smiled at Brida and then turned her head to Collin. "See you at the fair." She bid them both a swift goodbye, hugging Collin and smiled awkwardly at Brida wanting to hug her too, controlling her impulsiveness not wanting to embarrass herself. He watched as Lisa spun in their direction as she had to turn down a street, waving her hand enthusiastically, which made him smile. Assuring himself Lisa walked away safely, he turned to Brida.

"Are you liking the town?"

"I am. I didn't think I would."

"Why not?"

She kept her focus on the lake. "I simply didn't think I would."

"I think I can understand it. It's a quiet place and many expect it to stay that way. Who knows, change never asks for permission, as my mum says. When I was a child I used to hear the old ladies say this was a place of healing. Don't get me wrong, not that kind of healing people usually say when they want to find something new. This was- It is a place of healing. There are places like this around, they're not common, but they're there… like old marks, simmering and- Well, you know."

"The nuns mentioned something about that. How the lake was used for their rituals."

Collin studied her profile, shifting his gaze fixating it on the detective's stomach. He realized what he was doing, mortified, turning away. His own stomach twinged in the lower part and tried to control the sudden pain by taking a deep breath. "Right." He breathed out. "The library might have documents about it if you want to know more. I've never been interested in reading myself, all I know is by word of mouth."

"I might go."

Collin nodded, gritting his teeth at the throbbing sensation, scolding his face not wanting to show any discomfort. His body broke into a sweat and he almost hunched his body when the pain, as it came, disappeared. He salivated, letting go of the awful sensation that had assaulted him. He was probably falling ill, it was already the second time it had happened to him. He ran his hand down his jumper, brushing his sweat against the wool. "We should go back. The lake no longer looks calm."

Brida shot him a glance. Her eyes noted how one of his hands lingered on his stomach. He ignored how his mouth salivated once again under the gaze. Collin Fay passed his hand through his hair, glancing at the scenery where mist drifted through the trees and fell on the surface of the lake. He sighed, leaving the area with the detective. They reached the fair, where people were already waiting on each side of the street, staring in one direction, until soon flower-decorated trucks with children in white dresses began tossing petals decorating the street with them. On a tractor pushing a cart, teenagers dressed as pilgrims waved to the public. People of varying ages in colorful uniforms playing their instruments. Small groups strolled through the center showing other types of attires, until soon the main event arrived. The man who impersonated the founder. Mounted on a horse, clothed in black with a piteous countenance, behind him two rows of 'troops' in a similar uniform. The horse's hooves trampled on the petals left behind.

"It seems he was right," said Brida, staring at the 'founder.'

"Who was right?"

"Someone I knew."

His stomach lurched.

After the parade passed them, hearing the marching band in the distance, Collin spotted Lisa with her father, browsing through artsy figurines and small trinkets. Brida peered at a pair of beautiful, tatted lace earrings, bright in a green color. The woman at the stall caught her interest and drew their attention, prompting Collin to accompany Brida to see what appealed to her.

"Do you like them?" he asked, genuinely curious.

"I do," she responded neutrally.

"If the lady likes them that much, I can give her a discount if she buys another pair. I have several here with different patterns that I can show, so even the boyfriend can pick one out for her," said the woman, already pulling out a box, letting them see intricate patterns with distinct colors.

Brida smiled, lifting her eyebrows. "Alright, let's see them."

He also found that it wasn't important to correct the woman, although hearing that the detective might be connected to him in such a way made him tingle inwardly, in the deepest recesses of his heart. Heaving a breath, stilling his mind, he spotted a pair of earrings that caught his eye. It was similar to the color of Brida's eyes. "We'll take these ones." He quickly took his wallet out and paid for the two pairs.

"He has a good eye," the woman appraised, putting the earrings in a small paper bag, and handing it to the detective, wishing them a good day. Brida pulled out her wallet and was stopped by Collin who refused the money. He had paid because he had wanted to, nothing more.

"You didn't have to," Brida said.

"I wanted to. They'll look good on you."

Brida smiled, triggering *that* tingle to reappear. Not long after, they joined the Gallardo's and Lisa, upon noticing them, gently pulled Brida's arm and led her to meet her father, where the two exchanged a handshake and the gratitude of finally meeting. Collin clasped Lisa's shoulders, smiling a little at the girl who quickly hugged his side. Martin looked good with his hair down, neatly combed, dressed comfortably with a blanket covering his legs. On his lap were butterfly figures handmade from clay. Each butterfly had a different size and color.

"I hope you're having a good time here," Martin said.

"I am, thank you," said Brida.

"There will be different events throughout the week if you plan to stay longer. The town has always liked to hold this particular celebration. I'm sure there'll be no problem if you attend tomorrow's ceremony with us. Lisa has told me so much about you that I would like you to sit with us," he glanced at his daughter, smiling at her evident shyness. "Have you seen our martyrs?"

"Martyrs?"

"Our martyrs depicted in the church. Each painting has a story. The monastery cares for them and maintains them along with everything that resides within. There are many stories that might interest you. I know a few in case you want to join me for coffee someday. I expect to continue to remain in good health these days," he laughed, with a small twinge of self-contempt. "Anyway, it's better to enjoy it now while I can. I promised Lisa to go to the dances with her, would you both like to join us?"

Collin heard the detective accept the invitation and Lisa, like a hound dog, straightened up, grasped the back handles of the wheelchair, and headed for the casino. The casino was a historic landmark, typical of any building in town, maintaining an air of grandeur as they entered through the wide doors. Many would be surprised to know the history of the place, as it used to be a residence for a general. After the owner's death, it became a meeting point for chiefs and officers, founded the casino and, by simple luck, survived several internal conflicts. He could picture wealthy families arriving in those old carriages, dressed in their finery, eager to celebrate. Inside the reception area they were directed to the dance contest, observing the participating couples ready to begin. Everyone awaited for the emcee to kick off the competition, including the band, ready with their instruments in hand. The ballroom had rows of chairs surrounding the corners, leaving the center completely clear. Across from them was the judges' table, one of whom was Rhys, who greeted them from afar. Collin took seat next to the detective, while Lisa sat in the corner of the row, next to her father. He leaned back in the chair, tilting his head slightly toward Brida.

"Do you like to dance?"

"If the rhythm is slow, yes."

Collin gave a low chuckle. He couldn't imagine a woman like Brida, so earnestly pirouetting as they did in polkas. Slow rhythms suited her well. So did he. "Why am I not surprised?"

Brida turned to smile at him, squinting her eyes. "You're asking me to dance?"

"If I asked you, would you say yes?"

"You'll know until you ask me right."

"Guess we'll have to wait."

They turned their attention to the emcee beginning his speech, yet Collin couldn't stay focused on the presentation. The band playing polkas, the taps on the microphone when the presenter called another couple to dance, the stomping of the contestants, the applause when they finished their number couldn't hold his attention for long. His eyes strayed to the woman beside him. He let out a breath, running his hands down his jumper, refocusing on the dances. He turned his gaze to Lisa, who was totally absorbed in the dancing couples. He smiled at her expression, at least something good came out of it for that poor girl. Collin even found himself enjoying the dancing competition.

Arriving at his apartment after spending the evening with the Gallardo's, he prepared for bed. The knowledge he had gotten Brida some earrings elicited a thrill he didn't recognize all that well. He had believed he would never be one for details like that, but evidently he could. Settling into his bed, he fell asleep instantly, surprising himself when a thud woke him up. He hadn't even realized he'd fallen asleep. Collin felt irritation, covering his ears, whoever was outside he expected them to stop. The noise persisted, driving him out of bed. He left his apartment with a flashlight in hand, locking the door behind him and stepped outside to see what the noise was or who was causing it. Glancing at both sides, irritation morphs into concern. As he neared the entrance, the distinctly fluttering of wings was heard along with something scraping against the pavement coupled with other noises he couldn't identify. He pulled his keys out to open the gate, careful to not alert whoever was outside. In an instant a thunderous cry resounded. The hair on his arms stood on end at the sight of a small form running in flames. Scorched feathers were visible from where he stood, leaving a trail of smoke.

XX

The hooting echoed. Brida struggled to fall asleep, maintaining her eyes closed, keeping the rhythm of her breathing steady. Her mind was restless, buzzing with noise, quarrels, brawls, shouting, the indistinct sounds of traffic accompanied by an electric hum, all reminiscent of her city. Motionless, Brida focused her senses on the rustling of the trees, listening at one point the snap of a falling branch. The hooting continued. Now she tried to imagine landscapes. Lastly, she began to ruminate from memory the cases left on her desk, recalling details, autopsies, images, statements. Eventually, she heard the hooting recede along with all the sounds outside and inside her head.

She awoke after sensing something wet land on her face. She stirred, touching where the wet sensation was and opened her eyes. A damp patch had formed on the ceiling, which gradually spread, forming droplets that fell on the bed and on her, feeling another drop fall on her face. She studied her fingers and observed her digits stained by a dark substance. A breath echoed close by, followed by several others. Rhythmic. Someone was breathing somewhere near her. A voice with the gentlest timbre murmured in her ear, her own breathing becoming labored as she looked up.

The spot had a face.

Maroon eyes reflecting specks of red stared back at her. Brida tightened her teeth. The face smiled. The voice shifted to a low, smooth voice beckoning her to be comforted in its care. Reaching an arm out to that unusual beauty, her hand felt a naked body. A body lay on top of her, obscured by the shadows of the room. She breathed in and the scent of damp plants and fresh cut roots assaulted her senses, suddenly feeling a hand on her stomach. She stiffened at the touch. The hand remained on her stomach, slowly running its fingernails over the blanket, feeling them on her skin. The nails prodded and felt piercing pain on where it exerted pressure. Her hands constricted the neck of the body, tightening with absolute force to the point where the body quivered. A deep, raw burning entered her heart, controlling her mind with absolute dedication to a single emotion, her ire.

She saw herself. She was hurting herself.

Brida opened her eyes. The room grew dim and felt a heaviness in her muscles. She stayed awake until morning came, where she prepared for the new day, relieving herself from the intense dream. She grabbed the paper bag and pulled out the earrings Collin had bought for her. They were beautiful and reminded her of the earrings her grandmother wore. Brida put on the ones Collin choose for her. The new weight in her ears was welcomed. She adjusted the high collar of her shirt in front of the bathroom mirror, highlighting the green of her earrings against the dark colors of her clothing. Staring at her reflection, the image of her father came to mind. A man who always maintained a tense face, rarely smiling. Everyone in the family knew why. Her mother's death had affected him completely. The only distinct memory she had of her mother was her funeral. Holding her father's hand, standing next to the open casket adorned with white flowers and purple ribbons. The families separated after her mother's death. The Castillo's were few and had solemn looks, while the Gallagher's were ashamed of the whole ordeal. Several people had mentioned her father had the most stunning eyes ever seen, many were glad she had inherited them, but after her mother's death, that striking green had been covered by a pale cloak, leaving vacant eyes that at certain times the richest green returned to him. He had been proud when she became an officer, recalling when she took him out to dinner to celebrate, giving him azalea flowers and a gold chain her father had liked right away.

Her relationship with her father had been quiet. The house never broke its stillness, not even when her father returned from work. Her grandmother, with the same green eyes as theirs, was almost always sitting in her spot on the living room, silently embroidering intricate designs to sell later at the Sunday market. It had been her grandfather who broke the silence with his singing, being called 'pajaro' by his friends, and unlike them, he had brown eyes. A warm color she appreciated seeing under the sun, shining like copper. As years went by, only them were left, without the warmth of that old man who loved to sing and the great lady who passed away the same year her husband.

Her father had never been one to show affection, much less in public. She knew the man was afraid. It took time for his heart to shed the walls he had built up leaving a man in so much heartache. She was grateful her father wasn't alive to know what had happened to her. How close she had come to dying. Another anguish like that, her father wouldn't have endured. His death had been peaceful. He had took a nap one afternoon and never woke up. Abandoning her reflection, she left her delusions locked in that dark and humid room. She took her umbrella and stepped out.

Outside, the sky was foggy and the wind carried a strong damp smell. Passing through the festival market, she arrived at the town's public library. The design was similar to the one they had back in the city. The entrance adorned by Corinthian style columns in pink quarry stone, half columns ornamenting the façade, reached by steps leading to the old access door. The surrounding area was covered by lush trees, along with stone paths leading to the statue of an unknown poet. She knew a building like this, each mosaic on its floor could tell a different story. The girl at the counter indicated where she would find archives of the town's history and thanked the girl for her assistance. The archives were in the back, protected by old brown covers, and with utmost care of the old, yellowed pages, she began to read their contents. There were different types of articles, many of which talked about the town's infrastructure, until her gaze fell on a particular book.

An old record by an unnamed judge.

The paper was neglected, folded at certain corners, stained, and crumpled, various parts no longer legible. The writings of this judge lacked any semblance of grace. His narrative becoming haphazard at the end of each entry, recounting certain episodes of the town's history, as if this man had become vexed with the place. Instead of being enthralled by finding the memoirs of a character lost in history, her reaction was one of contempt. The first page was an entire brief in defense of the judge against witchcraft.

> *This site is in flux. Since I was made acquainted with the cases of witchcraft and Evil Spirits in this place, people became afraid in their hearts. Our church is full of His saintly images and scared objects to keep the Evil Spirits away of those women. The Devil is preying on us, corrupting is with his hollow promises, casting the fire of Hell unto our souls. Many tongues and dark hearts are residing near our quiet residence, troubling us. Anyone who opposes the Law from our Lord is void. Time will be out truth. The truth will cure us, prerogative of our Lord and his Glory against the matter of Witchcraft and their Works of pure Darkness, creating havoc amongst the Children of men. It is known to us that the Judgment of God is being inflicted unto our societies,*

> *binding us into his Holy rule, controlling the impulses Satan Work can do amongst us. The Lord was pleased with our work. There is no doubt about our actions. With this book the Works of God may be known; so he can be adored in his Justice and in his Truth. God will reveal the path for us, helpers of the truth. His greatness contains mysteries which require us finding out, bringing us to Glory; to the mysteries of Satan will only bring us Ruin. Witchcraft is the most mysterious of them all, letting loose upon us the Devil. The Anger of God will be cast upon us while we live alongside the Coven, diminishing our Harvest, driving our animals into panic, putting strange ideas to our daughters and sons, to the men of God, creating miscarriages and violent deaths. We fear it will be too late for us, we wonder if our Lord will have Mercy when the Time comes. We will remove the Wicked from the land of the Righteous. I will not fear what they can do unto me, for I am in Eternal service for his Glory, and his People […].*

She had to admit it was fascinating to read how someone from that time expressed themselves in their writings. Turning over the first letter of the unnamed judge referencing the old English laws. The legal process that took place in town was long and corrupt at the same time. Since then, record keeping was mandatory, which didn't come as a surprise to her. You have a society, therefore, there are records. Browsing swiftly through the cases of arrests of several individuals, apparently even including the imprisonment of animals. Before long she found a case of interest. Continuing to be mindful of the old pages, carefully smoothing them at the edges.

> *Warrant for apprehension of Charles Gorwin, Sr.*
> *[September 14, 1622]*
> *Complaint has been made by William Grenville & Humphrey Busse sen'r, against Charles Gorwin sen'r to have afflicted & abused residents of Dam'born' by witchcraft, contrarian to the peace of o'r sovereign land, against o'r sovereigne Lord [King] James I King of England & to the Majes'ts Laws-- Therefore in the Majes'ts name it's required to apprehend & seize the body of Charles Gorwin of Dam'born' & return him safely to the Majes'ts justice of the peace to be examined & proceeded according to law, for which this shall be – given und' -- & --*

> *Examination of Charles Gorwin, Sr., as Recorded by –.*
> *[September 19, 1622.]*
> *29. September. 22. Charles Gorwin examination & confession.*
> *He confesses to be in love with the witch woman for four yeares, the devil appeared to him lyke a woman, dressed in green, beautiful as a doll. The woman asked of him to surrender, which Sr Charles Gorwin promesed. He said the woman told him he would live contentedly. – Sr Charles Gorwin confesses to love the witch woman. That he did rituals to bless their union, syne their souls on the lake. He*

confesses he met the witch woman every day, meeting on a green peece neare the deepest part of the forest. He confessed he mett her to plan their lives together, erasing any division of theire souls. Sr Charles Gorwin has worshiped devil's design for four yeares, abolishing all rules of the church in the land. He sayth the witch woman promeised to live in equall bravery at his side, no punishment, no shame, no judgement, no sin. – Their union held in spring, a yeare ago. – Sr Charles Gorwin saith he is sorry –

[Yet he saith to not waste prayes on him. Sr Charles Gorwin desyres his witch woman, desyres to live and renounce them to live with his – love. He saith he will take the punishment and prayes for God to see the harme. The Truth wittnese-- -- Charles Gorwin]

Indictment of Charles Gorwin, Sr. for Covenanting.
[September 26, 1622]
The Juro'rs our Sov'— p'rsent Charles Gorwin sen'r of Dam'born' – wickedly mallitiously & -- with the witch woman & the Devill, Signe his name to the witch woman, and & gave himself to her in Soule & body to her – Sayth Charles Gorwin is become A detestable Witch—

Warrant for Execution of Charles Gorwin, Sr.
[November 9, 1622]
To Henry Warren high Sherriffe of Darm'folk. Greeting—
Charles Gorwin was found guilty of the felonyes and Witchcraft—sentence to Death accordingly passed ag't her as the Law directs in the Name of their Maj'tie James I King of England & Comand you—to be hanged by the neck [Burn the f--- like them] This shall be Sufficient Warrant Given under the hand of Jur' – of November—1622. [Hanged until Hee was dead, buried in--] [Trai—Make him confess.]

The pages had been damaged by the exposure of time, erasing certain words and even entire parts of the antique court records. In the middle of the pages, she unexpectedly came across a folded brochure of the town. It was old, with cream-colored pictures. The first image depicted a view of the lake with the only stone bridge it had, decorated with flowers and lanterns. On the bridge a nun was crossing it. Staring at the image of the nun, she couldn't give shape to her face due to the quality of the photo. The image dated August 9, 1962. Opening the brochure there was a concise introduction; *Welcome to Dameborne, a small but austere town where true magic takes place, in every corner, in every path and, above all, in every person who resides within. You have to visit the great lake of Dameborne, Tonalia Lake, to fill your soul with eternal peace. The natural environment not only is a spectacle for the eyes, but we also have different kinds of activities such as dancing, biking, climbing, boat rides and more. Come to Dameborne, leave your activities for a while, and delight yourself with our events.*

Let your mind flow with us. Let nature unmask you. The following images were additional areas of the town not yet visited by her, with the text running across the bottom, creating a gray blotch. The town hadn't changed that much since then. She put aside the brochure and turned her attention back to the old book.

Releasing a quick exhale, reviewing the cases of 'witchcraft' that had occurred in Dameborne -not as infamous as others, not even mentioned in the history books she had grown up with at Saint Elkan's-, she found herself questioning the veracity of this antique record. The cases were systematically recorded with information that could be sustained if she conducted a thorough research. The clock inside the library resonated. Brida glanced at her wristwatch, noting the time. She closed the bizarre record, leaving it in its place to head to the ceremony. With every step she took in direction of the church the sky darkened and soon began to drizzle. Opening her umbrella, she observed as the lake was enveloped in white mist, covering the vast panorama, as if the fog enclosed the town in its mantle. At the church entrance, she met Collin. His auburn hair neatly combed, the low temperature giving him a natural blush on his cheeks, comfortably but formally dressed for the ceremony. Within the damp aroma, she perceived a faint pine scent and unconsciously stood closer to him.

"I was waiting for you," Collin said. "We can go in if you like."

"Waiting for me?"

Collin raised his eyebrows, blinked, and then smiled. "Well, I was also waiting for Lisa and her family, but you arrived first." The rain had intensified as Brida left her umbrella at the entrance. Collin stared at her ears and politely smiled once more as the woman turned to face him.

"Let's go inside."

The dogs at the doors were grinning despite having a ring on their muzzles, their eyes no longer furious, but narrowed as if they were laughing. Collin pushed the door, letting Brida enter first, then closed it behind him, slipping into the shadows of the church. Their steps mitigated by the green carpet spread in the center row. She peered at one of the wall paintings, acquainted with the ruin of those holy women, halting her pace, tearing her attention back to Collin as she felt his hand on her arm. Brida followed in his footsteps, beckoning her as if he were her own devoted light, till they sat on one of the benches.

"I knew they'd look good on you," said Collin.

Collin felt rather than heard Brida's low laugh. At the apse area, the quartz altar was decorated with a dark green mantle with engravings of serpents, below were decorations of white lilies and wheat. The smiling angels continued their punishment against the people, forever inflicting pain and anger, illuminated by the candles on the altar. The bells rang as more of the townsfolk arrived, taking their seats, staying silent as the first rite began. Two nuns walked down the center, each one carrying a thurible suspended in chains, swinging it back and forth. The elderly nun Brida recognized took her place behind the altar. Her eyes downcast.

"In silence, begin the *collection*."

The silence of the ceremony never broke. People were seated and others kneeled. Brida kept her attention on the nuns who were arranging the altar with baskets containing small pieces of bread and three chalices filled with wine. Brida spotted Lisa kneeling by her father's wheelchair, holding one of his hands, and smiled at the sight of her calm demeanor. At the end of the second rite. Some approached the altar, receiving on the tongue from the hands of the nuns the piece of bread dipped in the wine from the cup. Lisa had gotten up from her spot to receive her piece of bread, bumped into a lady who, clearly upset by the small accident, grabbed Lisa's arm in a tight grip. Brida heard Martin clear his throat and the altercation dissipated. The lady clicked her tongue, leaving an embarrassed Lisa in line with her hand clutching where the woman had grabbed it.

As everyone returned to their posts, they continued their prayers in silence. During the concluding rite, the same nuns holding the thurible passed by, filling the chamber with the smell of incense. The ceremony had been serene, as esoteric as the place itself. As they emerged from the church, the contrasting sound of the rain stunned their hearing sense, causing them discomfort. Collin took Brida's umbrella and before passing it to her, he asked:

"Would you like to join me at the lake?"

"Is it calm today?"

"It is. If you want I can hold the umbrella."

Brida agreed and passed him the umbrella. He held out his arm and Brida grabbed it, finding the action courteous. Collin smiled, bravely touching her hand, feeling like a proper gentleman walking beside the detective. Her hand reminded him of the coldness of Tonalia Lake, her fingers were cold at the tips. Brida's hand had calluses and small marks between the fingers, likely from her type of work. At the lake, the sound had increased in intensity from what it already was. Brida surveyed the surface of the lake being stunned by the rain.

"Did you like the ceremony?"

"It was quiet."

"Yes, that's what it's about," he said. "We must think about us. Meditate on our actions. Everyone here knows what to do. Knows how to become aware of oneself and accept that we aren't pious people, well, things like that." It felt awkward to talk this way. He didn't believe himself a smart man to be educating the detective in their customs, and yet this was something everyone in town knew. His mum had taught him at an early age their way of thinking and he knew Martin had also instilled it in Lisa as well. Many didn't take seriously the teachings of the congregation, unhappy to learn many weren't virtuous people. "Everyone has a different problem and we cannot ask for understanding or forgiveness in the same way. Not many understand it. Those who truly want to heal come here. Few still have the tradition to cleanse with the water of the lake." Collin stared at the surface. So many times he had observed this body of water so particular and, at the same time, equal to any lake in the world. His stomach heaved. "If one doesn't want to heal, then, there's nothing to be done," he murmured the last part.

"Isn't it always the case?"

Collin turned to Brida and smirked at the monotone response.

"I came here for a distraction," she began, shifting her heavy gaze to the young man beside her. "This town has given me a lot to think about since I arrived, although these aren't new thoughts. I know you've realized I'm not well."

"I-"

"It's alright. I don't mind it," she said, turning toward the lake. "Everyone processes certain episodes differently. I've been told that what I do is unhealthy because I don't show the right emotions, according to the first doctor who saw me. The emotion I experienced throughout that time with that doctor was a constant nagging irritation," she smiled and Collin found himself charmed by her trying to be humorous, failing, but endearing in her attempt. Soon she dropped the smile. "I've always lived with discipline and will continue to do so."

"What happened?"

"My friend calls it an accident."

"And it was an accident what happened to you?"

"No, it wasn't."

"How do you feel now?"

"Better," she glanced at Collin. "What I can control is my present." The exact words her father had said to his own parents. Perhaps her father watched her form where he was, on another plane of life, paradise, another realm -whatever it was called-, disappointed she had become him. The lake darkened, as if the depths were expanding, haunting them like a predator. She could tell what had happened frivolously, -the way she preferred-, straight to the point. Few liked that way. She gave Collin's arm a gentle squeeze, drawing his attention. "I may not have the ability to express myself in a delicate manner most of the time. My old relationship is the cause of the problems I have today, it hurt me and others as well. I can't say for sure we were in love, but something close to it. A comfort."

There was a moment of silence.

"When I woke up in the hospital, the first thing I heard was my own heartbeat. The wound was still swollen and prone to infection. I know my case was on the news," she said. "Gutted with a knife, slightly curved in my own home. A wonder I didn't die they said. The circumstances were strange. There was speculation of revenge, heartbreak, psychosis or simply violence. When I returned to my home, I would stare at the place they found me. At work, I didn't improve." She even thought of selling the house. The house her father had chosen for them. When the thought didn't persist after living in that dingy apartment, she had been relieved. "Being here, in this place, has helped me the most."

After what it felt like a minute, Collin breathed out. He reached for the hand on his arm, massaging her knuckles, running his thump over her knuckles, sensing some slight scars between her fingers. "Were you scared?" Collin felt her eyes examining him, searching for *something* on his face. He didn't know what it was. Then she turned back to the lake.

"I was angry more than scared."

He nodded. Brida gave no further details, leaving Collin thoughtful. The rain poured with the same intensity, battering the umbrella assailing his senses. The odds of surviving a wound like that were slim. "So, that's why you came here."

"Not exactly. I had no intention to leave the city."

"Until you met Lisa."

Brida inclined her head in agreement and looked down at their hands linked on Collin's arm. His touch wasn't abrasive; on the contrary, it didn't irritate her, nor did it make her uncomfortable. Her body didn't tense in Collin's presence. "I don't believe myself tough, but just enough to continue. Thank you for listening to me," she said, wondering why she decided to open to him. She was aware many people preferred to open up to strangers about their problems, however, she didn't foresee a day when she would resort to that. "It's not easy to share these kinds of issues without being too blunt."

"I don't think anyone knows how to share it."

She simply replied with a small smile.

The two walked steadily away from the lake in the direction of the church. The old court records came back to mind, and recalled one particular detail. Collin had commented women had been murdered here. "Collin," she called his attention. "When I went to the library this morning, I found judicial records of the town."

Collin lifted his eyebrows, quirking a sardonic smile. "Of all the things you could've read."

"I also read about infrastructure," she added, which caused him to laugh at her. Even his laughter wasn't boisterous, it was sympathetic and mirthful, just as one might imagine it to be for someone like him. "It was an old judicial record, where there were cases of arrests and executions for witchcraft. I remembered you had told me something similar before."

"I wouldn't know much about it. My mum was the one who used to tell me those stories, but I can't really tell you anything else. I don't go to the library and I don't like to go to there. I didn't even know there was a judicial record about, well, executions." He passed his other hand on his hair, licking his lips in that nervous gesture of his. "It doesn't seem important if no one mentions it. I mean, maybe it's not authentic information."

"Is that what you think?"

"I'm not an academic, I wouldn't know."

Seeing how he had closed on the subject, Brida said nothing more until they neared the church. Collin greeted the Gallardo's as Brida politely returned the gestures. Lisa held her arm awkwardly, giving them a little smile. The second phase of the ceremony was about to begin. Reentering, Brida separated from the group when she caught sight of the young nun passing near the confessionals located in a secluded part of the sanctuary. When she reached them and turned around, the nun was facing the door leading upstairs, as if waiting for her. Without needing to say a word, she followed the nun up the stairs until they were situated on the inner balcony, behind them the large stained-glass windows of wild animals casting a natural glow on their backs. The young nun had her ringed hands clasped in front of her, watching as people took their seats and then looked up at the detective.

"Did you find anything interesting?"

The soft and low timbre made Brida get close enough to catch the scent of plants emanating from the religious woman beside her. "You could say something like that." Brida turned to the young nun, stationary as her temple. The echoing murmurs of the crowd ensured she kept her voice subdued. "If this is a place of healing, then any soul can be healed here?"

The nun let out a soft chuckle. "Purgatory doesn't exist here."

"Then there is no punishment."

"No, there never was one."

"But there is salvation."

"No, there is no paradise here, only us."

"Us?"

"You, them," she said, glancing down at the people. "And us."

"And if they don't want to be healed?"

"Then they won't."

The ceremony begun once again, all in silence preparing for the first prayer of the second phase. Brida stood next to the young nun on the internal balcony. Listening to the murmured prayers of the crowd, wondering if her father would've appreciated this site. She questioned if perhaps, in this place, her father could've been healed.

"Have you been sleeping well?"

Brida maintained her serious demeanor at the polite inquiry. The vivacious dream came to her mind, the sensation of her fingers sinking into that body's neck made her fingers twitch. She pointedly ignored the tingling in her hands. In her most active dreams they were always aggressive, violent. From the moment that intense heat had seized her body, witnessing that curved knife come out of her stomach in one swift motion, her reaction hadn't been one of shock, nor of resignation. Staring at the knife, at the bloody hand. The next thing she did was lunge as a wild beast at *him*. Her ire hadn't diminished as the days passed, as if a curse fell upon her, coming to life in dreams where she allowed herself to abandon all rationality and devolve into an animal.

"I have."

The ceremony concluded, but neither Brida nor the young nun moved from their places. Collin searched for the detective with his eyes and located her in what was a private conversation with a nun of the reclused congregation. His attention shifted when he felt a hand on his arm, looking at Lisa.

"Do you want to come with us?" Lisa asked.

"Are you or your family inviting me?"

"My dad, actually."

"In that case, I'll go with you," said Collin, giving a last glance to Brida. He and the Gallardo's exited the church. He was helping with Martin's wheelchair, sensing Lisa moving closer to him and thinking that she had simply approached him because she could be quite affectionate at times, he spotted Mrs. Laura near them. Martin glanced at the woman who knew was hurting, but he also knew she had taken it out on his daughter. Laura may have been an acquaintance at one point in his life, but now she was someone he couldn't even recognize. Nobody was against her pain, yet it annoyed him that Lisa had been the one on the receiving end of snide comments, yelling when clearly this woman should've retaliated with a certain group of young people in town.

"Let's see if this ceremony helps *some* people," said Mrs. Livia as a comment to the air. She grabbed the handles of the wheelchair, pushing past Laura. Mrs. Livia was open with her disdain. She was a grown lady, so she didn't mind being direct with people she disliked.

"We'll see," Martin replied. "I do hope it helps them."

Mrs. Livia clicked her tongue.

He did hope that, in some way, it would help Laura manage the hurt her daughter had caused and that Elizabeth would deign to return home and stop worrying her mother. In the end, Martin could understand the pain.

XXI

On the other side, his reflection glared back at him within the shadows of the bathroom. He felt trepidation at the indifference he kept feeling over the past few days, preferring to feel bad rather than detached. Thomas sighed, combing his hair. At least his upcoming vacation made him look forward to having some time to himself. Sometimes he would get upset, but it always came to the same feeling he was already familiar with; his own wistfulness. He quickly changed into his uniform and left his room, descending the stairs without turning the lights on, grabbing his wool jacket at the entrance. He gave the house a once-over. The more he stared, the more unnatural it all seemed to him. Maybe it had always been that way. He exited the house with keys in hand.

He found himself staring at a dead cat on his porch.

XXII

It was three o'clock in the morning. He lay in bed with his eyes open, staring vacantly at the wall, listening to the tapping on his window. A loud howling could be heard in the surrounding area accompanied by the harsh rustling of the trees as they moved with the elements. Collin Fay shifted under the covers, touching his stomach. It had been so long since he had a dreamed of someone he knew, in this case, was getting to know. He saw those flowing eyes, turning the liveliest green he'd ever seen, offering landscapes only he knew, showing him his own desires. He had jolted awake, ashamed of what he had experienced, filled with an inner peace so unbelievable it frightened him. A voice had asked him to calm down within himself, strangely similar to his own. Before falling asleep, a peculiar warmth settled in his low stomach.

Collin saw a skylight above him in his dreams. A silhouette loomed over him. He knew his stomach was open, unable to move, worrying more about the wound, pressing it with his own hands. One of the man's hand was stained with blood, *his* blood. Flecks of red tingled with the light. Those eyes fixated on the wound. He kept the strength in his neck to keep staring at the man, gritting his teeth. No longer feeling the pain. That man hunched over him, openly crying. Resigning himself to the final blow, the last image, the last breath, the next words he heard steeled his body, recovering his lucidity, wrath beyond his own comprehension invaded him. His heart beating loudly in his ears.

I love you.

It was hard to get up that day. The constant sound of rain made him suspect it would pour all day and possibly the next. He wanted to sleep a little longer, pulling the blanket up to his chin. His mind felt drained, throbbing on each side. Unable to make sense of his dream, he shifted uneasily, closing his eyes trying to drift to sleep again. He was dreaming increasingly often, and it bothered him that his mind became so active all of a sudden. The first dreams had been just like the ones he'd had since he was a child, the same ones that never left him alone at night, but gradually they began to transform, identifying familiar faces. They made less sense. He didn't know if his conversation with Brida had stimulated his mind in trying to imagine what had happened to her. He breathed out, exhausted, wanting to disconnect his mind from the world in order to sleep. Before he knew how much time had passed, he suddenly, without realizing it, fell asleep.

He woke up again and checked the time as he headed to the bathroom to begin his routine. The temperature had dropped, covering his neck with a knitted scarf, picturing Lisa complaining about the weather. Adjusting his jacket, not wanting to get a cold shock on the way out. His parents always warned him to be careful of the cold when he was younger, as it could twist his face. They constantly reminded him of the story of a great-uncle he never knew, how part of his face had gone numb from the cold, giving crooked smiles when he had been happy. He headed to the inn, holding his umbrella over his head, and entered the office to see Lisa writing down numbers in a notebook. He smiled knowing what it meant, they had tenants. Music played in the background and he knew it was Martin.

"Good morning," greeted Lisa, glancing at Collin and then at the window. She had a quilt draped over her shoulders, keeping herself warm and cozy underneath. "I hope it only rains today. I wanted to enjoy the fair more. My dad is in the living room if you want to say hello."

"I will. How are you feeling?"

"My hands hurt when I write."

"Where are your gloves?"

"I don't like them, they make my hands uncomfortable," she sighed, wiggling her fingers. She stood up, rearranging the quilt, heading with Collin to the inner gate connecting the house. "I think I'd better make me a cup of hot chocolate, so the cup warms my hands better. Do you want me to make you coffee?"

"No, I'll do it myself, thank you," he smiled, tugging her ear.

Lisa let out a chuckle, covering her ears. Collin greeted Martin, who was sitting on the couch, doing quick math in a notebook. He knew Martin kept his mind active, having the belief everyone should do mental calculations. It was a bit of an exaggeration to him, but it wasn't a bad thing. The butterflies Martin had bought were on the table as center decorations. He took one of the butterflies, inspecting the painting, carefully returning it to its spot. The table looked better with those colorful additions.

"You can take one if you want," said Martin.

"No, no, just looking, thank you." The butterflies look best on that table, closer to them instead of with him. He excused himself, entering the kitchen and saw Lisa heating milk with pieces of chocolate on the stove. "I think I'll follow your example."

"I knew it," she said, almost rolling her eyes. She pulled out a box of shortbread cookies and arranged them on a plate. Ever since she'd woken up she felt odd, not like her usual self, but close to it. She saw Elizabeth's mother at the ceremony, but holding her father's hand or getting close to Collin, she had nothing to fear. Even managing to ignore the lady's stares, focusing on the ceremony instead. She had also seen Collin beside the detective. Passing Collin a cup, sharing the morning together until an angry Mrs. Livia called Collin's attention to check one of the rooms. Collin rolled his eyes while Lisa snorted. She hugged Collin swiftly, feeling so much affection for him as she did for a brother before he left. Her eyes teared up as he returned the hug. Even as Collin tousled her hair making her laugh, pulling away from him, she still felt her heart tender.

Collin stepped out of the office and brushed past Brida's room, suddenly having the urge to knock on the door and see if she was all right. He dismissed the idea as it came and went to check first what the problem was. Upon reaching at the room indicated, he pushed the door noiselessly. The room appeared to be fine to the naked eye. He turned on the light to determine what the problem might be. As he entered the bathroom, he distinctly heard a creaking sound and realized he had stepped on broken glass. There was a piece of brick near the small window, now shattered. He felt the beginnings of a headache, no wonder the old croon was mad. He fetched everything he was going to need to clean up the mess. Taking the trash can of the room, throwing in the brick along with the shards of glass, cutting his hand in the process and letting out a hiss. What had started out as something simple to clean up, he had complicated it by cutting his hand. He was such a fucking idiot.

After disinfecting the wound and dressing it, he returned to work, covering the broken window with cardboard, preventing the elements from getting in. For the moment there was nothing else to do. His head stung, causing him to grimace. Soon he found himself pruning the inn's garden, holding a pair of gardening shears in his right hand and with the other removed the weeds, pulling them and throwing them away. He had gloves on, so he had no fear of damaging his wound, it only gave him discomfort when he clenched his hand into a fist while picking up a weed. The frigid air occasionally hit him in the nose, making him cough. Working rapidly, unwilling to spend any more time in the damp cold with the drizzling rain. He saw his work finished for the day.

Brida strolled into the inn after revisiting the town's history in the library, only to find Collin leaving his toolbox in the storeroom. The rain camouflaged her footsteps, so that the young man gave a little jump when he noticed her presence as he turned around. His eyes went down her stomach for a second. She ignored that detail to better focus on the bloodstain on Collin's hand.

"What happened?"

"What?" he asked distractedly. "Ah, you mean my hand. Someone broke the window in one of the rooms and I wasn't careful when throwing out the shards. I've already disinfected it, if that's what you're worried about." He straightened up, taking care his hand didn't touch any surface.

"Do you have any inkling as to who it might've been?"

"It could've been anyone," he shrugged, sounding tired about the whole thing. His headache was subsiding with the detective's presence, giving a weak smile. Cautiously, he left all the tools and gloves in order at the storeroom. His body was tense for not having slept well. That's why he had preferred to drink the hot chocolate with Lisa instead of the coffee, he knew he could get jittery. When he turned around, the detective was already gone, seeing her light a cigarette under the roof of the inn's rooms.

He wanted to apologize for the way he had withdrawn from yesterday's conversation, but he guessed Brida only went to greet him and not to talk to him. He had intended to tell her about his dreams, but they were just that, dreams. His dad had always told him he had too much imagination, that it would eventually fade away like it did with everyone else. Childish imaginations. His mum had a different opinion. She always believed in certain things he didn't understand as a child, such as putting salt in the corners of the house, passing an egg over his body, putting red bracelets on his wrists to protect him from the 'evil eye'. He remembers his mum reminding him his dreams couldn't hurt him, no matter how much he woke up with strange sensations in his body.

Returning to his apartment at five in the afternoon, he unlocked the iron gate, giving a curt greeting to the lady outside, who only regarded him with indifference and returned her gaze to her newspaper. Collin shrugged his shoulders, opening apartment his door, letting out a deep breath which made his shoulder muscles loosen. The rain hadn't stopped all day. He rested on the sofa, staring blankly, suddenly falling asleep. A light slumber, populated by various images he couldn't quite understand, yet vivid, just like the dreams that always haunted him. Something gel-like gently pressed against his lower abdomen, causing him to shiver, yet he didn't wake up.

XXIII

Thomas came home from his long shift, hanging his jacket on the coat rack at the entrance. His tired eyes were drawn to the lines of the floor tiles. He still couldn't get a word with Alina and, truth be told, he was weary of trying. At least his superior made no comment when he asked for four days of vacation, just enough time to rest his mind, or so he believed. In his room, he sat on the corner of the bed, listening to the comforting sounds of the house. He wanted for things to change as if at the snap of a finger, but for Alina it was difficult and he understood. Change often frightened people. He heard the fluttering of a bird again and wondered if there was a nest nearby.

Later at night, already bathed and changed, he laid down to read a novel he never managed to finish. He had to reread paragraphs, his mind drifted, listening to the sounds of the house, Alina's footsteps in the other room, that bird, the thunder of the storm that had fallen so suddenly. He lay immobile in bed, his eyes fixed on the small print of the paper, contemplating the trip he was about to take to the old town. One of his colleagues had recommended him to go over the bridge Dameborne had, telling him that the view was breathtaking. Even his superior had made a comment about the lake, of how he and his family liked to vacation there. He had considered inviting his nonna, albeit on another occasion, when he felt more at ease and without the current weather. Tomorrow morning he would leave for town, thus beginning his little vacation. At one point in the night he fell asleep, with the book on his chest until his alarm went off at eight o'clock in the morning. He had opened his eyes at five o'clock being accustomed to his routine, but managed to get back to slumber later, for which he was grateful.

Alina had the television on an instrumental music channel. The sound was soothing and he wondered how long the peace of the house would last with the news of his vacation. He retrieved his small luggage from the closet, packed the necessary clothes and items, bathed, and changed and covered himself up so that the cold wouldn't get to him. As one gets older, one must take more care of oneself in the face of drastic weather changes. Life was like that and that was that. As he went downstairs, he found his soon-to-be ex-wife painting her nails in the living room, seated on the sofa, focused on her activity. Even so, she looked wonderful, but all the mistakes they had made were already extreme. It would be foolish to forgive everything and act as if nothing happened between them. They were things he couldn't forgive.

"Good morning," he greeted.

"Hi." A disinterested reply.

"Alina," he began, walking confidently towards the entrance. "Just a heads up that I'm taking a few days off and I'll be in town." Now he waited for her reaction. He saw her stiffen, stopping passing the small brooch across her fingernails. Alina turned with a frown, plainly upset. Thomas felt discomfort as he sensed within himself the beginnings of that specific indifference.

"And why are you telling me now?"

"I'm just letting you know, that's all."

"Right," she said sarcastically. "Whatever."

He didn't even know why he kept trying. The indifference returned with greater force, completely changing his demeanor, causing Alina to tense up even more. If he said anything, Alina would think she was winning by getting a response out of him. Ignoring her completely, he grabbed the car keys as well as his luggage and left the house, disregarding how Alina tried to get his attention. He got into the car and let the engine warm up, shortly taking the road into town. The day was cloudy, with a dense, humid air.

The road remained uneventful, admiring the relatively small mountain range they had on the island, still green and full of mostly cone-bearing trees. The forest surrounding the road became progressively thicker as he approached the old town. He supposed if someone got lost in the forest, they were susceptible to walk in circles and even more so if one didn't know the trees well. What an ironic thought. He wasn't even in the woods and he'd been feeling lost ever since he wanted a divorce. Before long, he sighted an old statue of a dog, smiling, baring all its stone teeth. Driving past the flat entrance of the town, gazing at the picturesque houses stagnant in time. Crossing a street, he was slightly surprised by the image of an old lady holding the neck of a struggling hen in her hand and a knife in her other. The cut of the neck was swift, killing the hen instantly.

He wasn't shocked by the act, for his nonno had taught him how to break a hen's neck for a cleaner death when he had been a child, but rather by the utter carelessness of the old woman. Ignoring the scene, downshifting the gear, he began searching the place Brida mentioned, till he spotted a Brougham he knew so well in a centrally located inn. He parked and got out, sweeping his gaze around. The town as a whole was a combination of extremely quaint, old English style and countryside. To Thomas, it was nothing out of this world, just another scenic town like most of the others he had seen in his life. He advanced to the office of Gallardo's Inn, opening the door where a doe-eyed girl startled at the sound of the door. Thomas smiled, trying to give a non-threatening image while greeting her, noticing the nervous gestures of the girl, who had her hands pressed against her abdomen.

"Do you have vacancy?"

"Yes, we do," she said, rapidly pulling the registration book out and handing him a pen. "We have two vacancies. Room five is close to the office compared to the other rooms, so the street noise won't bother you. Tomorrow the festival will continue, if you want to go see it and if you came to the ceremony, you missed the day."

"Ceremony?"

"Um, well, the one we do every year."

Thomas simply nodded, leaving the pen down beside the book. He paid for three days in one lump sum and the girl gave him the key to his room. Upon exiting the office, the rain had calmed down, the sky remaining a dark gray. He took his luggage from the trunk and went to his room, seemingly cozy at first glance. The walls were a pale green, with a pattern barely visible due to the pale color. There was a painting in the shape of an oval above the bed, depicting the figure of a snake. Sitting on the bed, he noticed all the details of the room and, in that instant, he felt more comfortable than being in that house with Alina. He didn't like being alone, not that kind of loneliness, but he couldn't stand the strain of that kind of company in his life either. Shrugging the thought, leaving his room to get a better look at the town, noticing how close the church and the park with all its trees were. There wasn't so much activity, given the nature of the day. Shortly, he saw a head so recognizable to him, passing through the park.

"Brida!"

She stopped her step and green eyes intercepted his own. He crossed the street quickly, arriving where Brida awaited him at the park and without a second thought he hugged her. Brida tensed at first before returning the hug with the same strength, patting him on the back making him feel like a child. It had been a time since he received a hug like that.

"How have you been?"

"As usual, you know how are right now," Thomas said. He pulled away, smiling at his friend as they sat down on one of the benches overlooking the gazebo. He didn't want to talk about his problems right then. Thomas couldn't help but continuing smiling, Brida let out a huff and then smiled, patting his shoulder. He straightened up on the bench. "You look better, with more color here," he said, pointing at his own cheek.

"I've been enjoying my stay."

If Brida had enjoyed the town, surely he would too. He still felt irritated by what had happened earlier with Alina, but it was better to let it go. If Alina really wanted to ignore him, then there was nothing he could do about it. "This town seems to be a very old place. Which places you recommend visiting?"

"Several places. Tomorrow I wanted to go see the bridge. Today I spent my morning in the library. Now that you're here, we can go together to see it. I found an old brochure with a picture of the bridge and got curious."

"You point and I follow. So you've been studying and seeing places. You should take pictures of your first trip," Thomas said, almost like a reprimand. "The good news is that I brought my camera, though it's in the suitcase at the moment. We'll take a picture later." At Brida's expression with her raised eyebrows, amused by what he was saying, he regained confidence. She looked more at peace.

"We can take one picture."

Thomas snorted, nodding. The sound of a radio with a metallic sound was suddenly heard, the music was somewhat distorted, drawing the attention of the two. A group of young men passed by, one of them was the one carrying the radio, another a case of beer, the others alternated between smoking cigarettes or having their hands in their pockets. Thomas shrugged off the distraction, turning to her friend, resuming their conversation. "I'm glad this place is doing you good."

"What about you?"

"Me?"

"You sounded tired on the call."

"What can I tell you that you don't already know," he sighed. "Sometimes I fear we'll fight tooth and nail over everything, over every penny. I don't know why the process is dragging on so long. I'm trying to understand so I don't explode, but at the same time it is hard not to let stress get the better of me. I don't want to stoop to that level." He took a long pause. He turned to Brida, swallowing the saliva that had accumulated in his mouth. "I'm afraid of going broke after the divorce. At work they started to tell me different stories about it and I know I shouldn't put them in my head, but I got scared. I don't want to end up like that."

"You won't."

"We don't know."

"I was thinking of returning home. If an extreme case happens you know you can stay with me. There's more than one room."

"Thank you, really."

Brida nodded, giving a small smile.

"We'll see what happens in the future."

"Thomas," began Brida, drawing his friend's attention. "I've been thinking a lot these days. That's all I can do for the moment. I'd like to apologize to you for everything. I'd like to… still have your friendship. I think it's time to let it all go. I'm tired of this, Thomas, I'd like to wipe the slate clean."

"Are you sure?"

"We're not young anymore."

"And we'll never be again," he said. What a frivolous thought, but that was their nature. Ephemeral. "To be honest, I'm tired of a lot of things. I guess everyone has noticed, even if I don't like it. That's why they started talking about divorce that day at work, telling me the family stories about this uncle, that cousin, this, and that. I didn't even know how to react. I think I was just nodding my head to everything they were saying. This is why I didn't want to talk about it over the phone."

"Now you know you have me if you fall."

Thomas let out a small laugh. It sounded so simple, but coming from Brida he knew it was not. He knew Brida would give him asylum the moment it all goes to hell. "I know I made mistakes too. I've made my peace with that, the problem is when the other party can't and it affects you. I have tried many times with Alina, but even the saintliest man has his limits."

"I know."

"It's simply that. It's affecting everything and sometimes I feel like I'm not in control. Rather, I'm not in control," he finished, looking down at the stone path. He felt relieved to finally open himself to someone, thankful that it was Brida listening to his ramblings, voicing his thoughts out loud didn't make him sound egotistical, just hurt, and tired. "Enough about me, tell me, what have you been thinking about lately?"

"About returning home."

He nodded. "That's good."

"I plan to grow flowers in the garden again."

"What kind?"

"Azaleas for my father."

"Sounds great."

"I also plan to change all the locks."

"I can help you with that, if you want."

Brida gave him a small smile. "I'm fine with that."

"Maybe coming here is what you needed."

Just as she was about to respond, they heard glass shatter against the pavement. They followed the sound to where it had come from. Thomas was the first to come out of the park only to see one of the same boys they saw earlier clutching his head while another one tried to carry him. A man was yelling at them, threatening them to leave or he would throw more stuff at them. Thomas didn't see any blood, guessing the object had bounced off and hit the ground. Brida stood next to him observing the scene. There was nothing they could do since they weren't on duty. One of the boys shouted back, till he threw his beer, missing the shot and allowing the others to run away, before the man could take a heavier action against them. Brida had enough of it and touched her friend's arm. "Let's go to the inn and from there we can go eat somewhere together."

"Yeah, sure."

Thomas followed her friend to the inn, slipping his hands into his jacket. It was striking to him how life took its twists and turns. At least now he had the assurance he wouldn't be alone. They had been in such uncertainty, he thought he lost one of the closest friendships he'd ever had, thankfully it turned out not to be so. In the evening, when they went to eat at a nearby restaurant, the sky kept its gray color for the entire time they were together. Returning to the inn, as Brida lit a cigarette, Thomas spotted the girl from the office outside, moving empty flower pots into a storage room, locking the door. The girl turned and greeted Brida enthusiastically.

"Lisa, this is Thomas, my friend. If you're looking for a guide, don't hire Lisa. She'll only show you two places and that'll be all the service," said Brida, maintaining her serious expression while the girl in front of them went red, starting to tell Brida a strings of 'that's not true' and 'don't listen to her'. Brida huffed a laugh.

Thomas smiled, a little surprised he was being presented to the girl from the office. The girl, who now knew her name was Lisa, looked at him with her mouth slightly open and then smiled as if she knew him, sporting dimples on each cheek.

"Brida told me a lot about you, nice to meet you."

Thomas returned the greeting. "Nice to meet you too, Lisa."

"I promise I'm a good guide."

"I believe you, don't worry. Brida can be mean sometimes."

Lisa shook her head, denying his remark. For her, Brida may be one of those people who would get a spider inside her home and instead of killing it, she would get it out. Although on second thought, maybe the detective would simply ignore the spider. Brida wasn't a mean person. Not to her. "Tomorrow the market will resume if you want to go. I'm excited because Dad gave me money to buy me something," she said, explaining it more to Brida than to Thomas. "I don't know what to get, I'll see tomorrow. I have to go back to help my grandma, but it was nice to finally meet you, Thomas. I hope you have a nice day, well, um, what's left of the day. See you then!"

He watched as the girl rushed into the office and closed the door. Thomas raised his eyebrows at Brida, wondering how they had met, especially when the girl seemed like such an energetic person. "She seems like a very spirited girl. How did you meet each other?"

"At Gustavo's bar. She's the girl from the disappearance case."

"Ah. It worked out in the end?"

"No, police haven't given any verdict here."

"Case probably already passed to the city, then."

Brida slightly inclined her head, emitting a hm-hm sound.

"You haven't seen Ortiz around here?"

"No, they may not come due to the several storms," said Brida.

He nodded, accepting the answer. He had looked forward to seeing his former superior, but then again, that'll be another time. Thomas eventually joined Brida, smoking a cigarette as he told everything that had happened on his shift, laughing at the misfortune of his patrol partner, who had stitches in his arm from the bite of that lunatic they had arrested. It felt like going back in time, giving him a great feeling of nostalgia. Brida laughed low, enjoying the story. For the time being, he planned to disconnect from his problems and enjoy his stay in town. He still felt tired, but all right.

Late at night, Thomas felt his body naturally slackening bordering on the unnatural, which worried him a little. Perhaps his muscles were too tense. He felt pain in his extremities, as when one stretches a thread tightly and it deforms and breaks at the end due to the great tension.

Lying there, listening to the ambient sounds surrounding the town as opposed to the industrial noises of Saint Elkan, Thomas couldn't sleep. The same thought that had invaded him when he had been in the hospital watching over Brida suddenly gained full force. This was his only life. What broke him was the thought that life is not the past, nor is it the future. Seeing Brida at the hospital bed, he thought about how swiftly everything can be taken away from you. When he pressed her stomach- When he tried to keep everything inside when it was already outside. He saw *them* outside her body. He had tried to keep her body closed. Thomas sat down on the bed in one rapid movement, running his hands frantically across the bed.

He was afraid of many things. He feared that it would all be in vain. Thoughts like these tormented him constantly and the only one who heard them -first by accident- had been Brida and when he saw her dying, he selfishly thought he didn't want to be left alone. He couldn't talk to Alina, he had tried so many times and he simply couldn't. It was always about her and her emotions and never about his own. He had mistakenly believed he was being selfish, but then, she was supposed to be a life partner, a pillar, and she never felt like one. Perhaps initially there had been the falsity of a foundation, but the 'incident' happened and Thomas opened his eyes to everything he had been sweeping under the rug. He felt helpless because he just couldn't fix it like a crack in the wall. No. Nothing with Alina is easy. He almost always had to take the first step, to wait for her to agree to talk, wait for her to understand where his thoughts were coming from, hope it wouldn't end in yet another fight -discussion, argument, whatever they did-, to feel understood and know there were no misunderstandings between them.

No, everything had to be complicated.

He had wondered several times what it was that Alina had against him specifically, but then, as if in a flash, the answer came to him. When he had grieved for himself, when Thomas had completely collapsed from sheer nervous stress, Alina had misinterpreted his emotions *again*. He wanted to get away from everyone and at the same time be in the company of people. He hated that his coworkers knew about his problems. He hated the fact that the nurses overhead when Alina began another fight in the middle of the reception area and the head nurse glared at him, as if it was his problem that his wife was yelling. He felt ashamed when someone saw him and gave him 'support' so everything would end well in his divorce. He wanted privacy and didn't want anyone to know his private life, but no, Alina lately loved to point her little finger at him, yell and make her problems known. Thomas loathed to let others know anything private.

When he felt better, he laid back down, closing his eyes and forcing his body to sleep. His hands no longer felt clammy. Part of his mind was still troubled by the thoughts he kept on having and the other was exhausted. It was already rare the person who didn't know about his problems and he had to accept the fact his private life became public in that sense. What happened had already happened. He let out a sigh, annoyed with himself. He shouldn't think like that either. Thomas didn't want to hold any resentment against Alina, not wanting to hate her for he knew how deep her insecurities were.

What a shitshow.

XXIV

The sky hadn't cleared, although it wasn't raining heavily as the last few days. The market had reassembled and in less than an hour she would be out looking for something to buy. Her excitement at the thought of what she might be able to get kept her good humor. She combed her hair into a half ponytail, taking one of her ribbons and tied a pale green one in the hair tie, forming a long bow. Lisa had been immediately charmed by Thomas' presence, understanding why Brida appreciated the man so much. He had a genuinely nice smile. She had witnessed how Brida interacted with Thomas and almost cried when attempting to remember a time when Elizabeth had treated her kindly. Of course they had gotten along, but she couldn't quite recall a time Elzabeth had ever *listened* to her. It was always Elizabeth's and at first she didn't want to say anything, until she simply stopped trying. She was embarrassed to learn her dad had noticed and hadn't even been there with them to see it. Had everyone noticed but her?

Ever since the day of the ceremony she had dreamed disturbing things. Little things that made no sense to her and yet they made her hair stand on end. Teddy bears she strangely recognized. Notes she couldn't read. Broken things on the floor. A forest. The last dream she managed to make out was about the lake, the light hitting the surface brightly. She didn't understand any of it, not wanting to keep dreaming as the contents gave her a sense of foreboding. Every time she woke up, she felt short of breath, as if someone had tried to strangle her. In her most anxious state she had consulted her dad to see if there were marks on her neck, but he assured her that everything was fine. Her neck was fine. Lisa pursed her lips, combing her hair, concentrating on the sound the brush makes as she runs it through her hair. Her gaze drifted to her reflection in the dressing mirror, wondering about the kind of friendship she'd had with Elizabeth. Had it all been bad? She didn't know. She was afraid to know the whole truth. Afraid to know what she wasn't seeing. Deep in her heart she knew Elizabeth mattered a great deal to her and still did, even after everything. She squeezed the brush in her hand, hurting her palm with the spikes. She wasn't sure Elizabeth left town.

She stood up suddenly, putting on a knitted sweater and picking up a small purse adorned with beads. Saying goodbye to her dad, she gave him a kiss on his cheek, doing the same to her grandmother who was knitting, stopping at the front entrance of the house, peering through the fisheye outside. The street seemed quiet. There was nothing, nothing at all. Just the street she knew so well. Sighing, lowering her gaze momentarily, soon she heard a quick, almost choking breath, jumping up and peering again through the fisheye. She opened the door, expecting to see who had breathed that way near the door, but no one was there, causing her to feel a bit foolish.

On the way to where the fair market was, glancing around in hopes of spotting Collin, seemingly nowhere to be found. She didn't want to be alone and hadn't thought to call him to see if he wanted to join her. The one she did spot looking at a couple of crafts was Thomas. She got apprehensive about approaching him since he was older than her and she didn't want to bother him, but the fear of being alone in the street got the better of her. "Hello," she said to him with a shaky smile.

Thomas turned curiously to whoever was greeting him and smiled when he recognized the spirited girl. "Hello," he greeted, only to notice how she gripped the drawstring of her purse, white-knuckled. "Did something happened?"

"No, nothing happened." She ran a hand through her hair, combing it with her fingers controlling her nervousness. "It's just that every time I go out I get scared to be alone in the street, it'll pass soon."

"In that case, you can stay close until it passes."

Lisa nodded, thanking him. "Where's Brida?"

"She went to buy something, she didn't tell me what."

"Maybe it's a gift," she said enthusiastically.

Thomas laughed, charmed by how honest the young girl was. Her excitement wasn't strong, rather, it evoked the old innocence of his childhood. He was beginning to suspect Lisa was an overprotected girl by her family. "Who knows, but I don't think she'll be long now."

Lisa stood politely close to Thomas, calming the nerves that always formed when she went out. Sometimes she had the bravado and other times she had none. Today was one of those days where she didn't have it. She glanced at the stalls and then at the man beside her. "Brida told me about the time you had to arrest a man who was afraid of heights. Does that happen a lot?"

"Arresting people afraid of heights?" Thomas smiled, knowing what story Brida had told. It was one of the anecdotes he most enjoyed telling among many he had from work. "I don't even know how I got him down from there. The poor guy was clinging to the window so tightly that I had to grapple with him for a bit. I had to promise nothing was going to happen to him, but whenever I moved him, he would clung to the window again. The neighbors had to help me."

"I can imagine," she laughed, loving that story. She still couldn't picture an officer trying to retrieve a grown man clinging to a window. "And nothing else happened after he was down?"

"No, nothing happened after that. He was quiet until we got to the station." Thomas glanced at Lisa. He still found it curious how Brida had met this girl. All he knew was about the disappearance case. "So, how did you and Brida meet?"

"Well, I bumped into her one night and I already know it was stupid of me," she said, squinting at Thomas as if he was going to reproach her as well. She had it in her favor Thomas was unaware of the situation that night. "I don't know if Brida told you, but I'm looking for my friend. She left after a fight and hasn't returned. Brida already explained to me how to search without having to put myself in danger and above all to be patient, although it's hard."

"Yeah, that's the hard part. Brida told me a little about it."

"A little?" she asked teasingly.

He huffed a laugh, apparently the girl had already spent enough time with Brida to know how his friend managed information. "She told me about the case and that it could come to our attention, but that was all," he said, changing the subject, not wanting to diminish the girl's good spirits. Besides, their conversation was more about his work than the disappearance case itself. "Now that I know Brida tells stories about me and our work, what would you like to know?"

"Do you *really* like your job?"

Thomas gave it some thought, the question had been quick. "I'm not going to lie to you, yes, at times. I believe there's a range of emotions, you see, depending on what you have to do that day or well, see. We have paperwork and it can become routine at points, but most of the time I have no clue where I'm going to end up. I think you can get an idea if I tell you that one woman almost gave birth in the patrol car." Thomas smiled, excepting the tidbit of information would make the girl smile and understand some of the situations officers might be in. He couldn't tell her how the suicide rate was rising each year in the department. How there are times when arriving at a car crash to see the person struggling to stay alive, trying to reassure them and then, die on the moment. How many times he saw firsthand the fact many adults shouldn't be parents. He couldn't let the shock of certain situations get the better of him, he had to keep working. Everyone had to complete their work schedules. Thomas ran his hand over his chin. "I like my job, after all."

"What about a detective's job?"

"I prefer the rush of being the first responder."

"Emergencies?"

"That's right. I watch Brida work her cases and I prefer the blank slate of the day to an office full of cases waiting to be pieced together until they're completed or reach a dead end. I don't know if Brida told you, but she works in the homicide division. She was first assigned to the burglary division and then three years later she was transferred to the homicide unit." He recalled that day and how they celebrated. A big dinner where even his nonna congratulated her. Brida got lucky that two seasoned detectives retired, so she along with a colleague of hers filled the vacant places.

Lisa grimaced at hearing the word 'homicide'.

Thomas cleared his throat, changing the subject. He didn't know what else he could discuss with the young girl, however he knew Lisa appreciated her friend's presence. He didn't wish to discomfort the girl and even less so when she seemed anxious, clutching the drawstring of her purse. "Has Brida been doing well here?"

"I think so," she said, controlling the different emotions that came up all at once. She wondered if Elizabeth had ever asked a question like that for her, finding it hard to believe. She had realized afterward that she didn't talk much when she had been with Elizabeth, and if she did, it didn't last long. Still, she wanted her to go home safely to her mom. "I think I'm the one who bothered her most of the time." She said it out of habit, aware her presence didn't really bother the detective, which often reassured her. It would be embarrassing to tell Thomas she had personally seen how Brida became livelier since they arrived in town. Exactly as Thomas had said, Brida returned with two small paper bags on her arm. Brida offered the young girl a small smile and adjusted the collar of Lisa's sweater with her free hand, making the girl gain a sense of security, thanking her in a soft voice. "Now that Brida's here, I'd better go see what I can buy."

Thomas turned to Lisa with a pensive air. He didn't think it was a good idea for a girl like Lisa to go around the market alone. The town appeared quiet, but as in any place, anything could happen, especially remembering the group of boys from yesterday, who were attacked by a man near the park. He didn't think something like that would happen to Lisa, but one never knows. Better to be safe. "You can stay with us, of course, if you want."

Lisa eventually accepted when Brida stared at her with 'you will stay with us' eyes. It turned out to be the smarter decision, because now she could hear more anecdotes from the two of them, about their life and work, and simultaneously feeling secure. She was reminded of her friendship with Collin, how they saw each other as siblings. Lisa recalled one afternoon she admitted it to him and Collin just ruffled her hair to tease her, but she knew that Collin had taken the comment with fondness. Her heart clenched as she listened. It was almost noon and she hadn't bought anything. Some things had caught her eye, but on reflection it was better to save the money. She bid them goodbye, thanking them for their company. She arrived home at a brisk pace and went straight to the kitchen to get a glass of water. She stood there idly till she went to tell her family she was back. Her dad received her with a hug unknowingly helping her feel better. She kissed his cheek, hugging him tightly prompting her dad to let out a stifled chuckle, patting her on the back.

"Did you get anything?"

"No, maybe I'll see something better later. Nothing caught my eye. Maybe Collin would like to go with me tomorrow. I'll ask him when he comes to the house." Lisa straightened up, stretching her arms. "I'm going to take a nap. I don't know why I feel drained all of a sudden. "Do you need anything begore I sleep?"

Martin smiled. "No, don't worry. Go sleep."

Lisa gave him another kiss on the cheek before going to her room. She stood beside the bed, leaving her small bag on the dresser. Whether she wanted to rest her eyes or just sleep, she didn't know. Sighing, she lay down on the coverlet in fetal position, part of her face rested on her hands, staring at the wall of her room. She closed her eyes. *Lisa*, a voice called for her, feeling her body respond to it. As if the voice was near instead of far away. She wanted to respond to the voice, yet her mouth didn't move. Something cold settled at the base of her neck, which gradually began to tighten. She felt her body twitch, only to relax unnaturally. Whatever was on her neck maintained the same strength.

XXV

Brida stared at the surface of Tonalia Lake over the bridge. Reflecting on the ire she continued reliving in her dreams. The possibility of re-experiencing that kind of searing emotion, which burned like ice against the mind and could make anyone give up their rationality. Her anger appeared to be distant and yet close at hand. Perhaps it was only her imagination playing against her, nothing more than inventions of her psyche attempting to make sense of what had happened to her. The ring remained hidden in her pocket, she no longer wore it, nevertheless, that specific weight lingered behind all of her thoughts. She wondered if Thomas felt the gaze of the lake like pins of light upon them.

"The lake seems quiet."

"Looks like it," Thomas said.

All these days she has been in town, a sense of enlightenment came over her. As they both stood sentinel on the bridge, Brida felt an inner dam of emotions break. She had never been good with emotional reactions, even when was younger, a characteristic of the Castillo family itself. Thus, specific memories came to mind, moments when her anger surfaced when she had been hospitalized. She controlled herself from reacting to Thomas, nor to the others who visited her, which had been few, some colleagues from her division and Gustavo. Recalling how Gustavo presented her a large bouquet of camellias, saying that she had been fortunate enough to be alive. It had been the doctors who, in such an astonishing way, exhausted her patience, asking endless questions, so much so that it made her annoyance noticeable. Her father's voice resounded in her head, reminding her to control her actions, ashamed by her behavior she reverted to her serious demeanor. Appearing detached when in truth, she wanted to shut everyone out. The last 'doctor', who had been nothing more than a young man unqualified to treat her case, visited her, looking at her with contempt and uneasiness. Soon that intern also became noise, insignificant until such visits soon ceased to occur. "Who would have thought something like this would happen," she said without much thought. "When you leave town, what will you do?"

"What do you mean?"

"Will we stagnate again?"

"I don't know, hopefully not."

She disliked the answer, regarding Thomas out of the corner of her eye. Her gaze refocused on the view. She didn't realize she had frowned before she felt a touch on her arm, instantly relaxing her facial muscles, bringing her attention back to the presence at her side.

"What's wrong?" he asked.

"I'm thinking, that's all."

"Why do you think we'll stagnate?"

"I don't think we'll stagnate, I asked if we *would*," she remarked, which caused Thomas to let out a laugh. She felt him move her arm, earning a smile from her. Thomas was indeed a charming man. Unlike others, Thomas had no problem expressing these kinds of emotions, always maintaining a barrier of privacy, but if he had something to admire he was unrestrained with his words and actions. "I asked because I wouldn't forgive myself for getting listless again. I don't plan to go on living like this." She wasn't going to become her father. She wasn't going to let time strip away her layers to leave behind a wounded soul behind, waiting for the final day with so many regrets weighing on the heart. "I wouldn't forgive myself, Thomas."

"There's no way for you to get stuck like you were. I'll tell you the truth. I still worry about you in some ways. I thought my presence was enough at work, but it's partly my fault for thinking everything was going to be okay so soon," he shrugged. It felt cowardly not admitting he also stepped aside to try to keep some sort of balance with Alina, a nonexistent comfort level between them. He had distanced himself from coworkers and even from his few friends. A completely foolish decision, seeing how everything had gone downhill. "When you said we hadn't been friends for a while that day, I got angry. At myself, not at you. Not at you."

"I was too direct-"

"No, I needed to hear it."

"We've hurt each other enough."

Thomas nodded, smiling softly gazing at the lake. "The truth is that I distanced myself from many people, including my family. I don't understand how you can forgive me after all, but I appreciate it." He could get an inkling about it, considering Brida had him and Gustavo as her only close friends, and maybe she didn't want to be alone either.

"I forgive you because you forgave me."

"What?"

"What I want so say is thank you for caring about me," Brida said in a low, almost hoarse tone. She averted her gaze, forcing the words out. "I know I haven't been there for you either. All in all, I think we managed as best we could. If we really wanted to separate, we would've done it by now. I don't resent being left alone if that was your decision in the end. What bothered me is that it didn't come from you."

Embarrassed, the only thing he could say was an: "I'm sorry."

"It no matters anymore."

"I think it does."

"Nothing can be done about it, it's in the past."

"And I'm still sorry about it." He grimaced at Brida's resistance in accepting an apology. It was times like these that he disliked her stoic personality, but she was that the estrangement hadn't been by his own choice. "I know it won't be the same, but, I don't want to lose another friend, Brida. Maybe it's selfish of me." He forced himself not to say anything else, his stomach twisting with nerves. Standing there he felt like a *boy*, as if once again he was too immature with his own feelings, not knowing how to grasp them until too late. He shoved his hands in his pockets, staring out at the lake, with the nagging feeling that something was still wrong. He wasn't going to instigate something that was already forgiven on Brida's part, nor he was going to repeat himself. "It's starting to cool down."

Brida acknowledged him with a little hum, picking up the two small paper bags she had placed on the high, thick balustrade of the bridge. "I don't remember if I ever properly thanked you for taking care of me when I was in the hospital," she paused, pondering what to say next. "I know that couch wasn't comfortable."

"Hospitals aren't comfortable overall." Thomas smiled. This afternoon had reminded him of when they were younger, with fewer problems, head filled with ideas for a different future. It was odd how everything came to be. "You don't have to thank me Brida, not on this. Besides, you already did, several times."

They knew each other for so long he knew Brida would've done the same for him. However, they would never know, for they both had the same thought, neither wanted to see the other in that situation; Brida didn't want to see Thomas prostrated, nor did Thomas want to revive one of his most tumultuous experiences. At the inn they said goodbye, Brida gave him a squeeze on the shoulder and wished him goodnight. Thomas smiled at her and wished her the same. As she glanced towards his room, no light came through the heavy curtains of the window, giving the impression of no one being in there when she plainly saw Thomas enter. At that moment, she reached out to the door, wanting to reassure herself that Thomas was there.

She scowled and turned away from the door. Upon stepping into her room without turning the light, she carefully placed what she had bought on the bureau. She sat on the corner of the bed, fixing her eyes on the hare which always stood vigil, wondering if that animal would protect her dreams tonight as if it were a guardian. Preparing for sleep, she lay down, once again feeling her mind becoming restless, vivid memories came flooding back without warning, disturbing her as she was unable to control them. Her body tensed, her eyelids drooping every time she opened her eyes until she stopped, finally loosening her muscles. A male voice echoed in the background along with an ululation. Her ears reacted to the voice, yet the rest of her body was already too loose to become fully alert, falling asleep.

She was under the skylight again.

Tomasso "Thomas" Cipriani didn't dream often, and if he did, he never remembered it upon awakening. When he slept it was like disconnecting from the world. This time it was too vivid, too light. He could discern colors, lights, and faces. He woke up startled, never having experienced his conscious realizing he was inside a dream. Dreams weren't supposed to feel that way, not that he knew of. He felt drained, blinking in the pitch blackness of the room, guessing it was still night. Each minute spent in town comforted him, though it was only temporary. Soon it would be back to business as usual. Brida's words now made sense to him, he didn't want to stagnate either, wanting to go back to the city with something new, something that would soothe him when he felt short of breath. He felt on the verge of some kind of breakdown, he didn't know what kind, yet he sensed he would soon experience it by the way his heart pounded the last few nights. He was certain the accumulated stress had finally broken through his barrier.

His reflections swiftly drifted to yesterday's conversation, ashamed he had been annoyed with Brida even for a fleeting moment, knowing exactly at what point that vexation had sprung up. He had felt it when

Brida had been hospitalized, noting how she didn't externalize her emotions to the point of worrying about when she would explode. Her mask of indifference cracked every time she grew irritable whenever someone asked too many questions, when they tried to overanalyze her leading Brida to have specific episodes of anger making her stay silent for so long worrying him for her health. Those long silences, where he couldn't get a word out of her, made him self-conscious, pretending the silence didn't affect him by continuing to talk to her until eventually she would reply, first with a small hum, then a word, then a short sentence and finally Brida would reassemble her mask. He resented and, at the same time, he was grateful for the false normalcy.

Then, they reached the evening where he broke down reflecting on himself, crying for many different reasons he had never allowed himself to be open about, unfurling like a cocoon where the core had been plagued. A sense of loss overwhelmed him. He knew Brida could feel him tremble, as he tried to hold back the tears without letting out the slightest sound, only for his own nose force him to inhale sharply, making that typical sound when one cries. He already suspected what was going to happen, sensing his foundation crumble under the sheer stress and quick decisions, but that night everything came crashing down on him and the one who picking up the pieces had been Brida, who lay prostrate on a stretcher, hugging him as if Thomas' weight wasn't uncomfortable. He broke away from the hug, cleaning his face and neither of them commented on it. The medication had tired Brida again and Thomas was left alone thinking that he had to get a divorce. He loved Alina, she was a beautiful woman, but he began to lose hope in their union. A painful decision, but necessary.

What a shitty life they were leading.

The day she was discharged from the hospital, he and his nonna had prepared to escort her to that house, the nurses left them waiting awkwardly until they were given the 'all clear'. He helped her get into the car, causing her to huff, but she accepted the help as she settled in the copilot seat. Brida had no family nearby, she had never actually discussed it nor mentioned any relatives other than her late father, so he and his nonna were the ones who moved for her. His nonna had prepared food in containers for Brida, so she wouldn't even think about what to eat, having everything ready. By now the house was no longer under investigation, all evidence had been documented and collected. Thomas knew a cleaning company had left the place as if nothing had happened, although he noticed several objects arranged in different places. Every time he visited, he checked the place expecting to find blood stains, a small puddle, Brida on the floor, him.

He hadn't been the only one visiting her, a close-to-retire Ortiz also went to see her along with Gene helping with any chores she couldn't do with the injury. Even Brida's colleague, with whom he didn't speak but knew the man could talk his ear off, Pete Valdes, had visited her. He didn't know much about Pete to have an opinion of him. The only comment Brida made was that he had talked about the usual stuff. Another sense of false normalcy for everyone. It became apparent one day when he visited her that Brida showed her true fatigue. Her eyes had gone pale, unfocused as she rested. He disliked leaving her alone, fearing that man would return and finished what he failed, but he had to return to his own home.

One day, after finishing his shift, he visited Brida to see what she might need, finding her in the indoor garden, which was withering. The flowers he knew Mr. Castillo had grown, plants that Brida kept with discipline, had dried up. Thomas observed as Brida uprooted the dead plants, hearing her labored breathing. "Don't tire yourself out so much," he had told her, setting a particular chair nearby so Brida could sit and watch the dying garden. The chair was made of wood decorated with castanet leaves, with velvet green linings on the armrests held in place by metal buttons. The seat was of the same color and was also accompanied by an extra cushion, as Brida was still in a weakened state. That chair had belonged to Mr. Castillo. So many times he had spotted him sitting near the garden, listening to his music, reading, or simply looking at the flowers, absorbed in his own private world. It had given him an eerie sensation to see Brida in the same position as her father.

Brida had sat down, feeling pangs in her lower abdomen, heaving a great sigh as she gazed at the garden. Thomas noticed Brida's clothes beginning to stain with blood, signifying that she may have stretched her sutures. Thomas checked the wound with her permission. His hands shook knowing he had to help in removing the gauze. He forced himself to examine the stitches, otherwise they would have to go to the hospital, peering at the wound, it was closed, or rather, it was closing. The stitches were fine. Her stomach was closed. Thomas assisted in cleansing the wound and throwing away the bloody gauzes. The house always maintained its dark nature, making the corners of the rooms disappear. The gelid, damp air of the site made him break out in a cold sweat constantly, thinking it wouldn't do Brida no good to stay in this house, especially when she was healing and prone to falling ill with all the medication she had to take.

Days went by, turning into weeks, then months and by the time he realized all the mistakes he had made with all his friends and family, distance had already taken its toll. Then, one morning at the station, he had been puzzled to learn Brida wasn't staying at her own home. They hadn't spoken since they had grown apart. He inquired if she was going to sell the house and Brida stated that she was taking some time away, nothing else. She didn't explain her reasoning. He wondered if she had made that decision for security. He was aware she led a straightforward lifestyle, so he wasn't worried Brida would have financial trouble in the foreseeable future. Since Mr. Castillo's death, Brida received his insurance money, quickly saving it along with her earnings. But he didn't know much about her actual situation either, so who knows.

He reconnected with his coworkers, but became irritated whenever they mentioned his divorce or any of his problems that should be private. He almost always argued with Alina, sleeping in separate rooms, because they wouldn't stand each other. They had tried to 'talk' several times, attempting to communicate, yet it was useless when they were both going to be upset and uneasy the next day. Thomas might've thought they were well enough, but then Alina would withdraw her hand away when he had wanted to initiate a display of affection. And then it was he who -as he felt his wife's delicate arms around him-, got awkward, unable to pretend. He understood Alina, but it didn't mean he was going to repeat the same thing over and over again because she was the one who didn't want to see her own insecurities. It was tiring.

He knew he wouldn't be able to sleep again, his mind was too active, so he changed his clothes to enjoy his last day, since tomorrow he'll return to the city, to all his troubles. As he left the room, the light from the overcast sky made him squint. Thomas walked through town, till reaching the lake enjoying the view. Strolling back through the park brought on an episode of drowsiness. At the entrance of the park, he noticed a man staggering with bottle in hand, following in his footsteps but thought nothing of it. He sat down near the statue of Elkan, hearing the sounds of insects crawling up the legs of the rusty bronze horse, he glanced up and, like a memory of his childhood from his old school, Elkan's face blackened due to the accumulating insects. He noticed how some of them fell, hitting the statue and then the pavement, only to climb back up, crawling along the horse's legs. Anyone might feel unsettled by such image, but one who had grown up with this phenomenon felt nostalgic, letting out a wistful sigh. His eyes closed unwillingly, forcing them to open. He shouldn't fall asleep in the park, snorting by the thought, he walked back to the inn. Verdant eyes locked on him. Brida sat on one of the benches in the inn, closer to the entrance than the other ones, legs crossed, arms folded and a cigarette in one hand.

"What are you doing up so early?"

Brida didn't change her expression, seeming to be looking something behind him. From the way she was sitting, it looked like she'd been monitoring him. He didn't know what to think if that was the case. "I was awakened by some sounds," she said.

"What kinds of sounds?"

"A cat, perhaps," she responded standing up. "You look tired."

"I didn't sleep much."

"Hm." Brida dropped her cigarette, stepping on it, walking along with him. He didn't comment on the odd behavior, his eyes flickering each time slower, being brought back to attention when he felt a hand on the small of his back. "Go to sleep. I plan to visit the lighthouse if you want to join me later." Thomas smiled, nodding and entered his room, ignorant how Brida kept her eyes sharp behind them.

XXVI

Collin sipped his coffee, unintentionally listening to the bickering of the couple living next door to his apartment. Initially it had been faint sounds, someone scurrying around the small place followed by a door slamming. Collin assumed that would be all for the day when additional footsteps were heard, gradually the voices turned to shouts. The couple were annoying as neighbors and uncomfortable to watch. He wasn't even enjoying his damn coffee because of them. Ignoring the screams, he finished his coffee and prepared to leave. As he locked the door to his apartment, another door opened and closed. The woman who had come out hastily left, cupping her face in her hands. Collin raised his eyes and turned a blind eye. It was half past seven in the morning and the day already felt tiresome. As he shut the entrance gate, the same woman was crying, hidden from everyone's scrutiny, in the alley next to the complex, at the side of the dumpster. It was none of his business.

To him, it was stupid to tackle a problem that isn't his. He had seen this kind of scenario with his old friends. One thinks they're helping in the right way, falling into the white knight position when in reality what you get is a stab in the side for meddling into trouble that isn't yours. Plus, there's also the fact that couples in such relationships are fucking weird. It's always best to roll the eyes and walk away.

Upon entering the inn, the first thing he sighted was Brida sitting on a bench near the neglected garden, staring at the weeds and small bushes that were drying up in parts, leaving darkened green and brown leaves between the living ones. Undecided whether to approach the detective, he clicked his tongue and walked over. The sound caught Brida's attention, who apparently wasn't as deep in thought as he had assumed. He felt conflicted to see she wasn't wearing the earrings she wore at the ceremony, dismissing the thought as soon as it arose.

"Hey," he awkwardly greeted her. "Good morning."

"Morning." She smiled, noting his awkward stance.

Collin let out a breath, shrugging his shoulders. He sat down next to the detective. He almost crossed his arms, aborting the notion to quickly change his posture with his back against the bench, not wanting to look weird, failing in the attempt. All this was noticed by Brida, who merely raised her eyebrows.

"Something the matter?"

"No, nothing. I woke up tired today."

"Hm."

"So," he began. "How have you been?"

Brida glanced at him, seemingly taking pity on him. "Better, thank you. A friend came to sightsee."

He recognized an olive branch when presented to him and took it. "Sounds good." Collin almost wanted to groan at his uncertainty. He didn't know why he was acting like that. Better to get it over with and say what he wanted to say. "About the other day, I feel like I should apologize for being closing myself off. I'm not used to opening up about certain things." Somehow he cared about Brida's opinion. They hadn't known each other long and she was already uppermost in his mind. "You get used to not talking about it that it becomes difficult."

"I didn't think much of it, but I'll accept your apology."

Collin snorted. "How kind of you."

"Be thankful I didn't demand more."

"I can handle anything just fine."

Brida turned to him, watching as Collin maintained his cocky smile. Leaning toward Collin, catching his unmistakable pine scent, slightly tilting her head to one side, enclosing him among the green tides of her eyes. "I know you couldn't handle what I would want from you."

He almost had a knee-jerk reaction.

Brida laughed, straightening up. "I see your hand is better."

"Ah, yes," he laughed, coughing a bit at the end. He licked his lips. She laughed in a certain manner that made him want to hear it every chance he got, the sound vibrating in his ears, tingling his skin. It wasn't like what he often heard when he flirted with women his age, high-pitched. This sound was mature, assertive, and he wondered if Brida-He'd better stop that train of thought. "Feels much better. Anything interesting happened these days?"

"A friend came by and I'll be going back to the city soon."

He blinked. "How soon?"

"In two days."

"You sound awfully excited about returning home," he pointed out sarcastically. He knew better than to get his hopes up, he had forgotten it was all temporary. He shrugged, oblivious to the detective's silence, until a crashing sound made them turn toward the inn entrance. There was a drunk man. A bottle had been thrown into the street. The man had his head pressed against the park wall connected to the entrance's metal gate. Collin was about to get up from the bench, but halted when he heard the intoxicated man yelling something he didn't comprehend and slamming his clenched fists against his head. Collin grimaced at the display and looked away. Brida hadn't even moved, her gaze back to the dying plants. The man had stopped shouting to give way to a childish sobbing, reaching a point where it became inaudible, turning to see the man asleep on the sidewalk. "At least he's a sad drunk."

Brida made no comment, glancing over as she heard the click of a doorknob, seeing how Thomas looked both ways, bewildered. Thomas exchanged a look with Brida, who merely shrugged, rising from the bench. She wasn't going to comment on how that man had been staring and following his friend earlier. "Be careful if you go out."

"You too."

Collin saw the detective smile at him, triggering an almost natural reaction in response that left him questioning the extent to which he relished Brida's company, finding himself hypocritical for advising Lisa to be guarded while he was falling into the pitfall he had warned about. He always believed that trust was a privilege gained by sheer effort, unassailable by most. Trusting as quickly as he was doing with Brida, it put him on alert, as he never had the need to share his private thoughts. His dreams. He had always relied on his instincts and would continue to do so. He'll take the initiative later not wanting to miss the opportunity for a connection he knew could be worthwhile. As the two friends engaged in hushed tones, Collin entered the office greeted by a weary Lisa. Her eyes were puffy and reddened.

"What was that sound earlier?" asked Lisa.

"A drunk threw his bottle."

"On the street?"

"Yes." He saw Lisa massaging her neck, wincing. "What's wrong?"

Lisa cleared her throat, coughing, covering her mouth with her hand. Wiping her other hand across her irritated eyes. She felt the signs of getting sick again. "I haven't been sleeping well and I keep waking up with pain in my neck. My dad already checked my neck and says everything is fine."

"Looks normal to me."

"Would you like to have your coffee with me?"

"I've already had it, but I can join you."

He accompanied Lisa to the kitchen, watching her prepare a chamomile tea with honey as she told him what she had been reading, complaining about some characters of a story Lisa hadn't enjoyed. Collin didn't fully understand but let Lisa rant looking animated as she did so. Before long Collin saw Mrs. Livia and she asked him to check one of the rooms. Figuring it would be another mess like the brick incident, he turned to Lisa. "I'll be right back, then you can keep telling me about it."

"Okay, I'll wait. Maybe I'll take a nap."

"Go to sleep then. I'll see you later."

Lisa immediately felt better after seeing Collin finishing her tea, wiping her mouth with a napkin. She quickly checked on her father, who was watching TV, a western movie was airing, being in the middle of a fight listening to the sounds of gunshots and bottles breaking. Lisa went to her room, getting under the covers hugging one of the blankets she had put on top of the bed. Later she'd ask Collin to join her to the market, she had a hunch maybe she'd get something if he was with her. She let out a heavy sigh, loosening her body and closing her eyes. Waiting for sleep to come, imagining what she had read, picturing herself with the characters and scenes she had enjoyed reading, an image of what resembled a woman in the forest assaulted her, causing her to open her eyes. She shut her eyes and started to fantasize again, only to be startled by the image of the same forest. She heard a cry and suddenly her neck snapped shut, gasping for air, jumping out of bed, coughing, and clutching her neck.

Hastily entering the bathroom, coughing into the sink, nauseated by the sensation. When she managed to control the feeling, reflected in the mirror, a strange red line was seen, forming a V under her chin connecting with her neck. As she touched it, the pain was as sharp as needles piercing her skin. She stopped touching it, preferring to rinse her face and wait for Collin. She didn't want to be by herself and simultaneously didn't want to disturb her father, though at this rate her fear of sleeping alone was getting on her nerves.

Martin watched as his daughter returned with teary eyes, pale and smaller than she was. It concerned him she looked so crestfallen. His daughter settled down next to him, snuggling under the covers. Martin smiled and hugged her with one arm, turning his eyes back to the movie. He heard Lisa let out a sigh, hiding her face in his side. "What's wrong?"

"I can't sleep."

"You're already having trouble sleeping at this age?"

Lisa chuckled, giving a small no. "I keep having dreams."

"What kind of dreams?"

"Weird dreams."

Martin turned to his daughter, shortly noticing an odd line on the jaw connective to the ear. A red line, contrasting hideously with Lisa's fair skin. He moved to see that line better, noting the raised skin. He touched the back of her ear causing Lisa to recoil from the stinging she felt. "What happened to your neck?" Martin felt the concern rise in him, indicating Lisa to take the ointment he had for irritated skin. Spreading the cream, he observed how in certain areas the skin was so chafed it had red spots where the blood had tried to come out. His mind blanked as he wondered how this could've been done.

"I woke up with it."

"Tell me truth."

"I am!" she exclaimed, grimacing as her neck ached.

Martin stood quietly, applying the cream behind her ears, observing his finger had become stained with dried blood. It wasn't too much to push his worries over the edge, but it was enough to consternate him. "I wonder how you did this."

"I don't know."

Seeing how her eyes closed, he let her nap, he would check that line later. His mother checked on them and then went back to the inn office with her knitting tools to pass the time. By noon he finished watching another movie while reviewing bills and jotting down numbers in his notebook. Reflecting on his daughter, he recognized it wasn't doing her any good to be so cooped up, with no friends other than Collin, and he knew Collin wasn't so much her friend as he noticed Collin treat Lisa with the same familiarity with which one treats a younger sibling. This type of confinement wasn't good for anyone. At one o'clock Lisa was awake, still lying in bed with her eyes open. Martin patted her cheek making her laugh covering her face. "Feeling better?"

Lisa nodded. "I'll go help Grandma." Yawning, she got out of bed, her brain still drowsy. She kissed her father's cheek before going to the kitchen to find her grandmother already preparing the meal. Lisa stepped closer, becoming a little awkward at her grandmother's silence before she instructed her to make lemonade for them. Lisa quickly took out everything she was going to need, grabbing one of the pitchers, placing it on the kitchen counter. This time she hadn't dreamed anything strange. Nothing. Her brain had finally switched off, giving her a break. She didn't like those dreams, they were odd and vague, like puzzle pieces that had no shape. She stared at the cut lemons. Those dreams frightened her. She didn't believe dreams hurt people, it was impossible.

She heard the gate opening and closing.

Collin entered the kitchen, greeting them. Mrs. Livia returned the greeting and went to get Martin's wheelchair. Lisa smiled, passing him a glass of lemonade which Collin appreciated, wiping the sweat from his brow. "Did you have a good nap?"

"I did, thank you."

"That's good."

"Um, Collin," she took her time, waiting for him to finish his drink. "Do you want to go with me to the market? I didn't get anything last time and I'd like to buy something this time."

"Yeah, sure. When I finish work, I'll come with you."

"Thank you, I didn't want to go alone."

Lisa smiled, brought out the plates and served the food. Collin thanked her, placed the silverware and poured himself another glass of lemonade, now waiting for Martin and Mrs. Livia. Collin turned to Lisa to ask her to pass him the glasses and noticed the line of her neck.

"What happened to your neck?"

"I don't know, I woke up with this. Dad didn't believe me at first, he thinks I did it to myself with something, but I swear I woke up with it," she said, turning her head to the side, letting Collin get a better look at the line. "I don't know what could cause it, but it really hurts."

"Did you put some ointment on it yet?"

"Yeah, Dad put some of his on it."

Collin nodded. They left the subject of the line as Martin and Mrs. Livia joined them at the table. Collin wasn't going to interrogate Lisa in front of her family, instead he chatted with Martin about the cost of the broken window and that he had already found a guy who could give them a low price for it.

Lisa listened quietly to the conversation her family and Collin were having, all the while concentrating on finishing the food on her plate. She wanted to ponder on what she could get at the market and that's what she did, every time she began to wander in her imaginations, she always went back to the thought of what she could buy. It didn't matter her head hurt in the end.

XXVII

Thomas breathed in the salty scent of the coast, standing near the lighthouse, which was only about fifteen minutes from Dameborne, listening to the waves lapping against the elevated rocks. They had taken a picture in the somber atmosphere of the lighthouse, the shore and the sea, courtesy of a kind man passing by. Since childhood he had been fascinated by the stories of the sea thanks to his nonno, who had been part of the navy in his youth back in Italy. "Imagine staying here," he said, leaning on the railing, looking out at the waves. Imagining all the tales related to the island's lighthouse.

"You would've made a fine lightkeeper."

He could do nothing but smile at the blunt comment, it always caught him by surprise when Brida openly complimented him. He held his camera in hand, mindful not to let it slip away to the ocean in one false move. Thomas accepted his situation wouldn't change any time soon as he would've liked, everything has its time. He had no reason to be angry, preferring to maintain his mind calm and be gentle rather than explosive. Neither did he have to rationalize Alina's behavior anymore. There was no point, better to be at ease with oneself. He had truly loved that woman, the thought would return to him whenever they shared a quiet day, the way her lips pouted, uttering that little cupid's bow, he had always thought that was the loveliest part of her. Alina was a woman who loved her looks and he never saw an issue with it, anytime she had a nail accident and her polish fell off and she got frustrated and Thomas thought it was lovely. The women in his family took great care of their image, even the men, he remembered how his nonno wore his best gold chains, even owning glasses with leather lined handles. His mother often went to the hairdresser, maintaining her natural curls. The fact that Alina shared the same trait as his family had endeared him to her. In the end, he decided to conclude his musings by stating that all would be well.

All thoughts were put aside when he realized Brida went to chat with the museum tour guide. He could tell the guide had a sympathetic nature by the way he talked and moved his hands. What he gathered from the conversation was that they had recently automated the lighthouse, so a keeper was no longer needed. "A normal day here consisted of cleaning, fixing, of course, standing guard, making sure the lenses were clean and the light was operating properly. There was a lot of work…" the man trailed off, gesturing for them to follow him, pulling his round, electric blue glasses from the sweater vest and placed them on the bridge of his nose. Thomas walked in behind Brida as the attendant continued his explanation, holding the door open and closing it as they entered the museum. They quickly jotted their names in the log book, following the lively man as he told the nautical history of the island. Thomas looked around, picturing the families who had lived in this place far from town. As he listened to the guide, Thomas felt his curiosity piqued.

"Many would say it was men who ran the lighthouse, but in reality it was the whole family, depending on the location, of course. In this lighthouse it was preferable for the keeper to be married at least. Liquor was forbidden here, that's why families were preferred over a group of men. Yes, there were several accidents in this place, but what place doesn't have at least one?" the man shrugged, letting out a small laugh. "One of the last keepers we had here was a recently windowed man with his little girl; Norman and Joan Griffith. Their picture should be around here somewhere. Norman died of a heart attack and the young lady was left in charge of the light while others took care of the funeral. From there she petitioned to be the lighthouse keeper like her father. We like to tell that story unlike the others this place has. I don't like depressing stories."

"It does sound better," said Thomas. "No ghosts here?"

"No, I don't like taking the historical value of the lighthouse away from ghost stories," he said, dismissive. "So, no ghosts here, only old items with sentimental value."

Brida concurred, also preferring information to fantasy. The guide wrapped up the small tour and left them to explore the museum at their leisure. Thomas watched the man move as he heard the door open to make way for an elderly couple. He searched through the photographs that had been donated to the museum and found the photo of Mr. Norman Griffith with Joan in his arms above the white fireplace in what had been the living room. Mr. Norman sported a long beard with a mustache curling at the sides, dressed in uniform, and little Joan showed the typical curls of the period, wearing a light dress. They looked cheerful in front of the lighthouse. It was a somewhat unique photo, as they looked exultant compared to other antique photos they were used to seeing, with somber suits, more serious faces. This family had been happy in their new home. Brida seemed to have liked that particular photo. He turned to check on the guide, who was elsewhere explaining the working of a lighthouse to the elderly couple.

"Compared to the façade, it looks comfortable here."

"Hm." Was all Brida said to his comment. She stopped inspecting the photo to focus all her attention on her friend. "How have you been feeling here?"

"Better, I needed to get away from it all for a while. Your comment yesterday got me thinking, about whether we'll stagnate when we get back home." Thomas plucked up the courage to open up on the matter, aware if he didn't speak up now, he won't have another chance. "The truth is, I never felt like drowning myself in alcohol, nor to keep arguing with Alina, I just don't feel like being conflicted every day. I keep thinking that I want to go back to the routine I had before, work, exercise, visit my family more and try some family recipes. I don't know how much longer I'll have my nonna. She doesn't get any younger with each passing day. I need to change my priorities."

"I know Mrs. Serafina would be delighted to see you more."

Thomas smiled, sheepishly. "Yeah, I enjoyed dining with her last time I visited. Anyways, I know I don't want to try again with Alina, it would only make us miserable. What bothers me is that she can't seem to understand it and it gets on my nerves. That's when I lose my patience. The last few days I started to feel indifferent to everything and I don't like it. I don't like being like this. I can't be comfortable in that house. Lately I dread knowing I have to be there when I get off work and I'm done dealing with someone who won't listen. Maybe at first I thought we would work it out, but not anymore. I know Alina has her problems too and I don't know, Brida, I'm tired."

"Do you feel drained?"

"I do, I'm exhausted."

Brida stopped glancing at the details of the room, to focus on him again. She was the worst choice to come with this type of problem, as her first relationship resulted in an open stomach. She had no opinion of Alina, as she had become irrelevant as other people she didn't care about, yet she didn't believe Alina to be so spiteful. Alina, for her, was someone who needed to mature, to understand that they were already at a point in life where one had to be responsible with their words and actions, even if it was difficult to accept. Brida glanced at the Griffith's photo. "I don't believe Alina would want to stay either."

"You think?"

"I don't know her, though I doubt she'd want to live like that."

"Well, I hope you're right." Though inwardly he reasoned that perhaps Alina was one of those people who stayed in a relationship for the false comfort it provided. Personally, he couldn't stand it. He couldn't pretend. He didn't want to and wasn't going to, not even for Alina. Being able to share his troubles without judgment eased his mind, cooled his thoughts. He cleared his throat and smiled. "Thank you for listening to everything, Brida."

"You have to pay for the session."

"I thought we were friends."

"One doesn't befriend one's client."

Thomas snorted. They thoroughly enjoyed the museum and even had the opportunity to climb up the spiral staircase to the metal balcony of the lighthouse. Thomas was delighted with the view and asked Brida to take his picture. The tour guide offered to take a picture of them, a nice souvenir from the lighthouse, Brida consented by giving him the camera and now they had another picture together. His heart felt itself softening, although he was aware this was only one step of many to come. He had thought this place had been good for Brida, but now he realized it was good for him, too. Away from the pressures of their daily lives, giving way for the mind to open up completely, exposing even the most unpleasant parts of oneself. Outside the museum, once again gazing out to sea, a question occurred to him all of a sudden: "Brida, were you ever afraid?"

"About what?"

"Dying, I guess."

"Our death is inevitable. It's normal to fear it," she said dryly. Brida regarded him, let out a sigh and lowered her gaze to the rocky shore. It was such a human question. A question that in its time made her see life for what it was, making her reflect on the importance of how she used her time. "More than the fear of dying, what made me revaluate everything was-" She frowned, soon shifting her expression to one of weariness. "It's not that I don't have fears, but dying isn't one of them.

I do not worry about it. My father used to tell me to live well. I wasn't living well. It became routine to live."

Thomas contemplated his friend, glancing to where he knew the scar was. Whenever he reflected on that scar, he restrained his thoughts from wandering to that man who he hoped was dead. Being forgotten by all. *He* had left his mark on them and Thomas hoped life would do its work so that, when that man died, no one would remember him, leaving him in complete oblivion without even being recognized by Brida herself. It was a futile thought, he knew, yet he didn't care. "What about… What about *him*?"

"He's only a bad memory."

"How are you so sure about this?"

"I want to live well."

Thomas stopped what he was about to say. All the words left him, to fully understand what Brida was alluding to. It was useless to beat one's chest over something that couldn't be controlled. They cannot control what has already happened, only the now. As they had said before, they were no longer young, they couldn't afford to waste time. Sounds easy to say, but what choice did they have? "So, why didn't you throw that ring away?"

"I had a lot to think about."

"About the ring?"

"No, a ring is just a ring."

"Then about him."

"About me, Thomas," Brida said in a low tone. Her hands rested on the railing, revealing to Thomas her lack of a ring. "The ring helped me channel my thoughts, that's why I couldn't throw it away. I know it was wrong of me to keep it, but I needed something tangible to focus my mind." It had been one of the most expensive gifts she had received from him. In her innermost moments she pondered his decision to pick up that knife. She'll never know. "I want to live well," she repeated, gazing at the waves lapping against the high rocky shore. "We will," she corrected.

He believed her.

Thomas smiled, sensing a burden release his shoulders as he learned the true reason for that ring. It hadn't been what he'd assumed it to be. He was grateful to be wrong. The big picture opened up before him, finally finding sense in many of Brida's actions. It was one thing to assume and quite another when sufficient information had been provided so as not to fall into conjecture. "Yeah, we will," he conceited. "It's the best we can do." He admitted it gave him peace to know not everything was going to change. "Let me tell you that after the divorce, I don't plan to be in a relationship again. At least not for a good while."

"Sounds good."

"It does, doesn't it?" A sudden realization dawned on him. He had pondered whether he'd truly knew Alina, but he didn't know himself either. Take away his profession, and he's just Thomas; take away his name, and what's left of him? He recognized the impossibility of completely knowing himself, but before he knew enough, now it was almost nothing. His throat constricted, struggling to pass saliva down, his mouth pasty. "At one point I thought it would all work out. I believed that going to the sessions with Alina would help us," he said, clenching his hands on the rails, putting all his pride aside. "It made me realize that, well, that we behave as if we were children. My mom knew something about it, but maybe I was ignorant thinking that- Bah, there's no point anymore. It's pointless to repeat everything. All has been said and done."

"Ignorant in what?"

"No, no, it was a mistake to put it that way."

Brida didn't press for an answer, letting out a small hum.

"Naive, would be the correct word," he relented.

"Naive for supposing you'd be fine in your own marriage?"

Thomas almost flicked his eyes, slightly annoyed, though a playful mood welled up in him. He had needed these types of remarks from someone who could objectively point out his shortcomings, he didn't need anyone else to berate him, having enough with Alina and his own family. "It sounds so dumb when you say it like that. But that's why I decided to divorce, we were both unprepared and it's our fault. We crossed a line where we couldn't return."

Brida solemnly placed her hand on his arm. Amidst the silence, the two stood admiring the view, each in their own manner of appreciating the site. They were aware they had to return soon, noting the humid air becoming chillier. The reality of their predicaments appeared to be less of a burden now that they were able to recognize their situations for what they were, no longer affecting their psyches as much.

XXVIII

Collin felt twinges on the sides of his head. He had bought a bag of churros while Lisa searched for what to buy, turning every now and then keeping her in his sights as he waited for the lady to finish frying the last batch. Lisa was pale, her eyes downcast and dull, as if she had fallen ill again. She had put on a scarf to shield her neck from the frigid wind and also to keep others from seeing the strange line. He saw Lisa return to his side, leaning her head on his arm and let out a breath.

"Nothing catches my eye," she said dejectedly.

"We just got here." Collin took his churros as the lady passed them to him. He offered them to Lisa, who eagerly picked one, enjoying the warmth of the fried treat. Eating while accompanying Lisa around the market was helping his headache subside. When Lisa lowered her head to get a better look at some books, that red line grabbed his attention again. He wondered how she would've done it. Collin felt apprehensive for some reason. He knew it wasn't normal. "Do you have any idea what made you that line?"

"No, not really." She grabbed another book, reading the back. She was disillusioned to find out it was just a romance book with nothing interesting to her. She put the book down to pick up another one. She hadn't liked any of the jewelry enough to buy it, so in the end she opted for books, getting a little fidgety since she couldn't choose anything. On the bright side, Collin's presence kept her calm. Had she been alone, she wouldn't even been able to concentrate on reading the book summaries. After a while she found a book, a science fiction one, with an old cover. She loved the colors so much she bought it. The tension had left her body and mind holding the book in one hand, giving a quick hug to Collin who patted her back.

"Happy now?"

"Yes, I really like it."

"That's what matters."

"Can we go to the park?"

Collin was about to agree, but thought better of it when he remembered what had happened with that drunk earlier in the morning. It hadn't been a dangerous drunk, but the man still threw a glass bottle into the street. One never knows. "We'd better go to your house, so you won't get cold." As they passed through the park to get to Lisa's house, the drunk was still asleep in the same spot. Lisa grabbed his arm and leaned out to see the sleeping man from his side.

"Is it okay for him to be there?"

"I don't care. Not our problem." Collin shrugged and headed to the front of the Gallardo's house. He opened the door, opting to go to the kitchen, where Lisa took the opportunity to brew coffee. Collin set his bag of churros on the table, moving one of the chairs to sit down. "Go tell your dad that we're here. I'll take care of the coffee."

Lisa gave him a quick hug and went to check on her dad. Collin was left alone in the kitchen and turned to see the coffee pot on the stove and took out two cups. Days kept passing and there was no news from that girl. Frankly, it wasn't that he was interested, but she had been out of town for more than a month now. He had never liked Elizabeth. Lisa returned pulling him out of his thoughts.

"I showed my dad the book and he liked it," she said, setting the book on the table. She loosened the knot of her scarf, passing a cold hand down her neck, feeling for that line. She lowered her eyes to her new book and then to Collin, who held out the cookies she liked best. She smiled taking the package, opening it quickly and eating one. Collin served the coffee and poured milk into Lisa's cup. "Collin," she called, prompting him to look at her. "Can I tell you something?"

"Yeah, what's wrong?"

"I've been having weird dreams."

"Nightmares?"

"I don't know whether to call them nightmares. I haven't been able to sleep well since I started having them. I don't like them." She pulled a lock of her hair, combing it through her fingers. "I wake up every time I have them, but when I go back to sleep, they reappear. I can't remember them all. Have you ever had dreams like that?"

He dreams almost every night. It wasn't nothing new for him. "We all have weird dreams from time to time."

"Like these?"

"They'll stop bothering you if you don't pay attention to them."

"Really?"

"Yep, don't pay attention to them." It was pointless to pay attention to worthless dreams, however unsettling they might be to the spirit. It didn't matter if they felt real to the point he felt a curved knife dig into his skin and tug at his- It didn't matter. They were just dreams. They were of no consequence. His mind simply absorbed all the information and, as his dad had told him, he had too much imagination. On the other hand, he resented the words. If he had too much imagination, why did he know about the lake and the- It didn't matter. It didn't matter in the end. "Are you happy with your book?"

"Yes," she said, showing it to him. "I loved the cover."

"As long as you like it, it's fine."

Lisa nodded, smiling as she caressed the old cover.

Collin watched her handle the book as he sipped his coffee. He knew it wouldn't take Lisa long to devour that book, as she had done with others. In the past few days, she hadn't mentioned anything about Elizabeth and, more importantly, she hadn't done anything to worry everyone. Many were predicting the worst in Elizabeth's case. He knew what to expect in these cases, especially with girls. One wants the world to be less dangerous, but each passing year makes him think that maybe it had always been that way. His dreams were always surrounded by violence. A revolting violence that he had starred in different scenarios. He didn't need his dreams to know how dangerous the world was. Although there were some where he felt the tender caresses of another, whispered vows in his ear, intimate promises transcending the soul. The memory of those green eyes, morphing and luring him into their depths- He cleared his throat, concentrating on his coffee. "You should try writing a story. Distract yourself."

"I don't think I have any good ideas."

"You can try."

"Maybe, I don't know. I really don't think I have any good ideas for a story." She grew timid, fiddling with the corners of the book, gently poking at them. She'd never had the courage to write anything. Let alone something as personal as a story. "Although I'd like to try. Maybe it'll make better use of the time I spend at the office, besides studying. What should I write about?"

"Whatever you want," he said with a shrug.

"I'll give it a try."

Collin found her cheerier about the idea and was glad to see her less despondent. This way she'd be more concerned about writing a little story than about what she was going through. The grieving process was odd and different for everyone. He looked at the strange line, studying it. "Well, I'm off to rest now. Put more cream on your neck."

"I will, don't worry about it."

He bid the Gallardo's a polite goodbye and went to his apartment. Upon arrival, his neighbors were oddly silent. No crying, no shouting, no sign of their presence. All the better for everyone, who were only inconvenienced when situations like that arose. He locked his door and turned on the light. In the kitchen he began preparing a simple dinner, basking in the stillness filling the space. It dawned on him he should contact his family, let them know he was okay in town, that he was leading a quiet life. Collin knew his mum would ask him plenty of questions, most of which he was unprepared for, but then again, no one is ever fully prepared for all of life's twists and turns. He owed them many calls.

It took him a while to finish dinner. By the time he cleaned up, his mind blanked out. Outside, the wind whistled, rattling the windows of the apartment, forcing him to notice how lonesome he was. The insects were still at his window, but this time they weren't banging on it, just moving around the sealed frame. Following his routine, washing his face, brushing his teeth, and becoming comfortable for sleep, he turned off the light and closed the bathroom door. As he lay back on the bed, stroking his empty side, he contracted his hand to his chest conscious of his behavior. He frowned, irritated at himself. He glanced toward the ajar bathroom door. Initially he ignored it, but it kept distracting him to the point of irking him, clueless as to why he had left it open. He got up and closed the door, going back to bed intending on sleeping uninterrupted. Perhaps he hadn't closed the door properly, with that thought he fell asleep. A gentle press on his spine was felt, reaching all the way up to his neck, prickling his skin. He opened his eyes abruptly and turned his head. As usual, nothing was there.

He was too imaginative.

Sleep eluded him. A distant hooting kept him awake, listening to the tireless animal. A thump made him rise abruptly from the bed. Without turning on the lights, he left his room, hearing a groan behind the front door. From the peephole, he saw the neighbors' door open. He turned away from the door, irritated that the couple was back to their usual patterns. Frowning, grabbing a glass of water, he heard the thumping again. He ignored it and poured himself another glass of water. He returned to his room when he was sufficiently tired, his mind drifting, detaching from all his thoughts to let his mind zone out. As he lay down, he felt a damp patch on his lower back. He ran a hand across the bedsheet. Collin straightened up and ran his hand harder against the mattress. The bed was damp. His whole body stiffened as his stomach throbbed. He let out a groan, pressing a hand on his stomach as his bed became soiled. His movements slowed, eyes narrowing in pain, the objects in his room losing their shape.

His hair stuck to his forehead. He struggled to get out of bed, managing to do so with great effort, his body trembling uncontrollably. He entered the bathroom, leaning against the door, peering into the small mirror. There were two green dots at his back. Hastily he turned around. There was nothing. He was alone. He glanced in the mirror again and saw only himself drenched in his own cold sweat.

He was too imaginative.

XXIX

High in the night, Lisa Gallardo sat at her dressing table, concentrating on her writing. She pulled a blanket over her legs and opened a package of cinnamon cookies. The line on her neck remained, but it no longer discomforted her as before. It hadn't hurt as much to put the cream on as when her dad had put it on in the morning. The blood stains became less visible. She felt better to see her skin already healing.

She wasn't sleepy and took the opportunity to jot down ideas she'd had for a while. A simple story with a simple finale. A straightforward plot where she could unload her thoughts. She looked down at the new book and smiled at the idea of a world totally different from her own. She enjoyed reading the different worlds portrayed by various authors, often imaging ideas of her own, but it remained a private facet, not allowing herself to share any of it. She didn't have that kind of courage. Sometimes she would share with Collin the books she had read and what she liked and disliked about each segment. It embarrassed her how much she could lose herself in her daydreams, but it felt good to give herself a brief moment to indulge in whatever her mind wanted to create. Drawing without overthinking about what she was doing, envisioning an entire alien planet and its inhabitants, wanting to make them sensitive as she was. Lisa pressed her lips together and wiped a hand over her tearful eyes.

Thinking about her story made her focus on herself. Collin often makes her evaluate various aspects of life and among them was herself. In school she had struggled to make friends. And suddenly, Elizabeth connected with her. They had started off well, talking a little bit about everything, sharing jokes, learning from each other, and then little actions like tying her shoelaces, Elizabeth would keep walking leaving her behind or get frustrated with her for taking so long. If she talked too much about something she liked, Elizabeth wouldn't fully listen to her, often having to repeat herself. She didn't want to think badly of her knowing Elizabeth struggled with plenty of problems, but it didn't seem fair. She missed her and wanted her to come home, but now that she reflected on it, she didn't want to reconnect with Elizabeth.

Elizabeth did had her fair share of good times. At school, Lisa once received a love letter. She hadn't like it, leaving a strange feeling in her stomach. Elizabeth had laughed, taking the letter out of her hands, telling her she'd better stay away from that short of thing, it only brough trouble. Lisa simply didn't want to deal with any of it. In fact, she had considered that there was something wrong with her for being averse to the contents of the love letter, instead of being delighted, Lisa had felt pressured. Strangely, she had felt a sense of responsibility for someone else's feelings. Then days later at school, the boy from the letter tried to kiss her and she broke into nervous tears, scaring the boy and the people around them. Elizabeth saw her and helped her get out of school to go home. It had been her family who had reassured her that no one should pressure her and that if she didn't want anything, there were people in life who preferred to be alone.

Lisa had been stunned by such information. Her grandma had been furious by the whole ordeal and her dad gave her a stern talk about life, making Lisa reflect on his words, feeling better if she envisioned herself alone. After that episode, she didn't receive anything else. Something that had pleased her the most. Elizabeth had removed the letter from her locker because she hadn't known what to do with it. Elizabeth could be strange, but she'd had some good times too.

That's why she missed her so much.

Maybe Elizabeth hadn't been a good friend, but she wanted to see her return safely to her mother. She had wished Elizabeth to improve, to stop hanging out with those jerks, to leave that strange guy, blaming herself for not having an assertive personality to say everything she had wanted to say to her. She had tried to talk about it but it all turned into a big argument. Elizabeth had accused her of being jealous of her 'boyfriend', that according to Elizabeth, Lisa liked that guy when in reality Lisa was afraid of the whole group and specially of that strange boy. Lisa had remained silent not knowing what to say. That discussion ended badly when she told one of the many truths, that Elizabeth had changed for the worse when she started to hang out more with that weird group.

When Collin began working at the inn. Lisa, not knowing who to tell her problems to, broke down with him. Remembering with great embarrassment how hard she had sniffled her snot because she hadn't had a tissue on hand to wipe her nose till Collin had passed her one. He had listened to her and simply stated that she should find another friend. Lisa stopped her crying at his cold remark.

"You believe these problems are hard, but they're far simpler than you think," he had told her with a sardonic smile. "Really, when we are young we think the world closes in on us and that we are the center of the universe, that our problems are too incomprehensible for everyone else, but in reality we're just shit-" he had paused, clearing his throat. "We're just dumb to realize it's much easier."

"What?"

Collin had laughed at her reaction. As if her whole situation actually seemed funny to him. "It doesn't feel good when reality hits you, does it? Better now than later."

"Am I making it worse?"

"No, but you shouldn't let yourself fall for people like her either. Believe me, sometimes walking away completely is the best option you can choose." He had ruffled her hair making Lisa smile unintentionally. "Come on, don't cry. In many cases, the person who's the shittiest doesn't even know it. Do you understand what I'm saying?"

"A little," she had answered.

"Well, you'll soon understand."

From that moment on, she trusted him. She hadn't been entirely pleased with the answers, as she had wrongly believed it to be an attack on her only friend, yet she had appreciated his support. Collin could be harsh with his observations, but compared to her peers at school, he was honest. He had no reason to lie to her. She hadn't comprehended their conversation in its entirety until now. Looking back on it now, she found funny how Collin controlled himself from swearing, but one or two always slipped out. It was strange to realize how one could be attached to their own perspective and not perceive the harm that was actually happening. Even so, she didn't approve of people speaking ill of Elizabeth, for it wasn't right.

She glanced at the time and was startled at how late it was. Looking back at her writings and drawings, she broke into a tiny smile, already connected to her own world. She turned off the lamp and lay down hugging one of her pillows. Later she would tell Collin all about it. She wanted her protagonist to be like him, confident and clever. She also wanted someone like Brida in her story, with whom she had enjoyed her company so much she didn't want to forget her. She even wanted her dad in her little story. All the people she liked. Later she'd see how to do that, for now she was content, her heart full for the first time in so long.

That night nothing was felt in her neck.

XXX

He woke up tense, with his jaw clenched. Thomas stopped gritting his teeth, still feeling the pressure on them. His pulse beat erratically, taking deep breaths, not knowing what he had dreamt up to react so strongly, sensing a sharp discomfort in his neck, particularly in the jugular vein. He wasn't particularly eager to leave town, however, his vacation had ended. He massaged the area, dissipating the discomfort. Thomas had expected to be restless, but the opposite happened. He was at ease. He had no idea what would await him when returning to that house, although he didn't care much anymore. He had believed bad luck plagued them, that it had been unfair what had happened, but none of that mattered now. By the time he arrived at Saint Elkan, he'll have to contemplate on his next decisions, content with the new opportunity to improve himself. It seemed possible to reform himself without further issues. As he folded his clothes, he paused at the sound of a knock at the door, setting the suitcase aside to answer it. He smiled at the sight of Brida, who smiled back. He noticed the green earrings. They matched her eyes well.

"All set?"

"Soon," he answered.

Brida held a paper bag in one hand and passed it to Thomas, who was quick to note it held something delicate inside. He couldn't discern what it was from the shape alone, but from the probable material, it could easily break, knowing he had to tuck it into his clothes to keep it safe during the trip. "Open it when you're at home."

"What is it?"

"A gift."

Thomas raised his eyebrows. "Okay, I'll open it later." He would line it with his clothes, not wanting to break it even by accident. He lightly squeezed the object, realizing it had been a long time since he had received a gift. A gift where it wasn't out of politeness, nor obligatory, a gesture born out of the pure concept of giving. Thomas stowed his gift away in the suitcase and turned to Brida, who stood by the doorway. "Thank you. I don't have anything to give in return."

"It's a gift. I don't need anything."

He let out a chuckle, already having ideas on how he could return the gesture. He could make a lasagna after helping install the new locks, while Brida worked around the inner garden of her house, plating the flowers she mentioned for her late father. He remembered Brida had a good oven and never used it. It struck him how Brida had more than one green finger on her hands, whereas he was never good with plants, no matter how much he tended for them they died, and although Brida wasn't good at cooking, he was great at it. He loved to eat well just like his family, who were obsessed with their own recipes. His late nonno had always loved to talk about food, so much so his mother sometimes hadn't put up with him. All this was just a quaint thought that had come up unexpectedly, how everyone had their own talents. He zipped up his suitcase and went to put it in the trunk of his car. "Let me return the key."

Brida gave a small nod with her head. Thomas expected to see the cheerful girl at the office, encountering instead an old lady with a bored expression. The handling was swift and the lady wished him a safe trip. Thomas exited the office, smiling at Brida who waited for him by his car, looking in the direction of the central church. "Tomorrow you'll arrive then."

She turned her attention back to him. "Yes, I'll be at the apartment tomorrow morning. Then I'll go back to the house and get new locks." She pulled out her pack of cigarettes and passed one to Thomas, who accepted it, borrowing Brida's lighter. "Look for azaleas, too."

"You'll find everything quickly."

After finishing their cigarettes in peaceful silence, they hugged each other goodbye. Thomas smoothed his jacket and got into the car. Brida bent down to get a better look at him from the window, her arm resting on the car roof. The day was overcast, the clouds a dark gray, about to burst. The wind carried a strong musty smell. "Be careful on the road."

"I will. Drive slowly tomorrow, there may be another storm."

"Looks like it."

"I'll see you at work Brida, take care."

At the sight of Thomas' car pulling away, Brida released a sigh. The sky emitted a burst of light followed by a great thunderclap piercing to the bone. Reminiscing on all the dreams she'd had since she had set foot in town, contemplating they no longer had the same effect. She knew those dreams wouldn't leave her, but they weren't in control of her mind. Similar to the scar she bore, none of what happened in the past was going to fade away in it entirety.

Regarding the house, she did considered selling it, inquiring about the price, even if there were people interested in it. Ultimately, she couldn't bring herself to put a price on it. An outdated house filled with mementos of the Castillo's particularly. She couldn't discard her late father's efforts in acquiring it. The site where her father died in comfort that afternoon. When she would plant the azaleas, she wondered if the scent would reach her father's spirit and forgive her for considering getting rid of everything he'd worked hard for. She will continue to tend the garden and return to the old routine. She couldn't abandon the garden her father had tended for so long. Another flash of lighting made her narrow her eyes, waiting for the rumbling sound of thunder. She looked towards the church. A voice made her turn around.

"Good morning," Collin greeted her.

She examined him. He looked tired. "Morning."

"Ready to go back?"

"Hm. Tomorrow."

From his spot he glimpsed the earrings that best matched her eyes, sensing a peculiar satisfaction rising from the confines of his mind, settling down as a curious warmth in his chest. His eyes inadvertently lingered on her stomach, noticed by Brida, who stared at him and moved closer, causing Collin to inhale her unmistakable scent. The earrings jiggled drawing his attention.

"Is something the matter?"

Collin was slow to catch the question. He turned to stare at Brida with raised eyebrows, until his brain understood what the detective had asked. "Huh. No, nothing. I just slept poorly. The neighbors wouldn't let me sleep, you know how it is," he said swiftly. It sounded like he was excusing himself instead of engaging in a normal conversation. The gnawing sensation that he was losing something meaningful grew stronger. He shoved his hands into his pants pockets. Well, it was now or never. "Would you like to have dinner with me?" Apparently, his question had taken the detective by surprise, who then smiled.

"Do you have a place in mind?"

"My apartment, it's more comfortable."

"Do you want me to bring anything?"

"No, I have everything." He wasn't going to admit that he'd had everything ready for the dinner idea since yesterday. All he'd needed from her was a straightforward 'yes'. "Although, if you want to bring something you can." He noted Brida appeared pleased by the sudden invitation. Collin smiled sideways, evidently he wasn't the only one who felt interested. "How about seven o'clock?"

"Fine, I'll see you at that time then."

Collin wanted to draw a breathe a sigh of relief. He excused himself, heading to the inn's office. Upon entering, Mrs. Livia greeted him, ushering him into the kitchen, telling him the sink spout had clogged. He moved all the cleaning products from the bottom to have better access to the drain trap, shortly feeling a hand on his back and turned to see Lisa. She smiled showing her dimples, giving him a quick hug, prompting Collin to ruffle her hair. The line of her neck was less pronounced. "Feeling better?"

"Yes," she answered, combing her hands through her hair. "I had some ideas for a story. I got a little excited. So, um, I came up with a story about another world. It's a simple story." Lisa shrank inwardly, embarrassed to actually express her ideas. Feeling her face heat up, she coughed, trying to calm her nerves. "I slept better too. I didn't dream anything."

"Well, that's good," he replied simply. It was good Lisa distracted herself like this. He foresaw she was going to need it. "I expect to see that story finished later."

"But I've just started."

"And you're going to finish it."

Lisa laughed in disbelief that Collin was demanding a finished story. She gave him one last hug to go check on her father, leaving Collin to work in peace. She headed to her dad's bedroom, and on seeing he wasn't there, she turned to the living room where she found him. Her dad sat on the sofa watching television, grimacing as she heard the news anchor present the frivolous tragedies that happened on the island and across the country. "Hi, Dad."

"Hello, honey."

She rushed to hug him, kissing his cheek. "How did you sleep?"

"I had cramps at night, but fine." Martin settled in, hugged his daughter, and continued to watch the news, while Lisa looked the other way. In the end she preferred to hide her face in her dad's side. Martin gave her small pats on the back, pinching her vertebrae bone, which earned him a laugh from his daughter. His concern had diminished as he observed the line became less evident. He moved her ear to see the blood stains were also dissipating. "Are you going to study today?"

Lisa nodded. "I'll also read the book I bought."

"Good."

She stayed a while longer with her dad, thoroughly enjoying the outbreak of good health he was having. They spent a quiet morning. In the afternoon she took her place in the office, carrying several books and her private notebook, where she had begun to write her story. She still had thoughts about Elizabeth and where she might be. As much as she reflected on what kind of friendship they had, she still believed there had been good moments between them. She had given letters to her, thanking her for being in her life, where she portrayed about how she wanted them to grow old together while still remaining friends, but she had never received one in return, reasoning Elizabeth returned her affection through her presence alone. There was nothing tangible to remember Elizabeth by, not even a little drawing. She had witnessed at school how other classmates drew silly doodles in their friend's notebooks, passed letters and candy to each other. She had wanted to do the same with her one good friend, but Elizabeth distanced herself when she did all those things. She didn't understand why. Lisa heaved a sigh, looking down at her private notebook. Putting aside the history book she was no longer paying attention to, she picked up a pencil and began to write down a scene that had occurred to her. She was trying to draw a spaceship when she sensed another presence. Collin smiled, cocking his head to one side. "How long were you there?" she exclaimed, putting her hand over her writing.

"I called you, but you were too focused on your story."

"Well, It's just, um, I think I'm liking it."

Collin snorted. "It's okay. I'm done for the day."

"You're not having dinner with us?"

"No, I'll…" he trailed off, causing Lisa to narrow her eyes. Collin huffed, leaning on the desk. "I'll dine with Brida."

Lisa was surprised Collin deliberately sought to spend time with the detective. She wouldn't have imagined such a thing. Lisa visualized Collin next to the detective and thought they would look good. If they could connect. She smiled excitedly. "Enjoy your night then."

"Thank you. I'll see you tomorrow Lisa."

"Have a good night. Be careful out there," she said, escorting him to the door to lock it. Alone in the office again, she settled back in the chair, returning to her own little world. Writing down her thoughts and introspections might help her understand her own mind. The story itself wasn't fanciful. Nothing more than a story of beings from another planet coexisting with humans and being friends. Probably for others the concept was immature, but she loved how simple it was. *No, it's not true*, she thought. Friendship wasn't simple, or maybe she doesn't know how to be a friend. The sobering reflection brought everything she was doing to a halt, resting her head on her arms on the desk. What if she really had been the one who didn't know how to be a good friend? Since childhood she struggled to make friends. No one stayed and her dad assured her soon there would be someone who would. She believed him because Collin had told her the same thing.

The 'good friends' emerge when one truly values them, when one takes responsibility for their actions and words while communicating. When one wanted to be emotionally connected and grow to be a better version of themselves, attentive to the negative and the positive aspects of each other's personality. Collin had pointed out to her that there was no concept of a good friend or a bad friend, either you were a friend or nothing, simple as that.

She wondered again where Elizabeth could be and if she was happy. She sat still, her eyes fixed on the office door, wondering if at some point she could've changed anything. Whatever the answer was, Elizabeth wasn't with them, so it didn't matter.

XXXI

He had everything ready, only Brida's presence was missing. Collin decided to cook first and then take shower, expecting the detective to arrive punctually as she did before. He had opted for a comfortable yet casual look, arranging his hair the way he liked it. His natural waves were fuller when properly styled. Any hair looked good when it wasn't full of dirt, sweat and dust. He picked up his best cologne, sprayed his neck once and gently pressed his wrists against the damp area, spreading it evenly. The neighbors better be quiet this night, otherwise he'd shut them up himself. Collin checked at a glance that everything was in order. The doorbell rang and he noted it was four minutes past seven, without wasting any more time he went to greet Brida, who waited with a bottle in hand, from what he could see it appeared to be whiskey.

"I didn't know which one you liked," she succinctly said, letting him see the brand.

"This one is fine, thank you." He became fond of her bluntness of speech, which initially struck him as odd, but soon learned Brida had a straightforward character. She was courteous, just direct. He escorted her into his apartment and glanced where his most annoying neighbors resided, expecting his evening wouldn't be ruined by their irritating bickering. He changed his expression to a placid one as he closed the door. "Do you like smoked pork?"

"I do."

"Excellent, there's also salad and toasted bread with garlic."

"Thank you," she replied, taking her seat at the table.

Collin turned to the detective, seeing her take off her dark leather jacket, leaving it on the back of the chair, allowing those earrings to contrast with the black of her shirt. He told himself it was normal to like such details, although he had never been interested in those before. "What would you like to drink?"

"Water it's fine."

"Right, let me..." He went to pour two glasses of water and rested them on the table, hearing a low 'thank you' from Brida. He sat down and sketched a small smile, not knowing how to start the conversation without being crass. He didn't have much experience with *this*. He picked up the bowl where the salad was in, served it on his plate and then passed it to Brida. "So you're leaving town tomorrow. Going back to work?"

"Yes, back to my desk."

"It seems dull."

"It's work," she said, setting aside the salad bowl. "For my first time out of the city, it was a good experience." Brida looked down at the cutlery, specifically the knife in her right hand. "I plan to return to my old routine."

"What kind of routine?"

"The routine I had when my father was alive." She moved her hand away from the knife. "We enjoyed gardening, among other things."

"I never imaged you were into plants." He wanted to flick his eyes at his idiotic comment, but he had already said it. Besides, at first glance he didn't know what kind of tastes Brida could have for someone so earnest. "Sounds good. I'm better at maintaining a garden, not so much planting it and moving soil. I bought seeds once and nothing came out."

"It's just a matter of learning and patience."

"So your father loved gardening?"

"He enjoyed it."

Collin smiled, loosening his posture at the amiable exchange they were having. He was used to not having the need to fill the silence, but this time he wanted to ask many questions and get to know the woman in front of him better. Who knew talking about plants would relax him. From what he could see out of the corner of his eye, enough time had passed for the neighbors to act. Not a sound, scream or quarrel. A quiet night. "Tell me, what do you do in your spare time?"

"Depends on the day."

It was fun to wonder how she'd managed to get through life with that kind of personality. He soon remembered what the girls he'd dated before always told him. They always repeated two particular hobbies. "No drawing, no writing?"

"I don't have the artistic eye."

Collin cocked his head, smirking. "Not even a small poem?"

"I never had the talent for it."

"I can see that. I can't even imagine you singing."

Brida lifted her eyebrows, then averted her gaze. "I don't sing," she admitted.

He laughed, setting aside his glass of water. He thought it had been a lovely action. "That's where we're alike. When I was in school, my art teacher always made a face when I showed her my work. I was such a genius kid that she didn't understand my art." He snorted. A thump alerted him, cutting of whatever he was going to say, turning towards the door. The same sound as last night. Collin tensed his jaw, cursing those damn neighbors. A quiet night was all he'd asked for. Was it too much to ask for? He waited for the screams, but they didn't come. He expected the same thumping sound to be repeated. Nothing. "Well, don't worry, I don't sing either. Do you want more?"

"No, thank you."

Their dinner proceeded uneventfully. When they were pleasantly full, Brida helped him clear the table, taking the plates to the sink, but Collin stopped her when he saw what she was trying to do. He wasn't going to let her clean up. "Tomorrow I'll clean, let's play cards instead." He didn't care about cleaning up, that would be taken care of by future Collin. Brida returned to her seat. He took two glasses to pour the whiskey and grabbed his deck of cards he kept on his workbench. "You know how to play Poker?"

"I'm a little rusty on card games, but yes."

"Who knows, you might beat me."

"We'll see."

Collin poured the whiskey, smiling at the mute challenge they had set for themselves. He sat down, shuffling the cards with ease. "I remember the first time I played cards against my dad. He didn't let me win once. It only made me want to beat him more, until one day I did. I thought I was going to experience enormous satisfaction, but I felt nothing. In the end I preferred to play with him and that's it. I don't why I remembered that." Nor did he know why exactly he had shared it.

Brida gave a small smile. "You sound close to him."

"Ah, well, yes, I guess." Collin distributed the cards. He had yet to contact his parents and let them know he was living well, but in general, he maintained a good relationship with them. He knew his mum would accept him with open arms while his dad wouldn't have much of an opinion. Cautiously he asked: "Do you have any memories like that?"

"We were content in our own way."

"And that was enough for you."

"It was."

Collin lowered his gaze, smiling. They played enjoying each other's company, at times they were silent, just playing and drinking. He hadn't been aware they were already halfway through the bottle. Brida, without uttering a word, turned out to be competitive in the game. He could tell by the way she had paid attention, winning the last rounds. "You lied to me about your rusty hand."

"Or I've been lucky."

"I don't think so."

Collin reshuffled the cards. Perhaps the alcohol made him let his guard down as he gazed at Brida's stomach, right where he could guess the- No, he *knew* the scar was in that exact spot. He wondered about the scar. Not just anyone could have the same composure as Brida, and he questioned if it was all a farse. It had to be. Was it possible to leave it all behind? It couldn't be that easy. But then, what else was left? Life went on no matter how much one wanted everything stop. The world would keep on rolling, that's how insignificant they were.

"Why do you look at my stomach?"

He blinked. "Huh?"

"I've noticed you've been looking at my stomach lately."

"I haven't… I don't know." In that moment, Brida stared at him, keeping him alert amidst the green waves, erupting and transforming, engulfing him. He told himself it was just the light playing games with his perception, maybe even the whiskey. His mind scattered, unable to focus on a single thought. He wasn't sure what to say about it. "I didn't know I was doing it. Sorry it's just- How do you live with it?"

"With the scar?"

"With everything."

Brida had her hand on the glass, stirring the liquid leisurely. She looked down at the glass. No one cared about other people's problems. Many could empathize, but if the affected individual didn't put effort on their part, even the most charitable person would drop them. No one wants to be in the company of someone stagnate and even less so if that person knows about their problems, but does nothing to address them. Brida breathed out a sigh. "You have to." She wasn't going to be stalled by *him.* She wasn't going to waste her life's time. "Although I admit there are times when I go back to that moment. It no longer impacts me as it did before. The tricky part is to take the next steps."

"You didn't know what to do?"

"No, that's why I took this vacation."

"Did being here really help you?"

"It did," she said, sorting her cards. She paused the game, closed her deck, and placed it face down on the table. Collin mimicked the motion, taking the opportunity to fill the glasses. "I considered what to do next. I was close to selling the house my father chose for us. I gave myself some time away from that house and even met a couple who didn't care if the place had been a crime scene. I showed the house once and preferred not to do it anymore. My father died in that house and I knew I'd die there too. What I didn't anticipate was it would come so soon, but I survived." She shrugged and then frowned, halting her speech. She had to remind herself she shouldn't talk like that. It had no effect on her, but it had on others. Her counselor had recommended her to lighten her speech. The few observations she had agreed with. "I'm sorry, I'll try to be less blunt."

"Sounds like something you've thought of before."

"We may die tomorrow," she said, rather dryly. "It's only natural."

"I guess, I guess so." The subject of death unsettled him in comparison to Brida. As much as his dreams depicted the pure agony of various people he'd never met in his life, the moment his own body became unnaturally still, he always tried unsuccessfully to wake himself up. Death breathed down his neck every night, and it frightened him, because she was creative. He coldly thought that death was a great artist for making him undergo different lives. He loathed those nights. "I don't care about lots of things in life, but I want to be at peace. That's why I came back here, to my hometown. I knew I was being a burden to my parents, so I left. I haven't called them." He admitted softly, looking down at his hand, playing with the rim of the glass. "I planned to call them soon."

"You should."

"Yeah, I really should."

They resumed the game, a pleasant silence forming between them. She won the last round, making Collin laugh at the sight of her cards. Brida glanced at her wristwatch and noticed the time. She set the deck aside along with her glass. "It's too late and tomorrow I'll leave early."

What a sobering thing to say. "You came with your car, right?"

"I did," she said, putting on her jacket. "I knew I'd enjoy my time."

Feeling his stomach tighten with nerves, he smiled, controlling his emotions. He had also enjoyed it, perhaps too much. Collin quickly put the glasses in the sink, ignoring Brida pulling her pocket notebook out of her jacket and jotting something down, then leaving it on the table. Collin returned, checking the time. He hated having her go out at that high hour, but it would be too risky to say that out loud, so he took it upon himself to escort her to her car. Checking there were no shifty strangers watching them. "Be careful at the inn too."

"I will, thank you."

"I'm not joking."

She lifted her eyebrows. "Neither am I."

He immediately felt apologetic for speaking like that, only using that certain tone with Lisa. He heard Brida's husky laugh, which more than hearing it, he felt it. He blamed the alcohol for dispersing his wits, as the only thought to come forward was how much he liked to feel, rather than hear.

"I'll be careful, Collin. Have a good night."

"Have a safe strip tomorrow." He stood there, ensuring she was safe, until the car turned down the street to reach the inn. It didn't feel right. A deep dissatisfaction invaded him. He huffed, closing the gate, and returned to his apartment, accepting that it had been his last interaction with the detective. He was about to wipe the table until he spotted a piece of paper. A number alongside Brida's name. He froze with paper in his hand and then smiled, leaving the cleanup for later. It might not be the last interaction. He went to his room and tucked the paper safely in the top drawer of his nightstand.

After that there were no more thoughts, able to sleep soundly.

XXXII

Thomas had yet to open his gift. He was getting ready to head to work, but now that he wasn't distracted by the strange atmosphere in the house, he took the chance to open his suitcase, which he hadn't even unpacked. He picked up the paper bag protected between his clothes and opened it. It was a statue of a dog lying down with a snake between its paws. He found it curious, but loved it. He placed it beside the lamp on his nightstand, on top of the book he was reading at the time. He would thank Brida later.

XXXIII

When she awoke, there was nothing in the inn room. There were no stains on the ceiling. There were no familiar faces staring down at her, no fluttering of wings haunting her senses. There was only the painting of the hare with whom she had grown accustomed to see above her as a silent guardian, staring at the nocturnal animal, black eyes bore into her own. On her next visit, she'll search for a painting like this one for the house and put it in her bedroom, above the bed. The painting had no signature, therefore no point of reference. She began her morning routine, preparing for her trip. She donned a dark turtleneck shirt to protect her neck from the low temperature of the day. Seeing her expressionless reflection in the bathroom mirror, she found herself ready to return. Being in town had been like a long dream.

Her wristwatch stated it was close to eight in the morning, enough time to say goodbye to Lisa if she sees her at the office and visit the nuns for a final time. She put on her jacket as she went out, noticing the weather carried a certain humidity, the clouds were about to break covering the sky entirely. All her belongings were now in the trunk of the car and proceeded to leave the room key. Trying the handle, which was normally locked for security reasons it unlocked, opening the door. Lisa wasn't in the office, but surprisingly her father was. His shoulder-length hair had a healthy glow, his cheeks were flushed complimenting his skin, although his eyes were tired.

"Morning."

"Good morning." He greeted, clasping Brida's hand, instructing her to leave the key on the desk, aware that Brida had paid for her stay beforehand. He noted the detective glance at the gate guarding the hallway connecting to the house. "Lisa is asleep at the moment, but I can leave her a message if you want."

She didn't know what to say.

Martin smiled complicitly at the detective. "Don't worry, I'll tell her you looked for her before you left, that'll make her happy. Thank you for bringing my daughter back home and also taking care of her while being here. Lisa is going through a grieving process, but she has been calm these days. Whatever you explained to her, it made her understand a few things."

"I didn't do much."

"Little or much, it doesn't matter."

She gave a polite nod. "I trust you both continue to feel well."

"We will, thank you. It's going to rain soon, be careful on the road." Martin gave her a final handshake, smiling at the presence he didn't think he would appreciate. "If you ever decide to visit town again, you know the inn is here. There's also the hotel if you want the lake view, an old place with history as everything around here. You have to see it for yourself." He clicked his tongue. "I'm here talking to you about this and taking up your time. Have a safe trip. Visit the town when you get a chance."

"I will, thank you."

Returning to her car, she grabbed her umbrella from the trunk and headed for church. She passed through the park, ignoring the statue of Elkan, which emitted odd buzzing sounds until she caught sight of an insect crashing down with a dull thud near where she walked. She failed to identify which insect it was. Arriving at the entryway of the building, grabbing one of the hoops on the ancient door knocker, the image of the dogs biting on the hoop indefinitely in time, their grins welcoming her presence, she knocked on the heavily decorated door. The sound echoed. In those seconds, the antique door opened, revealing the image of the young nun. The sight of her contrasted against the stark darkness of the site, emanating her own light, allowing Brida focus only on her.

"You're leaving," pointed out the young nun.

"I came to say thank you."

The nun let her slip inside, closing the door, enveloping them in the dark naturalness of the nuns' home. Brida didn't move waiting for her eyes to adjust to the gloom, the sister's presence close by her side, invading her olfactory senses with the scent of roots and plants. It was curious how she now found herself inside a church, even as a child she never had the need. The forced routine of the confessional annoyed her greatly, getting into trouble with the nuns at school. The headmistress had called her father into her office. Brida recalled a smoldering sensation in her chest against the nuns and teachers for wasting her father's time, only to have him sternly stare at her. Brida had clenched her hands into fists. He had told her to lie next time or say the first thing that came to her mind. If they coerced her to confess by force, they would get stupid answers. She had done it for her father, not wanting to waste his time again by giving cynical confessions to the priests. Compared to her school chapel, this place possessed an ethereal impression unmatched by other buildings like this one.

"Perhaps my father would've liked it here."

The young nun smiled.

"Or perhaps not."

"What makes you say so?"

"Not many can bear their own self." Her father wouldn't have been able to, he had carried a severe burden of resentment and grief. Most of the Castillo's disregarded him and she couldn't become an anchor for him until reaching adulthood, even then, she hadn't feel like one. Her father always upheld more than one barrier. She gazed at the nun's face, searching for a devout light in those dark eyes. The young nun approached, guiding the detective to the monastery garden. Brida peered at the chiaroscuro paintings of the saintly women. Their agonies depicted forever, never forgotten as her own betrayal. The major divergence between them was that she carried on with her ephemeral life and wasn't trapped in a pit of tragedy for the rest of her existence. The aroma of humidity assaulted her, surroundings her senses.

"Accompany me, I won't take much of your time."

She had no trouble following the nun's lead, familiar with the path leading to the central courtyard. The garden was well tended except for the fountain, stained by patches of moss, filled with stagnant water presumably from the recent rains. The young nun sat on the edge of the fountain, positioning her ringed hands on her lap. Brida settled next to her, retaining a respectful distance. It was a beautiful garden.

"Do you feel qualified?" asked the young nun.

"I know what I have to do for now."

"We are glad to hear it."

"Thank you for taking care of me."

"We were pleased to do so."

She felt a hand touch hers. Brida stiffened, stating at the nun, who kept the gentle yet mysterious smile in her subtlety. The touch held her attentive, drawn to the nun's visage. There was a familiarity in her warmth soon dispelling the feeling. The skin bore the smoothness one appreciates when running a hand over a surface. The perfume of plants deepened, latching to her mind. This church and its congregation didn't conform to the typical idea Brida had growing up. She admitted she had developed a fondness for the inmate nuns. "I don't care much about the future." Brida glanced at their joined hands, particularly the nun's hand, studying the dull veins like brush strokes, down to the rings that glistened with the light. "It's not indifference."

"We know it's not."

"Thank you for letting me into your home."

The nun returned the sentiment by tightening her grip on Brida's hand, digging her nails into her skin like an animal's talons. Brida didn't react as the pain never came. "We were delighted by your visit. It has been a long time since we've shared our presence with someone else." The sharp, cutting autumn wind whistled, stirring the shrubs and trees in the garden. Brida narrowed her eyes while the nun kept her gaze fixed on her companion. "Your eyes bring old memories to me. When you raised your eyes to the altar, I didn't hesitate to love them. They remind me of what was taken from me so long ago."

Brida regarded the nun silently.

"The past is already gone."

And the future will always be out of reach. Brida heard a flutter and noticed the older nun in the open corridor connected to the courtyard. The nun bowed her head in greeting and faded into the shadows of the corridors. Brida took the young nun's hand in hers as she rose from her place. "I'll take my leave, thank you again."

"*Ve con cuidado, mi azalea.*"

She took one step, becoming two, till she was close enough to count every eyelash in those eyes seeming to consume the very light, to note the texture of the skin, the verdant gems shifted with every breath. The nun had lifted her head, holding her stare. Hearing that old nickname accompanied by the nun's tender gaze made her posture soften, inhaling the perfumed air. Brida tilted her head, regarding the nun. "Did I let that name slip when I stayed here?"

"Several times."

Brida looked at her expressionless. Soon she smiled. "*Gracias.*" The nun smiled back. A flood of serenity surged through her, not knowing how to react to this force that possessed her mind, transmitting itself to the soul. With no further words, aware the nuns had their routine and Brida had to return to her own, she gently released the nun's hand. Serenity persisted within her even after the parting.

She stepped out of the church, slipping from the shadows into the static world outside. Brida reached into her pocket, where the ring had remained hidden since she had arrived in town. After she had managed to shape her thoughts, the ring became weightless, a consequence of her reflections constructing a new foundation. Leaves from the nearby trees swirled and fell in distinct points. The town remained eerily quiet even at the hands of nature.

A decision had already been made regarding the ring.

XXXIV

Packing and moving her minimal belongings from the apartment to the house had been effortless, only having the necessary in that dingy place. She had thanked the landlord and he had blessed her.

"I hope nothing happens to you now," he had said.

Brida huffed out a laugh. Who knows what would happen to her in the future. It wasn't something she was concerned with. Nonetheless she had thanked him for the kind wishes and left the place to go home. Upon arrival, she had lingered in the doorway, the stillness immersing her in memories of her father who, as solemn as he had been, received her every time she arrived. Although she had grown accustomed to the mournful quiet of the corridors, Brida searched for the image of her father, envisioning him welcoming her. The apparition of him loomed as she passed the inner garden, halting her steps. Several fragments of her dreams invaded her mind, enough to create heaviness in her chest. Soon she'll plant azaleas for him.

Time elapsed while Brida arranged her clothes and picked up the statuette she had bought from the market. Two barn owls standing on a log. She positioned it in her office, on the walnut desk, upholstered by a glass top. As she sat down in the leather chair she let out a heavy sigh. With her work schedule she'll have to work the garden at night and wet it at four o'clock in the morning. She'll see on those days how her schedule accommodates her. From the middle drawer of the desk she pulled out a framed sepia-colored photo and placed it next to the statue. Her grandfather was the only one with a broad smile marking his crow's feet, even her grandmother had a lightened expression. Both of them holding her father's shoulders. Her father held her in his arms at a young age, she may have been five years old in that picture. Her father had been a good-looking man, yet after her mother's death, it left him marked. He had become a surly man, who couldn't stand the touch of other people. She didn't recall why they were smiling in that picture, being more credible they were forcing it given it had been after her mother's death. She leaned her back against the chair, her eyes no longer gazing at the faces of her relatives, their features became absent as her eyes unfocused.

At nightfall, the sky became fully overcast and a few moments later thunder made its presence known, rattling the windows of the house. Rain pelted straight down, gaining speed with the wind, now pouring vertically, battering the glass of the windows. She didn't need to consult the weather to know it was going to rain throughout the night and probably the following day. The glass had fogged up, blurring the view of the city. Brida who remained in the office, perusing family photos she stored in the bottom drawers of the desk. She glanced at the door, setting down the photos and headed out into the frigid corridor.

She stood still under the skylight.

Twilight cascaded in a bent line contrasting with the gloom of the rest of the house. The place where she fell to the ground and could no longer get up, staining the floor with her blood. She had stained more than just the floor tiles. How could she have considered to dispose of the house when it owned her father's soul and her own blood?

In that second, Brida saw *him*.

She had no emotion at the sight of him, kneeling there, crying over her inert body. How he had taken her face in a way as if it were such a sensitive moment between them. Passing a hand along the side of her face, combing her hair, memorizing each of her facets. Tenderness. It would be a word to describe the scene from his perspective.

"*What I feel for you is deeper than any romance people think they understand,*" he had whispered, staring at her. She recalls his words with vivid accuracy. How one night, between sips of wine, he told her how people think love as a mockery, when love is an unconditional force. How love itself could be such a grotesque, misunderstood and violent force. "*Don't you crave it?*"

She had no answer to his question which made him smile. She had stared at him in a sharp manner, discerning his words. But he planted a seed of doubt in her being. Brida pictured that jovial man, with his almost too complicit eyes and his engulfing pine scent. Love could be transformative.

Perhaps it was her who didn't understand it.

Brida headed to the bedroom, pushing the door open smoothly without emitting a sound, where she undressed and changed into a comfortable set of pajamas, laying her head on the silk-covered pillow, staring at the ceiling with her hands resting on her abdomen. She closed her eyes, mimicking sleep. The image of her face emerged behind her eyelids. It was her face and simultaneously it was not. Her father stared and at the same time she stared at herself. A pattern of her own self.

She contemplated her visage, the hidden face. Unchanged and also changed. Her eyes opened as the hooting became present, this time she listened to its call without the need to be aware of her own existence.

She knew she would be back to the place who became aware of her, possibly from her own beginning.

XXXV

It rained almost every day, at times in pauses, other times so heavily to the point of blocking the vision of the windshield when driving. Snowfalls were rare on the island, but it didn't mean that they couldn't see it in winter, especially in late December and early January. So far it had only rained, which increased the cold temperature and made the streets prone to accidents. Brida parked her Brougham at the station parking lot. The Saint Elkan Police Station was an antique building with gothic and contemporary details mixing in a juxtaposition of eras. The entrance was the best example of this, with Corinthian columns on the sides supporting the pediment depicting birds, angels and nature surrounding the divine beings, yet the interior was modern, changing multiple areas over time to enhance the overall security of the building. The desk sergeant greeted her behind the bullet- proof glass, unlocking the security door to let her enter into the offices. She thanked him, returning the greeting courtly, and opened the second door to head to her division. Walking through the corridors, her footsteps echoed on the polished tiled floor, the walls were a pale yellow with a wide brown stripe underneath, decorated by the occasional plant, wooden bench, or filling cabinet. Upon reaching her division, of the total number they were, only two were at their desks. She took off her scarf, leaving it on the chair. Her desk was organized just as she had left it. An hour went by in which she already had her coffee, concentrated on rereading the file in her hand till a newspaper blocked her view. She looked up to see Thomas in his winter jacket smiling, his cheeks rosy from the cold, humid air, passing her the day's newspaper.

"Morning."

"Good morning. I saw this coming here and I thought you might be interested," Thomas said. He particularly looked better these winter days. After the last conversation with Alina, he had improved.

Brida knew Thomas often visited Mrs. Serafina. He went out more with colleagues from work to have a few beers and regaining his social life. Gradually pursuing everything he had mentioned when they visited the lighthouse, jogging in the evenings, going out to social gatherings, and visiting his grandmother. She had also considered visiting the kind lady who had helped her when she couldn't even go near the stove due to her type of medication. Later she would ask what type of present she could arrange for Mrs. Serafina. Brida unfolded the newspaper to facilitate reading it, following Thomas' direction, flipping through the advertisements and other articles. Two in particular dealt with the town and cases of domestic violence. She turned the page and looked at the following article:

> *SAINT ELKAN. Published December 15. Saint Elkan Police Department (SEPD) dispatched a K9 team to facilitate the search for Elizabeth Montebrook Davis. The body was discovered by a police dog on Wednesday, at about 12:08 p.m. The young girl had tied a rope to a sturdy branch and the other end to her neck. Subsequently, personnel from the Forensic Services arrived at the site to begin their diligences and to arrange for the removal of the body. Police said the death wasn't suspicious, suspecting Elizabeth Montebrook committed suicide. Carolyn Davis, mother of the deceased girl, said her daughter had often struggled, but always maintained herself positive. Carolyn said: "She was a good girl, caring, loving with her family and friends [...].*

She put the newspaper on the desk. "Suicide."

"Mystery solved."

Brida nodded absently. One of many. There was still the matter of who that man in the park had been. It may have been her paranoia now that she considered it. Briefly rereading some segments of the article, the words echoing in her mind, she wondered about Lisa and her possible reaction to the news. "At least it's been resolved."

"It's certainly not good news, but now the family knows."

At the very least Mrs. Carolyn Davis had her daughter's body, that's for sure. Most families eventually resign themselves to simply wanting the bodies of their loved ones returned to them, but unfortunately this didn't usually happen, resulting in the dreadful mystery of where their remains would be. But this time, a mother is aware her daughter's body has remained intact and that it was the daughter's decision to take her own life. These kinds of losses changed parents in extreme ways. It was a frivolous thought to have, yet there were far worse fates in this world. Brida concurred with Thomas' comment. "The family knows."

"Well, how's the garden coming along?"

"I'll plant the azaleas in early spring."

"I thought you'd plant them already."

"No, I'll look for other plants for now."

"Don't know much about it, but sounds good," he said, giving a smile. He straightened his posture, adjusting his wool jacket, running a hand over it, removing a few wrinkles in the process. He didn't know how to ask the next question without sounding rude or too interested, it was simple curiosity. "Brida," he began, clearing his throat. "About the ring. Do you still have it?"

"No, I don't."

Thomas blinked, staring at his friend. He didn't even know what to say, but he was reassured to know that the object was no longer nearby. He wasn't going to ask more, it was enough he had asked if she had it. "Well, that sounds good too." He sounded a bit awkward. Relief was evident on his face. Thomas checked the time and had to start his shift. "I have to go. Just wanted to show you the news, I'll see you later."

"Be careful, Thomas."

"I will, thank you."

She folded the newspaper and put it aside, refocusing her attention to the file she had been holding earlier. Her coffee had gone cold. She rose from the desk to reheat the mug, meeting her colleague at the break room, the one she had been promoted with to fill the division's position, Pete Valdes. A curly haired man of whom the old ladies used to say every curl was a mischief, and with all the stories Pete had up his sleeve, she could believe the old ladies. Pete was a vivacious man who enjoyed chatting a bit about everything. Brida preferred to listen, so they made good friends: one being a chatterbox and the other listening. He was preparing his coffee, taking one of the sweet breads that were available and smiled when he noticed Brida's presence. "We're in for a long day," he greeted, shaking off the sugar that stuck to his fingers. "How are you doing today?"

"Fine, thank you."

"I almost got hit on the main avenue," Pete began his tale, without minding the curtly reply, taking the opportunity to talk knowing Brida would listen to him. "They don't know how to drive and it's always raining on this damn island. Don't you think that's fucking stupid? I'm telling you, one of these days they'll come crashing down on me. I'm going to go crazy if they hit my new car."

"They?"

"Yes, they, not me."

Brida tilted her head, smiling at the indignant answer. Anyone could understand Pete and his rant. A new car was a big investment only to have some moron ram it and generate another expense. Brida reheated her mug and leaned against the counter, listening to everything Pete had to say. Later, they would be on their own cases, working all day till the end of their respective schedules. Maybe in the evening she might go to Gustavo's bar, invite Thomas over and the three of them could have a drink together. Gustavo might be genuinely pleased at the sight of his two friends, discussing work and life with him as they had done before. It had been a long time since the three of them had met alone. The day went by briskly and Brida sought out Thomas aware he would be filling out his report for the day.

"Been a while since we had a reunion like that," Thomas said.

"About time," replied Brida.

Both agreed to spend a short moment and then rest from the long day they respectively had. The bar was nearly full, but quiet, bustling in the evenings, and then dying in the late hours of the night. Gustavo greeted them from the bar, smiling at his two friends, whom he hadn't seen together for a while.

"Look who deigned to show up," Gustavo said, leaning against the bar, putting his rag over his shoulder. He looked at Thomas who just smiled, shrugging his shoulders. "I had asked Brida about you, but you disappeared. No warning, no nothing. You're worse than Brida."

Thomas had no excuse there. "Well, but I'm here now."

"Aha, a miracle," replied Gustavo sarcastically. Gustavo turned to Brida, who was clearly enjoying the interaction. "Can you believe him? And then he's the one complaining about us not connecting and not seeing each other-"

"That's not true," interrupted Thomas. "And you know it."

"You know we love you, now, now, don't get upset. Don't you see we missed you around here?" Gustavo snorted, patting Thomas' arm. He liked to annoy him to the point of arguing for quite a while. "What would you like to drink tonight? I'm in the mood for tequila today."

"Whiskey for me," said Brida.

"For me a Martini, thank you," muttered Thomas, still reflecting on Gustavo's comment. He was right, because compared to Brida, who had come to the bar several times to see Gustavo and spend time here, he hadn't. He had gotten so far into his own problems that he was now ashamed to realize he should've been the one to point the finger at instead of telling Brida that she had been the difficult one to talk to.

"You know he didn't say that to hurt you."

"No, I just realized something."

"Alright," relented Brida.

Thomas smiled and squeezed Brida's shoulder, shaking her a little, laughing when Brida let herself be moved but squinted at him. Gustavo returned with the beverages and accompanied them with his tequila glass. Brida listened to the spirited discussion they were having about soccer, nursing the frosty glass of whiskey. They couldn't linger long, since they had to work the next day, although the brief time they did have was enjoyed as if it had been an eternity.

"Really, you should come here more often," said Gustavo, hugging Thomas and patting him on the back, then hugged Brida, who accepted the gesture. "I was thinking of doing a small reunion at my house soon, what do you say?"

"Sounds good," accepted Brida. "You tell us what to bring."

"Just your presence."

"We'll see what to bring later," said Thomas, more to Brida than to Gustavo, causing the other to roll his eyes and want to take a swing at his friend, but they were just playing around. They said goodbye to each other and left for their destinations, two to rest and the other to continue working late into the night.

XXXVI

At midday on Sunday, the phone rang. Half an hour ago it had stopped sparkling, giving way to a bone-chilling wet cold. Brida had been tending to the inner garden, moving the new soil in the utter silence of the house. The advantage of having an indoor garden was being able to take care of it without inconveniences, sheltering it from the high temperatures and when the day was agreeable for the plants, they enjoyed the light and shade all at once. She took off the gloves covering her hands and walked over to the phone, picking it up and putting it to her ear. "Who is this?"

"Hello?" Brida knew to whom that lovely voice belonged. She had grown accustomed to his soft timbre, at times becoming versatile voice in tune with his jovial nature. "It's me, Collin. Am I… Am I speaking to Brida?"

"Yes, Collin, you are. How have you been?"

"Me? Fine, everything's fine here as far as I can tell. I don't know if you saw the news recently or if someone told you at work about, well, about Elizabeth. Lisa was hurt by the news, but I think she knew somehow. She left flowers at the funeral. Mrs. Livia argued with that woman and let Lisa enter. What an asshole. After all, that woman still has her shitty attitudes, but hey, who knows what went through those people's minds. Anyway, how did it feel to be back to monotony?"

"As usual. I'm gardening today."

"That sounds better than what I was imagining." Collin couldn't suppress a smile from creeping onto his face at the sound of Brida's voice. Truth be told, Lisa hadn't been doing good knowing Elizabeth had hanged herself, much less when there was no message left behind and thus all secrets stayed with her corpse. "I'd like to see that garden."

"Soon you will."

"All right, sounds like a plan to me."

"Give my condolences to Lisa, may she recover these days."

"I will, thank you. It'll make her happy to hear from you," he said, passing a hand through his hair and licked his lips in that nervous tic of his. "I didn't mention to her that I have your number." Rather Brida had given him her number, but semantics. "Well, we'll see how these days go. It was good to hear you."

"I'm also glad to hear from you too, Collin."

Collin was stunned by her sincerity. Unfortunately, he couldn't stay on the payphone too long, nor did he want to take up Brida's time. He hung up after giving Brida his number. He knew she'd return to town. Something whispered deep inside him the detective was going to return to the place where her own psyche had reflected as a ray of light against a surface such as this very town. That was why he had returned as well. Knowing he had plenty of time to visit Lisa and continue with his plans for the day, he went to check on her. Arriving at the Gallardo's house, Collin knocked on the front door and was greeted by Mrs. Livia.

"How are you, Collin?"

"Fine, ma'am, thank you. Is Lisa awake?"

"Lisa!" Mrs. Livia shouted. "Collin came to see you!" She turned to Collin, crossing her arms. "She's been crestfallen these days, but we'll see if she'll get over it soon. It doesn't do anyone any good to be like this for a long time. I'll leave you two, thank you for checking on her."

"It's nothing." Collin almost wanted to roll his eyes, but didn't out of politeness. Lisa was still in the grieving process and they had to let her go through it, not to let her give up entirely, but to come to terms with the loss. "We'll see how she reacts later."

Mrs. Livia huffed and left to continue her own routine.

Then he saw Lisa peek out at the entrance and briskly walked over to hug him, hiding her face in his chest. Collin hugged her back tightly making Lisa squeal, but he smiled when he heard her muffled giggle. She pulled away and wiped a hand across her eyes. Collin squeezed her arm, allowing her to compose herself. "I wanted to see how you were doing."

"Well, not great, but it's not the same as yesterday."

"That's good, that's good."

"I know it's strange, but I think I already knew."

"What do you mean?"

"I don't know. I really don't know. Elizabeth didn't look good the last few days she was here and I don't think anything was good for her. Not her friends, not that strange guy, not her family and neither me.

I've been talking a lot with Dad these days about why someone might take away their own life and I'll never understand why. But, I don't know, I don't feel it was the right thing to do. Not like that. I would've liked a lot of things, but they don't matter anymore. Not with Elizabeth gone," Lisa said with a shrug.

"We'll never know what's in people's hearts."

"I'll never get to know someone at all?"

"No, not really." Collin smiled. "But you can get to know enough."

Lisa sighed tiredly. "I think I want to be alone for a while."

"That's okay, you know I'm here if you need anything."

She nodded, feeling the urge to cry but she controlled it by hugging him, listening to the rhythmic beat of his heart, calming her nerves. She gave him a small kiss on his cheek as they said goodbye, giving each other another tight hug. Collin felt the impulse to protect her from everyone and everything, away from this damned world they lived in, but it was best to let her learn on her own. He smiled warmly telling her that tomorrow they would go to the lake and Lisa agreed. They felt better as each went off to their own plans for the day.

After going out with two of the new acquaintances he had made, he returned to his apartment to prepare dinner. He ate mechanically, vacantly, his eyes lost, nearly in a hypnotic state at the table that in what was his small dining room. He wiped his lips and left the dishes for later. As he entered his room, he breathed in a fragrant aroma that awakened even the most primitive instincts of his being. He changed in the same way he had eaten and lay down, lost in his reverie. Collin was unable to fall asleep, until the moment he shut his eyes, he heard someone's breathing. His mind was strangely silent.

He didn't know when he fell asleep.

He opened his eyes and turned his head to find Brida's presence, never on her side, always lying on her back, as if she was uncomfortable in any other position. He watched her, counting those bent eyelashes that made such an attractive image. He couldn't control his impulse and touched those eyelashes making her open her eyes. The green ocean captured him and drowned the fisherman.

Upon waking up, he felt his empty side. Melancholy oppressed him, his dreams revealed endless scenes he longed for, yet he slept in his solitude, far from the soul that had and kept consuming him. He began his routine, calming his senses, dampening the sensations with which he awoke. He had dreamed once again of passing peacefully in his sleep with Brida beside him, watching him while he closed his eyes and felt too much peace, his heart settled, quieting. Letting the tides of her eyes engulf him, filling his soul to the point of fear of connecting to another soul. He took those dreams as a good omen, feeling for the first time at ease with his dreams.

A hooting echoed.

www.ingramcontent.com/pod-product-compliance
Lightning Source LLC
Chambersburg PA
CBHW051247250726
48656CB00004B/1176

9798323910267